Following God

WOMAN to Woman

LIFE PRINCIPLES FROM TITUS 2

WOMAN to Woman

LIFE PRINCIPLES FROM TITUS 2

A Bible Study by

Barbara Henry

Advancing the Ministries of the Gospel

AMG *Publishers*™

God's Word to you is our highest calling.

Following God

WOMAN TO WOMAN: LIFE PRINCIPLES FROM TITUS 2

Fifth Printing, 2006

ISBN: 0-89957-250-2

Unless otherwise noted,
Scripture is taken from the *New American Standard Bible*®. Copyright © 1960, 1962, 1963, 1968, 1971, 1972, 1973, 1975, 1977 by The Lockman Foundation. Used by permission. (www.Lockman.org)

Scripture quotations marked (NKJV) are taken from the New King James Version, Copyright ©1982 by Thomas Nelson, Inc. Used by permission. All rights reserved.

Scripture quotations marked (NLT) are taken from the *Holy Bible,* New Living Translation, copyright ©1996. Used by permission of Tyndale House Publishers, Inc., Wheaton, Illinois 60189. All rights reserved.

Scripture quotations marked (NIV) are taken from the HOLY BIBLE, NEW INTERNATIONAL VERSION®. NIV®. Copyright © 1973, 1978, 1984 by International Bible Society. Used by permission of Zondervan Publishing House. All rights reserved.

Cover design by Jennifer Ross
Layout by Rick Steele
Editing by Christy Andrepont, Jody El-Assadi, and Rick Steele

Printed in the United States of America
11 10 09 08 07 06 –EB– 10 9 8 7 6 5

This book is dedicated to

the eleven women

who were my Titus 2 women,
who shared their lives
and their wisdom
with me and allowed me
to tell their stories.

Acknowledgments

I first want to give praise to the Father who called me to be one of His own, and to His Son, the Word, whose life and teaching is the basis of all that is in this book. Then I want to thank the Holy Spirit whose work in me and in the many women who contributed ideas and truth to this study made the writing of this book possible. Beyond the eleven women to whom this book is dedicated, there are many more who have enriched my life and contributed to this study, both by their prayers and their insights. I especially want to thank Kim Felder and Alona Eastland, who believed I was on the right track from the beginning and encouraged me to persevere. Other women at Living Way Fellowship in Littleton, Colorado helped me in my early attempts to find Paul's meaning and related Scripture. When I moved to Seattle, the women at Green Lake Presbyterian picked up the baton and spent hours discussing and praying over the various sections of the book. Special thanks go to Shiree Harbick, Judy Bodmer, Barbara Goebel, and Jeanne Gray for editing and proofreading the manuscript. I loved going over it together. Thanks, too, goes to my pastors, Michael Kelly and Kevin Vanden Brink, and elder Ed Nudelman who gave me needed encouragement and spiritual covering. I am especially grateful for Dan Penwell, who believed I had something to say, and helped me say it better; and the same for my editors Rick Steele and Christy Andrepont.

Finally, I want to thank my family: my daughters, B.J. and Sara, for reading, critiquing, and even rewriting some of my words; their husbands, Dan and David, whose expertise with computers rescued me many times; my sons Dan and Nathan and Nathan's wife, Rami, for their support and prayers; my sister Rebecca and her husband David, my brother Terry and his wife Anna for giving comfort and encouragement in the hard times; my parents Al and Betty for sharing their home with me so I could focus on my writing; and my five grandchildren, Emma, Fin, Owen, Ione, and Liam, for bringing joy, love, and diversion to their doting Nana.

 BARBARA HENRY

About the Author

Barbara Henry received her B.A. in Education from Covenant College and her M.A. in biblical counseling from Colorado Christian University. She has been involved in women's ministries for over thirty years—leading and writing Bible studies for the local church and spiritual direction for individuals. Her passion for equipping others for ministry makes her a popular speaker in churches across America.

Barbara has four children and for the last ten years has served as a single parent. Both of her daughters are stay-at-home moms, and her sons are active in music ministry. Barbara is blessed with five beautiful grandchildren and hopes to have many more. For more on Barbara, check out her Web site at:

www.barbarahenry.org

About the Following God Series

Three authors and fellow ministers, Wayne Barber, Eddie Rasnake, and Rick Shepherd, teamed up in 1998 to write a character-based Bible study for AMG Publishers. Their collaboration developed into the title, *Life Principles from the Old Testament.* Since 1998, these same authors and AMG Publishers have produced four more character-based studies—each consisting of twelve lessons geared around a five-day study of a particular Bible personality. More studies of this type are in the works. New authors have recently been acquired, and new types of studies have been published in an ongoing effort to add fresh perspectives as to what it means to follow God. However, the interactive study format that readers have come to love remains constant in all of our newest titles. As new Bible studies are being planned, our focus remains the same: to provide excellent Bible study materials that point people to God's Word in ways that allow them to apply truths to their own lives. More information on this groundbreaking series can be found on the following web page:

www.amgpublishers.com

Preface

You are about to embark upon the study of the three most definitive verses in the Bible for women's ministry. In a letter to Titus, a pastor Paul is mentoring, he describes the ministry he envisions for the women of Titus' church. He begins by describing the kind of women who are to lead the ministry and then goes on to list the topics they need to address. As is true of all Scripture, these verses not only speak to Titus, but also to all of us. They are as relevant in our culture as they were in Paul's day. They are for the pastors like Titus who oversee women's ministry, for the older women who are wondering how they can help the women they are discipling, and for the younger women struggling with deep issues and not knowing where to turn.

The last phrase of Titus 2:5 gives us our reason to study and obey this mandate for women, *"that the word of God may not be dishonored."* We want to honor the Word of God. When older women deal with their sins of self-centeredness, gossip, silence, addictions, and busyness in order to become involved in the lives of younger women, they are honoring the Word of God. When younger women realize others have wisdom to share and humbly seek and submit to the training they offer, they honor the Word of God. As women study His words together and seek to obey them, they not only honor the Word of God, their lives will be greatly enriched.

Women today have fewer natural opportunities for connection and need to be more intentional in their efforts to get together and see this training accomplished. Our lifestyles often become too isolated, and cross-generational relationships are rare. The Holy Spirit has much to do in and through the Church to bring about *"the building up of itself in love"* (Ephesians 4:16). As we study together, He will reveal changes that need to be made both individually and corporately. I pray we will all be open to His work in us and follow where He leads us.

This book is designed to be used either as a Bible study guide or a mentoring guide. For those of you who have chosen it to be a guide for your weekly Bible study, it is a systematic way of working through all of the categories listed in Titus 2:3–5. If the study is conducted in a twelve-week format, it will at least introduce the topics and key Scripture passages that speak to those topics. If your group chooses to take longer, it will provide enough discussion material to keep them going for a full year or more.

As a mentoring guide, this book can serve as a resource for questions and verses to use in a Socratic method of training. In other words, when a younger woman asks a specific question or brings a situation to your attention, you can find in this manual other questions to give back to her which will help her find the answers she seeks. The Holy Spirit has identified and listed for us in these few short verses in Titus the key topics you, as a mentor, will be questioned about. The Word of God, as our only rule of faith and practice, supplies the answers. This relational approach to the text may not get to all the topics, but the desperate need for answers adds what we call "hunger sauce" to make what they receive more satisfying. If they aren't asking the questions, the answers may not seem pertinent to their lives.

If your mentoring relationship lasts several years, life will have a way of bringing up most of these topics. Under His sovereign direction, God will ordain situations that may eventually cover it all. God knows what women want and need to talk about. However, you, as a mentor, need to be familiar with each category and be able to recognize a topic when it surfaces. You may want to meet with a group of other women who are also mentoring younger women to discuss the topics and encourage one another in your mentoring ministry.

Counselors may also find specific sections helpful as homework assignments to give to their clients when one of these issues comes up in the counseling hour. The Scripture passages will provide verses for meditation and the questions will give food for thought and journaling.

Following Christ,

Barbara Henry

Table of Contents

How to Use This Study

1. **Don't do it alone.** This book is about building relationships where ministry can occur. If you read this study alone and never talk about it to anyone else, it has failed in its purpose.

2. **Let it be a starting point.** Focus more on the Scripture than my comments or the quotes. God will use this study to the degree we allow His Word to penetrate our lives. Look for other passages that address the topic—read and discuss them, too.

3. **Try to have access to a New American Standard Bible,** since most of the questions are based on the words used in that version. It will be helpful to use other versions as well, but the questions might be a little confusing when the wording is different.

4. **Some of the words Paul chose to use in these three verses are unique.** By that I mean that certain words that Paul uses are not found anywhere else in Scripture. That opens the door to differing translations and interpretations. Do your own word study and see where it takes you. There is room on the shelves for many more commentaries on this passage—preferably written by women.

5. **The application question sections at the end of each day's reading** (highlighted by the red "stop" signs) are meant to help you assimilate what you have studied and leave you with things to meditate on throughout your day. These questions are for personal use, to highlight what the Lord may be teaching you or convicting you about. Perhaps what you write in the short space provided may only reflect key ideas you develop more thoroughly in a journal.

6. **Mentors or discussion group leaders will find the Leader's Guidebook indispensable.** It includes:
   - ✓ a memory verse to help focus your mind
   - ✓ instructions for leaders so that they know what to do to fully prepare for each session
   - ✓ information on what leaders should expect in each session
   - ✓ the main point of each lesson
   - ✓ the main objective in each section
   - ✓ additional discussion questions for each passage (A good leader will not simply provide the answers, but ask questions that will guide the women to discover the answers for themselves.)
   - ✓ an "In Case They Ask" section providing additional comment on difficult questions

7. **If God highlights a certain topic in your life, explore it even more.** Make it a point to talk with others who have studied it more thoroughly. Read some of the books I quote and do additional study. Then let your director of women's ministries know you are willing to help others who may be struggling in that area.

Part One

Preparing for Ministry

1

Lifestyles of Older Women

She had no degrees, no training, no title, and no recognition from the church, but she was chosen by God to model for me what a Titus 2 woman looks like. An eighty-year-old widow, Lucille was weak in health but strong in the Spirit. Her quiet ministry to me would revolutionize my thinking about women's ministry.

Feeling inadequate to speak to our women's study group on the topic of prayer, I asked several friends, "Do you know anyone in our church who could teach us about prayer? Any prayer warriors here?"

"Lucille is the one you want!" they all said.

I wasted no time in contacting her and asked her to come and tell us what she had learned about prayer and intercession.

"Oh, honey, I don't think I could do that," she responded humbly.

But after some encouragement, Lucille accepted my invitation and so moved us by her thoughts that a visiting friend told me, "If I were you, I would put her in my back pocket."

Following my friend's advice, I asked Lucille if she would pray with me and for me on a regular basis. Thrilled by my request, she freely offered her time and gifts to me. At the time I had no

Lucille . . .

. . . a prayer partner

> *"Older women likewise are to **live priestly lifestyles,** not to be malicious gossips, nor should they have any addictions, but should be teachers of beauty, so that they can train the younger women to love husbands, to love children, to be of sound mind, to be pure, to be keepers of the home, to be good and to be submissive to their own husbands that the word of God may not be dishonored."*
>
> **Titus 2:3–5 (Author's Paraphrase)**

Lifestyles of Older Women

DAY ONE

Word Study

OLDER WOMEN

The term *"older women"* in Titus 2:3 is translated from one word in the Greek (*presbútis*). This is the only time *presbútis* is used in Scripture. *Presbútis* is the feminine form of *presbútēs*, which is found only three times in Scripture. Both forms of this word are related to the more common word, *presbúteros*, which is the title for the office of elder in the leadership of the church.[2]

---

idea I was on the brink of disaster, but God knew how much I would need Lucille. For two years we met once a week to pray. Her simple love of Jesus and her faith in His faithfulness carried me through the most painful years of my life. Weekly visits kept me focused on Christ. Her relationship with Him painted a picture of my own longing for Jesus and called me to the beauty and peace He desires me to enjoy. Lucille's prayers built a bridge for me to Christ, ushering me into a deeper and sweeter communion with Him.

Years later, on hearing my story of Lucille, a well-known counselor and author, Larry Crabb, commented to me, "I am sure she gave more help to you than I could have offered in that difficult time in your life." Dr. Crabb and I both understood in that moment that witnessing a life of passion for Christ, intimacy in prayer, and wholehearted trust in Him can change us far more than the best insight or understanding of people ever could.

Even before I began to study Titus 2:3–5, God gave me a picture of its fulfillment in the life and ministry of Lucille. Although she never talked about these particular verses, God's work in her life made her a model for me. The first verse in this passage describes the kind of women Titus is to find to minister in his church. Paul tells him they are to be *reverent in their behavior* (see Titus 2:3a). We will explore what he meant by that, but first we will grapple with the big question of which women are older.

BEING OLDER

No one wants to admit to being an older woman. For some reason old age is a degrading attribute in American culture. In Paul's day it was a place of wisdom and honor. Today we will look at other verses that contain the word *presbútēs* or *presbútis* in an effort to discern why Paul chose this particular word. If he meant to say "geriatric women" he would have used *gēráskō,* or if he was referring to being old in the sense of being worn out or obsolete, he would have chosen *palaios.*[1] I believe he chose this word carefully and with specific intent. It is my hope that upon completion of this study every woman reading these words will want to be an older woman.

📖 Read Titus 2:2. How does Paul describe older men? Does his description paint a positive or negative picture of being older?

_____

_____

_____

_____

_____

📖 Read Luke 15:25. How is the word *presbúteros* used in this verse?

_____

_____

_____

It is obvious this is a comparative use, not a reference to the brother's old age. He was simply older than his younger brother. In the same way Paul may not have meant to categorize women into certain age groups. I suggest we should realize there are women who are older than we are and women who are younger. Each woman should see herself as both older and younger. She should be a mentor to those who are younger while remaining willing to learn from those who are older. Women of all ages are necessary in the body of Christ to pass on what they have learned as well as to see themselves as students, eager to learn new things from others.

📖 Read Philemon1:1–2 and 9. Whom do you think Paul was claiming to be older than? How old do you think he was, and what is the basis for your guess?

_____

_____

_____

The common greeting at the beginning of the letter implies Paul is writing to a family. Philemon is presumed to be the husband of Apphia and the father of Archippus. Since Archippus is an adult (a fellow soldier) it is assumed that Philemon is older in years than Paul. Possibly for this reason, some translators choose the word "ambassador" for *presbútes* instead of the *"the aged."* It seems that Paul is placing himself in a position from which he can make an appeal to Philemon. It may be that in some way his maturity in Christ or position in the church gives Paul a place to advise him, even though Philemon may be older.

Chronological age should not be the only factor in defining the older/younger question, for spiritual maturity and life experiences have much to do with what we have to offer and how we relate. In many circumstances, a woman who is younger *chronologically* can be considered older *experientially*. For example, a member in my church recently lost a husband after fifty-six years of marriage. Her loss reminds me that it may be entirely appropriate for a relatively young woman who has been a widow for several years to take on the role of an "older woman" in aiding an elderly woman who is just now experiencing the trauma of widowhood. You will notice in the stories that introduce each chapter that some of the women are older, some younger, and some are my age, yet they were all my mentors and in that sense, older women. It all depends on what God has taught us and how willing we are to share with one another.

📖 Read 1 Timothy 5:1–2. How did Paul tell Timothy to relate to older women (*presbúteras*)?

_____

_____

In treating older women as mothers, Timothy may have looked up to them for guidance or help and certainly would have given them respect. Ideally, our mothers are the ones we go to with our questions.

Although we have made the point that we are all older women, it is also true there are seasons of life that allow more time and maturity for some older women to be more involved in ministry than others. The leader's guidebook contains extra resources for women who have the time for study and deeper

> *Each woman should see herself as both older and younger. She should be a mentor to those who are younger while remaining willing to learn from those who are older.*

Older women bring with them mileage and experience that will help them gain credibility with younger women.

research. Older women who have moved out of the child-rearing season and may be retired from the work force have more time and opportunity to dig into some of the more difficult questions. They also bring with them mileage and experience that will help them gain credibility with younger women.

📖 Read Galatians 4:19. Paul is taking on the metaphor of motherhood in this verse. What is his goal?

_____

_____

_____

Paul considered discipleship as intense as the labor we experience in childbirth. It is not something we do unintentionally. But like childbirth, each experience is different depending on many factors. This study guide is designed to be used in a variety of ways but the goal is always the same—to encourage and equip women to help other women grow to be like Christ.

🛑 APPLY Below are some application questions. As you progress through this study book, you will notice that each day's reading will conclude with an application section easily identified by the "APPLY" stop sign symbol. Most of these application sections contain several questions. Use these questions for meditation and reflection throughout your day. Ask the Holy Spirit to convict you of the things He wants to change in you and to teach you the truth He wants you to learn. Some questions will pertain to you; some will not. Don't feel you have to write responses to every question.

Are you bothered by the reality of getting older? Why or why not?

_____

_____

_____

_____

As an older woman, what do you have to offer to those who are younger than you?

_____

_____

_____

_____

As a younger woman, what are you looking for in an older woman?

_____

_____

_____

_____

_____

A COMPOSITE PRIESTHOOD

Since the Reformation, Protestant churches have taught the doctrine of "the priesthood of all believers." The reformers taught that, according to Scripture, all believers are priests, making the Roman Catholic tradition of penance and confession to a priest unnecessary. But, for some, this has led to an independent spirit that has no need for other believers—the pervading thought is, *Since we have Christ, we do not need another person to be our priest.* The situation has become just the opposite of what God intended. He wants everyone to be a priest, but we have ended up with no priests. He wants each of us to embrace the call of ministry to others, but we see our personal priesthood as reason to need no one else.

In his description of older women, Paul chose two unique words in Titus 2:3 that are translated *"reverent"* and *"behavior"* in the New American Standard Bible. The Greek words are *hieroprepēs* and *katestema,* and they are used to describe the kind of older woman who can train younger women. As you can see from the word study sidebar on the right side of this page, Paul is literally challenging us as women to live "priestly lifestyles." Today we will begin our study of the priesthood, looking at God's explicit instructions for ministry and the examples we find in the Old Testament priests and the New Testament believers. This study will help us understand how **we** can live priestly lifestyles.

Word Study

REVERENT BEHAVIOR

The Greek word, *hieroprepēs,* literally means "proper to priests."[3] It is a unique word in Scripture, formed by the combination of two common words: *hierós* and *prépō. Hierós* means "sacred character," and *prépō* means "to become suitable, proper fit or right."[4]

Katestema is also a unique word and not the usual Greek word used for "behavior." A literal translation would be "lifestyle," or as the New International Version translates it, *"the way they live."*

📖 Compare Genesis 12:3; Exodus 19:5–6; and Revelation 1:5–6; 5:9–10. What do the following phrases reveal about God's continuing plan and purpose for His special people: *"in you all the families of the earth will be blessed"; "you shall be to Me a kingdom of priests;"* and *"He made us to be a Kingdom, priests to our God"*?

_____

_____

_____

_____

_____

THOUGHTS ON THE PRIESTHOOD

"The beauty of the word [priest] is that by its actual derivation it makes clear that "priest" is an active idea, its history revealed in a word of positive and powerful purpose. The real meaning lies in the original definition—bridge builder.... priesthood was always meant to be something practical—to help us "cross over" or to "get from here to there."[5]

—JACK HAYFORD

📖 Read Leviticus 6:6–7 and Exodus 28:29. How were the Old Testament priests bridgebuilders?

_____

_____

_____

_____

The priests brought the guilt offerings of the people to the Lord and returned with God's forgiveness to the people. They also carried the names of the tribes of Israel into the Holy Place. When God calls His people a *"kingdom of priests"* (Exodus 19:6), He refers to His plan that together we carry His truth and light to the rest of the world. He wants to make us part of the bridge that will help others come to God.

> *"...you also, as living stones, are being built up as a spiritual house for a holy priesthood...."*
>
> **1 Peter 2:5a**

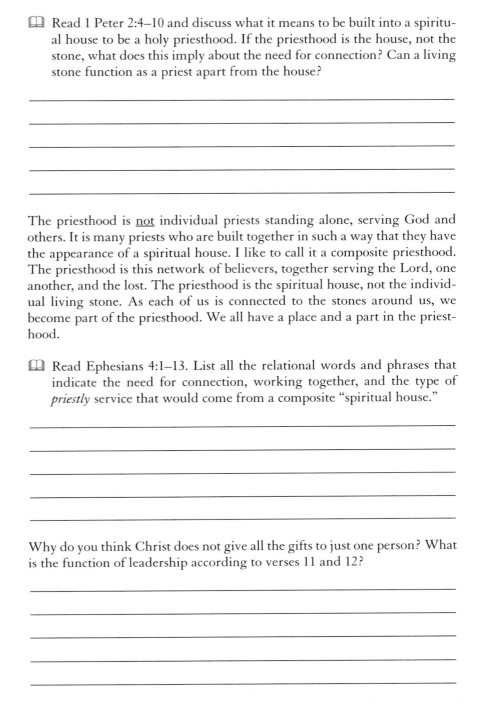

Read 1 Peter 2:4–10 and discuss what it means to be built into a spiritual house to be a holy priesthood. If the priesthood is the house, not the stone, what does this imply about the need for connection? Can a living stone function as a priest apart from the house?

_____

_____

_____

_____

_____

The priesthood is <u>not</u> individual priests standing alone, serving God and others. It is many priests who are built together in such a way that they have the appearance of a spiritual house. I like to call it a composite priesthood. The priesthood is this network of believers, together serving the Lord, one another, and the lost. The priesthood is the spiritual house, not the individual living stone. As each of us is connected to the stones around us, we become part of the priesthood. We all have a place and a part in the priesthood.

Read Ephesians 4:1–13. List all the relational words and phrases that indicate the need for connection, working together, and the type of *priestly* service that would come from a composite "spiritual house."

_____

_____

_____

_____

_____

Why do you think Christ does not give all the gifts to just one person? What is the function of leadership according to verses 11 and 12?

_____

_____

_____

_____

_____

Did You Know?
BODY LIFE

In 1972, Ray Stedman published the book, *Body Life*, which revolutionized many churches' understanding of lay ministry and the purpose of spiritual gifts. The passage in Ephesians 4 was a key to understanding that Christian life was to be lived as part of a body of believers—called to serve one another with the gifts Christ gave to each of us.

The comma after the word "saints" in the King James translation of Ephesians 4:12 is not in the original Greek. When the comma is added it makes the sentence into a list of three reasons why leaders in the church need gifts: so they can perfect the saints, do the work of the ministry, and edify the body. But when you take the comma out and change the word "perfect" to "equip" (as is done by most modern translations) it becomes a different paradigm. It now means that our teachers and pastors are to equip the saints to do the work of ministry rather than doing all the ministry themselves. This makes a huge difference in the way churches develop their ministry strategy.

Even though many churches have changed their overall strategy for ministry, sometimes their women's ministry programs are still patterned after the old understanding of Ephesians 4. If your women's ministry only consists of special events where a professional speaker (with gifts) comes to minister to your women and you have no plan to equip your women to minister to each other, you are essentially working under the old tradition. If so, it is time to make some changes.

Our ministry as priests is part of the work Christ is doing. He calls each one of us to fulfill our part. There are many women in your church who need what you have to offer. And, in order to become fully mature in Christ, you need what they have to offer. Each of us needs to be connected with more than just a few women. We get a taste of the importance God puts on relationships when we see how God the Father, God the Son, and God the Holy Spirit relate within the Trinity, and then how He calls the church to relate. Loving God and one another is what it is all about.

APPLY What do you see as "your part" in the body of Christ?

_____

_____

_____

_____

Does your church exemplify Peter's illustration of a spiritual house made of living stones?

_____

_____

_____

How effective is the leadership of your church in equipping the congregation to minister to one another and to those outside the church?

_____

_____

_____

_____

Word Study
MINISTER

"The church is people, equipped to serve, meeting needs everywhere in Jesus' name. . . . each believer is potentially capable of ministering just as surely as the pastor is. . . . [The role of leadership] is to teach everybody in the church how to minister."[6]

—JERRY COOK

MINISTRY TO THE LORD

Lifestyles of Older Women

DAY THREE

The first thing God told Moses concerning the priests was that their purpose was to *"minister as priests to Me."* The most effective ministry to other women begins with personal ministry to the Lord. Time spent in His presence prepares our hearts and minds to not only love Him more, but also to love others more. If our ministry flows from any lesser motive than the love of Christ, it will be of the flesh, and worthless in the sight of God. Fruit that lasts comes from intimacy with Christ and grows in an ongoing walk with Him. Whether older women act as friends, prayer partners, mentors, disciplers, teachers, or counselors, we can model our ministry to younger women by following the examples given in Scripture.

> ## "... they shall make holy garments for Aaron ... that he may minister as priest to Me."
>
> ### Exodus 28:4c

📖 Read Exodus 28:1–4. What do you think it means to minister to the Lord? Why did the priests' garments need to be holy? What can we learn from this?

_____

_____

_____

_____

_____

_____

Think of Aaron as a model who works for a great designer. His garments are produced according to exact specifications in order to reflect the genius of his employer. Verse 2 tells us his garments were to be _"made holy . . . for glory and for beauty."_ When we are dressed in Christ's righteousness, we reflect His glory and beauty. Just as Lucille's life was a picture of Christ's love and care for me, we can be models for the Lord, reflecting His glory and beauty as we minister to Him and to others.

📖 Read Hebrews 10:19–23. How did the priests of the Old Testament minister to the Lord in the Holy Place? (Exodus 40:22–28) What might these verses teach about the ministry of the New Testament priests?

_____

_____

_____

_____

_____

_____

A study of the Tabernacle is rich in symbolism, and Paul's reference to the Holy Place brings to mind the three pieces of furniture it contained and what the priests were to do each day. I would suggest keeping the oil in the lamp stand is symbolic of being continuously filled with the Holy Spirit; the bread on the table is symbolic of our daily need for Christ and His Word; and the altar of incense is a symbol of our daily prayers. Discuss this picture of our daily ministry to the Lord, or your own interpretation of the symbols.

> ## "Truly, truly, I say to you, he who believes in Me, the works that I do shall he do also."
>
> ### John 14:12

📖 Read Matthew 20:26–28. What are two of the ways Jesus carried out His priestly ministry mentioned here? What did He teach His disciples about ministry? What works do you think He was referring to in John 14:12?

_____

_____

_____

_____

_____

_____

As the High Priest, Christ offered His life as a sacrifice to ransom His people, and that is the part of a priestly ministry we cannot offer. But He also came to serve others, and this we can do. Our greatness in the kingdom is measured by how willing we are to serve others.

📖 Read Isaiah 61:1–3, 6. Jesus read this passage in a synagogue in Nazareth and revealed that He was a fulfillment of the prophecy (see Luke 4:18–21). Look for at least seven specific ways Jesus modeled the love of God. Do you think these are priestly duties?

_____

_____

_____

_____

_____

_____

_____

Although the prophecy in verse 6 is spoken to the Israelites, do you think it is also fulfilled in a sense when those in the Church are called "priests" (see Revelation 1:6 and 5:10)?

_____

_____

_____

📖 Read Matthew 25:40. What did Jesus teach about ministry to the Lord?

_____

_____

_____

_____

Jesus' warnings in this passage (Matthew 25:31–46) and the similar one in Matthew 7:21–23 clearly teach we minister to the Lord not so much by dramatic performance of miracles but by humble service to those in need. Christ's revelation of the surprise some will face on judgment day is a sobering thought.

APPLY Have you ever watched an older woman in worship or prayer and been drawn closer to God by the beauty of her example? If so, how did her example impact your walk with the Lord?

_____

_____

_____

_____

_____

_____

Put Yourself in Their Shoes
CAREGIVERS

Mother Teresa of Calcutta looked behind the eyes of the poor, the sick, and the needy, and said she saw the image of God. She learned to love God by loving others. . . . For caregivers, giving care isn't a chore but a form of worship. I've heard that Mother Teresa asked all prospective oblates, 'Does your work give you joy?' If the answer was 'No,' they didn't make it in.[7]

—GARY THOMAS

Jesus said—"For I have come down from heaven, not to do My own will, but the will of Him who sent Me" (John 6:38).

What does your ministry to the Lord consist of?

_____

_____

_____

_____

_____

How are you doing at loving your neighbor or serving the least of the brethren?

_____

_____

_____

_____

Have you ever been tempted to think "serving" was not your gift, so you could ignore any reference to this kind of ministry?

_____

_____

_____

_____

_____

How do you see yourself ministering to women who are younger than you are?

_____

_____

_____

_____

_____

Lifestyles of Older Women

DAY FOUR

INTERCESSION

The work of intercession is a primary means to live out the Titus 2 model of "lifestyles proper to priests." Intercession is building a bridge between God and those we love by praying for them. Interceding for one another not only strengthens the bond we have with one another, it brings the power and wisdom from above that we all desperately need. Andrew Murray wrote:

> *Of all the traits of a life like Christ's there is none higher and more glorious than conformity to Him in the work that now engages Him without ceasing in the Father's presence—His all-prevailing intercession. The more we abide in Him, and grow unto His likeness, will His priestly life work in us mightily, and our life become what His is, a life that ever pleads and prevails for men.*[8]

Over and over again the stories in Scripture illustrate the prominence and efficacy of prayer in the lives of the saints. This is most true in Christ's life. The stories are all models for us of the ministry of intercession. Some day our intercession will become a model for the women who are younger than we are.

📖 Read Isaiah 62:6–7. What can we learn from the ancient intercessors? What do you think they were watching for? How can we develop a lifestyle of watchfulness? What do these verses imply about the purpose of prayer?

_____

_____

_____

_____

_____

Although God's purpose in establishing prayer as part of His eternal plan is in part mysterious, this much is clear: He wants us to pray and intercede for others. For some reason He often waits to move until someone prays. He wants to be *reminded*. Because prayer is completely in the realm of faith it is a difficult task. We need all the help we can get. We need to be reminded as well. Reminders to pray are everywhere, if we look for them. Talk about how you can establish visual reminders for your prayer life.

📖 Read Exodus 30:7–8; Colossians 4:2; 1 Thessalonians 5:17; and Revelation 8:4. According to these verses, how often should we pray?

_____

_____

_____

_____

_____

📖 Read 1 John 5:14–15 and discuss how we can have confidence that our prayers will be heard and answered.

_____

_____

_____

_____

_____

We can have confidence that the prayers of Scripture are heard and answered because we know they are "according to His will," since they are inspired by His Spirit. Of course, there are no guarantees that a specific application is inspired, but we must trust that He hears our prayers and will answer them. Although God knows everything and can do anything, He still tells us to pray. We don't know why God set it up this way. We don't know why prayer was to be such a vital part of the priest's ministry. But, clearly, our part is to pray and to believe He will hear and answer. We must leave the "whys" and "wherefores" with Him.

Word Study
INTERCESSOR

An intercessor means one who is in such vital contact with God and with his fellow men that he is like a live wire closing the gap between the saving power of God and the sinful men who have been cut off from that power. An intercessor is the contacting link between the source of power (the life of the Lord Jesus Christ) and the objects needing that power and life.[9]

—HANNAH HURNARD

Did You Know?
PRAYING GOD'S WORD

Paul models intercession by including many of his prayers in the letters he wrote to the early churches. We can use the words and ideas of his prayers to structure our intercession for others. So, for example, I pray Ephesians 3:16–19 for the girl who needs to know the love of Christ, or Philippians 1:9–11 for a sister whose love is faltering, or Colossians 1:9–12 for a woman who is seeking God's will for something, and 2 Thessalonians 1:11–12 for all of you who are studying Titus 2.

How much time do you spend praying for others?

_____

_____

_____

_____

Have you ever promised to pray for someone and then realized later that you had completely forgotten? How did that make you feel?

_____

_____

_____

_____

_____

Have you tried keeping a prayer journal? If so, describe how it has helped.

_____

_____

_____

_____

_____

How might the following things remind you to pray: a stoplight; weeds in a garden; a child's toy; the breakfast dishes; the missionary's prayer card on the refrigerator; a homeless person; the evening news; a sleepless night; a verse in Scripture that brings a friend to mind?

_____

_____

_____

_____

Lifestyles of Older Women

DAY FIVE

SACRIFICE

Christ's sacrifice on the cross fulfilled all that is necessary for our atonement so there is no more need for the blood sacrifices the Old Testament priests offered. Christ's prophecy that the temple would be destroyed was fulfilled seventy years after His death and since that time the Hebrew people have not resumed the animal sacrifices. Yet, we are called to make some sacrifices in our lives—to lay down our selfish desires in order to take up the responsibilities we are given. Christ's clarion call to "take up our cross and follow Him" (see Mark 10:21) implies a measure of sacrifice. Today we will look at some of the ways we might need to sacrifice in order to be priests to one another.

📖 Read 1 Peter 2:5, 9, 12. What do you think the *"spiritual sacrifices"* are that the *"holy priesthood"* is to offer up?

_____

_____

_____

📖 Read Philippians 2:1–18. What kinds of sacrifices are implied by this call to humble service?

_____

_____

_____

Make a list of all of the words or phrases in this passage that would involve sacrifice.

_____

_____

_____

_____

_____

_____

In verse 17 Paul describes the type of sacrifice he was making as a priest for the Philippian believers. There is no doubt that his life was given that others would know Christ and grow in their faith. Paul promises that the joy he experienced in living that way was available for others who would do the same. I believe this is part of what Paul had in mind when he calls older women to be priests for younger women. The same promise of joy that Paul speaks of will be yours as a result of such sacrifice. The following quote by Oswald Chambers conveys Paul's vision and asks if we are ready to make the same kind of sacrifice Paul made:

> Are you ready to be poured out as an offering [as Paul was in Philippians 2:17]? Are you willing to sacrifice yourself for the work of another believer—to pour out your life sacrificially for the ministry and faith of others? Or do you say, "I am not willing to be poured out right now, and I don't want God to tell me how to serve Him. I want to choose the place of my own sacrifice."[10]
> — OSWALD CHAMBERS

📖 Read Romans 12:1–8. What is a living sacrifice? What kind of personal sacrifice does it take to recognize that you belong to all members of the body of Christ? What is the purpose of our spiritual gifts?

_____

_____

_____

_____

We often hear the first two verses of this passage quoted, but not always in the context of the verses that follow. A living sacrifice implies that our

A living sacrifice implies that our lifestyles should not be self-centered and comfort-oriented.

Being in community and offering ministry to others sometimes requires the sacrifice of our personal desires and agendas.

lifestyles should not be self-centered and comfort-oriented. Being in community and offering ministry to others sometimes requires the sacrifice of our personal desires and agendas. Think of examples of how others have sacrificed in order to minister to you. We need God's grace and transformation to enable us to break out of the world's mold of independence and self-sufficiency in order to become loving servants to one another.

APPLY What kind of sacrifice would it take for you to be a priest for another woman?

_____

_____

_____

_____

What women are you connected to in this type of relationship?

_____

_____

_____

Are you willing to sacrifice your own life so that the faith of others will grow? How do you respond to the questions posed by Oswald Chambers (see quotation on page 15)?

_____

_____

_____

_____

Have you ever experienced the kind of joy Paul refers to in Philippians 2:18? How has personal sacrifice led to an experience of joy for you?

_____

_____

_____

_____

Spend some time with the Lord right now in prayer.

 Heavenly Father, I praise You for your plan of salvation—not only for the complete work of Christ on my behalf, but also for making me a priest, that I can have a part in serving You and others. I praise You that You are sufficient in Yourself, yet You have chosen to love me, and to long for my love. Thank You for teaching me that though I am sometimes tempted to be self-sufficient, life is more abundant when I reach out to You and to others. Thank You for making Your church interdependent, for creating a composite priesthood, that can accomplish ministry only as we work together. Thank You for making me a living stone, and for placing me in the spiritual house of Your church. Help me, Lord, to find and do my part to serve You there.

Lord, I confess my self-centeredness. Please forgive me and make me more like You. I confess my prayerlessness also. Please forgive my independence and lack of concern for others. Too often, I forget how much I need You and forget my promises to others that I will pray for them. Please forgive my forgetfulness and help me remember. Teach me to pray without ceasing.

Lord, I pray for each woman doing this study with me. May You give them a Spirit of wisdom and revelation that they may know You better. I pray also that the eyes of their hearts be opened and enlightened to know the hope of their calling to be older women, the riches that are there for their enjoyment in the saints who are set as living stones all around them, and the power of Your mighty strength in them to accomplish all You have given to them to do.

Finally, I pray that You would protect me from the evil one. Uncover his lies and reveal his deception. May Your truth shine forth in my life, and may I be a light to all those around me as I reflect Your glory. Amen.

Write your own prayer or journal notation in the space provided below.

_____

_____

_____

_____

_____

_____

_____

_____

_____

_____

_____

_____

_____

_____

_____

_____

_____

_____

_____

_____

_____

_____

Notes

2

Earning Trust

I should have known she would not tell me about anyone else's sin or break any kind of confidentiality, even for a great illustration in a book. I had asked Ferne to think about her experiences on the mission field and try to remember a time when Satan used gossip to destroy a ministry. Rather than telling me about anyone else, she said, "There was a time early in my ministry when I spoke negative thoughts about another missionary. It was not unusual to grumble about those in charge, to complain about the decisions of the leaders, and to talk about all they said and did."

"Amazing," I thought, "I wonder how many stories she could have told me about others, but didn't!"

Ferne is one of those women everyone loves. She is so kind and gentle with never a harsh word and has an uncanny way of making others feel safe and secure. There is always a cup of tea ready whenever a woman needs to talk with her. The pace slows down and the warmth of her home and her smile invites openness and honesty. She is a woman of few words, but those words are filled with wisdom and kindness. She has friends all over the world who trust and confide in her. Her life as a missionary overseas has taken her into all kinds of circles—speaking with kings and beggars alike. People of all backgrounds feel great freedom to speak openly with her. God has used her in ministry all over the world because she knows the importance of confidentiality.

Ferne...

...a confidante

I asked Ferne why she thought women are singled out in this warning against slander and gossip. She said, "Maybe because we are naturally more verbal. Remember Proverbs 10:19 says, 'When words are many, sin is not absent, but he who holds his tongue is wise.'"

"How can we learn to hold our tongues?" I asked.

"The battle is in the mind. Rather than thinking negative things about a person, we need to think of ways we can build her up. We need the mind-set to edify not tear down. Colossians 4:6 tells us, *'Let your conversations be always full of grace, and seasoned with salt'* [NIV]. Sometimes we get the recipe mixed up so our conversations get full of salt and are only seasoned with grace."

Later I was talking to Donna, her daughter-in-law. "What is it like having Ferne for a mother-in-law? She seems so perfect." I said.

"If you are asking me to tell you anything negative about her, you will have to look elsewhere. She is the last person I would gossip about." She quipped. "Last year Ferne and I were in Nepal speaking at a women's leadership conference. The younger women of Nepal are forced to live with their mothers-in-law and many of them hate it. We were able to tell them about our relationship and explain how the love of Christ enables us to live together in harmony. The older women were lined up to speak with Ferne after the seminar wanting to know how they could win the love of their daughter-in-laws. I feel so blessed to have such a wonderful mother-in-law. How I wish to reciprocate that blessing to her and pass it on to the generation following me!"

Confidentiality

Without assurance of confidentiality there is no trust. Without trust there will be no Titus 2 ministry. Confidentiality is broken by gossip. Today we will look at one of the major sources of gossip. The Greek word *diabolos* is not always translated as "*slanderers*" or "*malicious gossips.*" It is more often translated as "*the devil.*" In essence, Satan is a slanderer. He is the one who is often behind the gossip that goes on in a church. As the accuser of the brethren, he uses other believers for his mouthpiece. By choosing the word *diabolos,* Paul emphasizes the importance of not letting Satan use us in this way. If we are going to develop a ministry that invites women to talk about serious topics, including their struggles and sin, we must have a strong commitment to be on guard at all times against the enemy's schemes to get us to gossip.

Read John 8:37–44 and Ephesians 6:11. What are some of the schemes of the devil and how do we stand against them?

_____

_____

_____

_____

_____

"Older women likewise are to live priestly lifestyles, **not to be malicious gossips,** nor should they have any addictions, but should be teachers of beauty, so that they can train the younger women to love husbands, to love children, to be of sound mind, to be pure, to be keepers of the home, to be good and to be submissive to their own husbands that the word of God may not be dishonored."

Titus 2:3–5 (AUTHOR'S PARAPHRASE)

The devil is a murderer and a liar, and he uses his "children" to do his dirty work. Although we are not his children, he can use believers to speak his lies when we are deceived by him. We must put on the armor of God in order to fight against being used.

📖 Read Revelation 12:7–11. What are the devil's major offenses according to these verses? How is he overcome?

_____

_____

_____

_____

Satan is all about deceiving—deceiving the whole world and accusing the brethren. At the end he will be thrown down, but for now we must do battle with him by wearing the armor of God, speaking the truth, and defending the brethren. He is overcome by the application of the blood of the Lamb to the sins of the saints. The gospel of forgiveness both in heaven and in the Church can overcome the destruction he plans.

📖 Read 1 John 1:5–10. Who walks in darkness? (To whom is John writing?) What do we say when we are in darkness (verse 8)? Who might be the source of that lie?

_____

_____

_____

_____

_____

_____

_____

Discuss the difference between secrecy and confidentiality. How does Satan use and confuse us with both gossip and secrecy?

_____

_____

_____

_____

_____

Part of walking in darkness is secrecy. The quote from Gary Collins in the side margin of this page was written for counselors but can easily be applied to older women in the church, as I have done in the brackets. Collins makes it clear that secrecy requires silence no matter what the circumstances. In some cases, confidentiality should be broken if the individual or the church will be helped by truth and light. Satan has confused many to think all sin must be kept in the dark. This enables him to isolate individuals in their sin and cut them off from the help they could have from the body of Christ. Both the extremes of gossip and secrecy must be avoided.

Word Study
SLANDERER

The Greek word, *diabolos*, in the context of our verse, would mean "given to finding fault with the demeanor and conduct of others, and spreading innuendos and criticisms in the church"[1]

Did You Know?
DIABOLOS

The word *diabolos* is translated as "the devil" thirty-five times in the New Testament, and is translated as "slanderer" only twice.

Word Study
SECRECY

Secrecy is the absolute promise to never reveal information to anyone, regardless of the circumstance. Confidentiality is the promise to hold information in trust and to share it with others only if this is in the best interest of the [younger woman] or sometimes in the interest of society [or the church.] On occasion the [older woman] needs to break confidence in order to take action that is likely to prevent violence [or other dangerous consequences].[2]

—GARY COLLINS

📖 Read Proverbs 10:17–21. How are both secrecy and slander addressed in these proverbs? Contrast the results of an open, honest women's ministry with one that lacks confidentiality.

_____

_____

_____

_____

_____

These proverbs contrast the righteous with the foolish, and touch on leadership, honesty, and confidentiality—all important factors in a Titus 2 ministry. An older woman with a _"righteous tongue"_ is as choice as silver—she can avoid both pitfalls of slander and secrecy as she deals openly and honestly with others. Satan will tempt her to gossip on one side and if he can't trip her up there, he will try to convince her she must say nothing at all. An effective Titus 2 ministry will walk the tight rope with great care to not fall off one side or the other.

APPLY Take some time for personal application. How has Satan tempted you to speak when you should be silent, and to be silent when you should speak?

_____

_____

_____

How can we know what to say and when to say it?

_____

_____

_____

What have been some consequences of gossip in your experience?

_____

_____

_____

Why is trust important to women's ministry at your church?

_____

_____

_____

Earning Trust

DAY TWO

OVERCOMING GOSSIP

The first step in overcoming gossip is to recognize the sins in us that cause us to gossip. We cannot just blame the devil. But gossip and its root sins are often hard to detect. We seldom plan to gossip or realize we are doing it until we look back at a conversation. We see it in others before we see it in ourselves. Sometimes our focus on others' sins is simply an effort to divert the searchlight from our own. The sins that lurk behind gossip are insidious and deep-rooted. They are the ones we don't want to see in ourselves, but get a strange satisfaction from identifying in others. But when we confess someone else's sin without her presence, no good can be accomplished—only pain and destruction. Gossip is a false concern for others. If we really cared, we would go to them and fight for them and do all that we could to help them to freedom and reconciliation.

📖 Read Leviticus 19:15–18. What eight sins do you find in this passage that can lead to gossip or slander?

_____

_____

_____

Discuss different ways each of these sins might lead to gossip. For example, an implied sin mentioned in verse 17 could be called failure to reprove or rebuke a guilty neighbor. The way we *"incur sin"* or share in her guilt is by avoiding a necessary conversation. In our fear of confrontation we allow hatred to grow in our hearts. Eventually, the unresolved conflict can leak out into gossip.

📖 Read James 4:11–12. How does gossip speak *"against the law and judge it"*? What parts of judicial law are ignored when we gossip (see Deuteronomy 19:15–19)? Where do you think our desire to judge others comes from?

_____

_____

_____

_____

These can be confusing verses, but they are helpful in understanding gossip, once we take them apart and look at each phrase carefully. God set up specific ways to deal with sin and spelled them out clearly, both in the Old Testament and in the New. When we don't follow His laws we are, in effect, judging them—saying we have a better way. The passage in Deuteronomy is referenced in Matthew 18:16. Both passages underline the importance of establishing the facts and hearing from people who know the truth before accusing or judging anyone. They both also look to God-ordained authority (priests, judges, or church leadership) to make the decisions regarding individual cases. When we gossip or make false accusations (usually because we don't know the whole story) we are sidestepping God's ways of *"purging the evil from among you."* Notice the severe punishment He gives to those who gossip. According to Deuteronomy 19:19 we face whatever punishment we feel the sinner deserves.

This passage implies the reason we are tempted to judge others. Gossip comes out of our desire to be God. Not only does it put us in the judgment seat, it also seems to move us closer to feigned omniscience. Gossip is inviting because we want to know it all, and be known as the one who knows it all, and the one to decide what is good and bad. Have you seen the bumper sticker that says, "I am doing God's work—judging others"? These verses

GOSSIP'S DESTRUCTIVE NATURE

Gossip is a dark way to gain a sense of control by crushing another's reputation with words.... Gossip repeatedly shows up in Scripture's lists of heinous sins (with adultery, murder, and theft) because it kills the heart of another human being.[3]

—SHARON HERSH

"If he has accused his brother falsely, then you shall do to him just as he had intended to do to his brother. Thus you shall purge the evil from among you."

Deuteronomy 19:18–19

make it clear that God is the only judge, and we need to leave judgment to Him and to those He has ordained to represent Him.

📖 Read James 3:14–16. How can jealousy and envy lead to gossip.

_____

_____

_____

_____

_____

Did You Know?
CHRONOLOGY OF PAUL'S SELF-IMAGE

Paul referred to himself as the _"least of the apostles"_ (I Corinthians 15:9) in approximately A.D. 55. Around A.D. 62, he called himself _"the least of all saints"_ (Ephesians 3:8), and, a year later as he sat in a prison cell in Rome, he saw himself as the "chief of sinners" (see I Timothy 1:15 KJV).

Christian maturity repents of pride and seeks humility. Rather than fearing insignificance, mature Christians embrace and glory in it. John the Baptist said about Christ, _"He must increase and I must decrease"_ (John 3:30). James, who could have boasted about being the brother of Christ, called himself His "bondslave." The progression of Paul's maturity went from seeing himself as _"the least of the apostles"_ (1 Corinthians 15:9) to the _"least of all saints"_ (Ephesians 3:8) to the chief of sinners (see 1 Timothy 1:15 KJV). Normally, when we compare ourselves to others we want to be the best and envy others when they seem better. Our flesh and the devil try to put them down by gossip. In contrast these three examples of Christian maturity fully understood their personal need of grace, and did not try to look better than others.

📖 Read Romans 1:28–29. What are some other sins that precede gossip?

_____

_____

_____

_____

Although this passage is speaking of agnostics or atheists, we can still see the progression of sins that lead to gossip. We are not filled with unrighteousness because we have been made righteous, but these sins can be occasional visitors to our souls. When we entertain such sins, we invite gossip in along with them.

📖 Read 2 Corinthians 12:20. What sins surround gossip in this verse?

_____

_____

_____

_____

The sins of pride, anger and fighting are always present in a church plagued by gossip. Jealousy is also common. How often we hear complaints about cliques or factions coming from those jealous of friendships they see in the body. Think about what needs to happen to foster a sense of belonging and loving compassion for every woman in your church.

Today we have studied various passages of Scripture that have identified many root sins which can lead to gossip. We need to be brutally honest with ourselves and recognize how often we fall in this area. As soon as we see our failure we must be quick to confess it and ask for forgiveness. A church filled with honest, repentant women will become a safe place to grow and mature in our Christianity.

APPLY What are the root sins in your heart that sometimes lead you to gossip?

_____

_____

_____

We often hear of gossip cloaked in prayer requests; what are some other devious ways you let things slip out?

_____

_____

_____

What do you envy in others that your gossip reveals?

_____

_____

_____

Why is the amount of gossip about a person usually proportional to that person's level of authority and impact?

_____

_____

_____

TAMING THE TONGUE

James warns in the first verse of Chapter 3 that not all of us should try to become teachers. I believe this applies to women who desire to train younger women. It speaks against the presumption that just because a woman is older she is prepared to be one of the "older women." We may have difficulty in finding trustworthy older women since the tongue is such a difficult thing to control. However, we should not see this as an excuse for some to disqualify themselves from the call of the Titus 2 mandate. We should see this as a principle that heightens the calling. We are not off the hook because we cannot control our tongues. I believe there is a universal call to **all** women to desire to be involved in ministry, and each of us should know that the pursuit of this calling involves a major struggle with our tongues and a great need for grace.

Make a list of all the warnings James gives about the tongue in 3:1–8. Do you think the end of verse 6 gives us an excuse for not controlling our tongues?

Earning Trust

DAY THREE

📖 *Doctrine*
THE POWER OF THE TONGUE

Words have power. We must set out to harness that power with a clear awareness that words can both tear down and build up. They are much like a sharp knife that in the hands of a surgeon can heal, but in the hands of a careless child can kill. *"Death and life are in the power of the tongue"* (Proverbs 18:21).[4]

—LARRY CRABB

_____

_____

_____

_____

_____

_____

The warning in verse 6, that the tongue is set on fire by hell, makes a clear statement that helps us see why we gossip. But rather than simply saying, "The devil made me do it," we need to see this as an area of spiritual warfare. As we saw earlier in this chapter, the Greek word for slander is also another name for Satan. Slander is what Satan is all about. We need to learn to expect his temptations, identify them for what they are, and seek God's grace and wisdom to resist them.

📖 Read James 3:9–13a. What do you think Paul is talking about in verses 9 and 10? What are the three questions he asks in 11–13?

_____

_____

_____

Paul is pointing out that it is unnatural for two opposites to come from the same source. He wants us to see if we have two kinds of water, or two types of produce in our lives. Then he goes on to answer his three questions in the verses that follow.

📖 Read James 3:13–18. How do these verses answer the questions asked in verses 11–13? What two kinds of wisdom can cause a Christian to produce two types of fruit? How does this lead to two kinds of water coming from our mouths?

_____

_____

_____

_____

James explains that there are two kinds of wisdom and implies that a Christian can choose to act and speak from either one. If we find that our tongue is stumbling, that it has been set aflame and is full of deadly poison, we must identify the bitter jealousy and selfish ambition that is in our hearts. He also mentions arrogance and lies that come from our evil human nature as well as from Satan.

As we seek to identify the older women in our midst who can minister to the younger women, it is very important that we look closely at how they use their tongues. While Titus 2 simply says that the older women should not be slanderers, James 3:17 lists the positive attributes of a woman who allows the "_clean water_" of God's wisdom to flow through her. Attributes like purity, gentleness, and reasonableness are antonyms of the attributes that lead to gossip. We can

> ### "Does a fountain send out . . . both fresh and bitter water? Can a fig tree produce olives? Who among you is wise?"
>
> ### James 3:11–13

best avoid gossip by allowing the Holy Spirit to produce this kind of fruit in our lives. Take time to reflect on the application questions below.

APPLY Even though James says *"these things ought not to be this way"* (3:10), have you experienced both blessing and cursing coming from your mouth?

_____

_____

_____

_____

What can you do to limit the flow of earthly, demonic wisdom and to increase the reception of wisdom from above?

_____

_____

_____

_____

Do *"purity, gentleness, and reasonableness"* describe the kind of fruit God is producing in you?

_____

_____

_____

_____

Do others describe you as "full of mercy and good fruits, unwavering and without hypocrisy"?

_____

_____

PEACEMAKING

Earning Trust

DAY FOUR

Peacemaking is a bold concept that needs further exploration. How do we become peacemakers? Peacemakers are the last in the list of beatitudes in Christ's "Sermon on the Mount." If the beatitudes progressively build on one another, we need to cultivate all the preceding qualities in order to become peacemakers. We must first recognize our spiritual poverty and know that we need God's grace to enable us to make peace. Then we mourn our sin, recognizing our own guilt before attempting to deal with someone else's sin. We hunger and thirst for righteousness, truly longing for justice and truth in every situation. We need meekness and gentleness in order to help others; then we are able to extend mercy to all involved. Our hearts must be purified and able to identify Satan's lies and our own self-deceit. Then, finally, we are ready to be peacemakers.

"The seed whose fruit is righteousness is sown in peace by those who make peace."

James 3:18

Read James 3:18. Discuss what you think the *seed* is, what the *fruit* is, and who the *sowers* are. What does this verse have to do with gossip?

_____

_____

_____

_____

_____

Read James 1:19. Why is this an important verse for peacemakers?

_____

_____

_____

_____

A peacemaker knows that in order to heal relationships there must be communication that is not fueled by anger.

A peacemaker knows that in order to heal relationships there must be communication that is not fueled by anger. Usually, the communication should be between the parties involved and no one else, unless a third person acts as peacemaker. The problem is, most of us will talk to other people rather than the one with whom we have the problem. We think we need another perspective or confirmation that we are "in the right." But, be careful at this point that the talking does not lead to gossip. If you happen to be a third person with whom someone chooses to talk about a particular person or conflict, rather than hearing their story and receiving it as gossip, consider the possibility that God has chosen you to be a peacemaker in the situation.

Compare Matthew 5:23–24 and Matthew 18:15 (NIV). When is it your responsibility to "go" to the other person?

❐ if I offended them
❐ if they offended me
❐ both

A peacemaker knows and believes that it is always *our* responsibility to go to the other person. This is true whether we have sinned against someone or someone has sinned against us. There is really no other choice but to **"go."** Waiting for others to come to us is not an option. Talking about it to someone else is gossip. Jesus said in Matthew 5:23–24 that if you remember someone has something against you, even if you are in the middle of worship, reconciliation precedes worship. He said, "**go** *your way—first be reconciled to your brother* [or sister]" (emphasis added) and then come back and finish worshiping. If we really took His words seriously, I wonder how many of us would be in church on any given Sunday. But there is more. It is not just when we have made someone else angry that we must **"go."** Jesus said in Matthew 18:15, "*If your brother* [or sister] *sins against you,* **go** *and show him his fault, just between the two of you*" (NIV [emphasis added]).

If someone tells you about a conflict she is having with someone else, what should you do:

❐ send her to that person
❐ "go" with her as a peacemaker
❐ tell someone else

As peacemakers, we must be quick to **go** when any conflict surfaces in our own lives, but also we facilitate the **go** when we hear of conflicts among others. We are the coaches who encourage and prepare the younger woman to speak to the person she has offended or who has offended her. We may need to **go** with her in order to help uncover the truth, encourage confession and forgiveness, and see that a complete reconciliation and restoration is accomplished. There is seldom a good reason or excuse for choice (c) unless we are carefully following the Matthew 18 principle.

Peacemakers use their tongues to bless, heal, and restore rather than to curse, hurt, and destroy. Many of the bridges we need to build require some work of preparation. At times we must remove the rubble and clear the way. Hebrews 12:15 warns us to "*see that no root of bitterness springing up causes trouble.*" Often bitterness comes from hurtful words that have been said or silence that has not been broken. Without peacemakers, many will "*be defiled*" and a Titus 2 ministry will not last long.

For those interested in learning more about it, Ken Sande has written an excellent book entitled *Peacemakers* (Grand Rapids, MI: Baker Books, 1991). In it he covers all the scriptural passages that describe for us what a peacemaker is and does. This would be an excellent resource for those who aspire to be Titus 2 women. However, as you will see in the quote below, Sande does not believe in a "peace at all costs" philosopy:

> Not all conflict is bad! Since God has created us as unique individuals, human beings will often have different opinions, convictions, desires, perspectives, and priorities. Many of these differences are not inherently right or wrong; they are simply the result of God-given diversity and personal preferences. When handled properly, disagreements in these areas can stimulate productive dialogue, encourage creativity, promote helpful change, and generally make life more interesting. Therefore, although we should seek **unity** in our relationships, we should not demand **uniformity**.[5]

APPLY   Is there unresolved conflict in your life today?

_____

To whom do you need to "go"?

_____

_____

What keeps you from "going"?

_____

_____

What would it take for you to become a peacemaker?

_____

_____

Where are you in the progression of the beatitudes?

_____

_____

_____

THE MATTHEW 18 PRINCIPLE

Galatians 6:1 tells *"those who are spiritual"* (the older women) to gently restore someone caught in a sin. Jesus taught us exactly how to do that in Matthew 18:15–17. These verses are occasionally used in serious cases of church discipline, but should be used on a regular basis, whenever we seek to help someone deal with her sin. In most cases the first step of just talking with her is all that is necessary. But too often we resort to the world's system and gossip rather than taking this biblical approach. Even though it is hard to confront someone we love because we fear rejection, Jesus gives no room for hiding from confrontation. His words are clear and should be applied to every situation of conflict or sin.

📖 Read Matthew 18:15–17. Review each step and think of various examples of what each step might look like in any given situation.

(Step 1) Why does Satan work so hard to keep us from taking the first step? Who is the only One we should talk to before going? How can finding out someone's true intentions clear up misunderstanding?

_____

_____

_____

_____

_____

(Step 2) Why are reinforcements necessary for this step? What are some possible advantages of having someone else involved when we get to this point? How might this be a safeguard from gossip and the isolation of silence?

_____

_____

_____

_____

(Step 3) Notice this step is reserved for hardened refusal to repent or total inability to recognize sin. Do you think "the church" is the whole church or just the leadership? Who should decide when the whole church should know? Do we tell the church so everyone can judge the person or so that the warfare against the sin can be taken to a new level? Is the goal still to see the person freed from the bondage of their sin? Why would the prayers of all the saints be needed?

_____

_____

_____

_____

> *"If your brother sins, go and reprove him in private . . . . If he does not listen to you, take one or two more with you. . . . If he refuses to listen to them, tell it to the church . . . . If he refuses to listen even to the church, let him be to you as a Gentile."*
>
> *Matthew 18:15–17*

(Step 4) How is the goal changed in this step? If it is not restoration, then what is it? Why does she need to be approached as an unsaved person? Again, this does not open the door to judgment or slander but simply changes the way we pray for and reach out to her.

_____

_____

_____

_____

📖 Read Ezekiel 3:17–21. In what ways could we be considered "watchwomen"? What happens when we fail to give warning to those who are acting wickedly?

_____

_____

_____

_____

Our calling to be "priests" to younger women requires that we give warning about the dangers of allowing sin to go unchecked in their lives. Our calling to be "confidential" requires that we be very careful not to say anything to anyone else about the sin or failures of those we are trying to help.

If you want to see a vital women's ministry developed in your church, one of the first things to address is how you are going to contain gossip. According to Titus 2:3, a chosen older woman cannot be a gossip, or the ministry will be destroyed even before it gets started. A younger woman will never open up to an older woman if the older woman has not earned the younger's trust. We must all be aware of Satan's schemes and surrender our tongues to the Holy Spirit. If we practice peacemaking skills and the Matthew 18 principle in our daily connections, the relationships we establish will have a better chance of being effectual in Christ's kingdom.

APPLY What specific situations has the Spirit brought to your mind as you have studied this lesson?

_____

_____

_____

How can you apply the Matthew 18 principle to someone who gossips with you?

_____

_____

_____

Have you ever seen the Matthew 18 principle practiced regularly?

_____

_____

_____

If all the women in a church agree that conversation about another woman's sin never takes place without her presence, much of the temptation to gossip could be avoided. In this way the focus is kept on restoration rather than judgment, because her presence reminds us of our real purpose.

What could you do to see it used more in your life? In your church?

_____

_____

_____

_____

Spend some time with the Lord in prayer.

Heavenly Father, I praise You for Your mighty power that is far greater than any other power in the universe. Praise You that Your truth is far brighter than the darkness Satan tries to spread over the earth. I give You honor and glory for Your excellence and majesty. I stand in awe of Your infinite beauty and grace. Thank You that Your grace is greater than all my sin.

I confess my tongue is unruly and loves to gossip. Father, please forgive me and so fill me with Your truth and grace, that I may speak more loving and kind words. I confess my envy of others, my judgmentalism, and my pride. Lord, please continue to reveal to me the heinousness of these sins, and give me a heart that longs to be totally cleansed of them all.

Lord, I pray for my sisters and ask that You would enable us all to be peacemakers. Would You, by Your grace, sow in each of us the seed whose fruit is righteousness that we might make peace in all our relationships and in all our homes. May we use our tongues to bless, heal, and restore, rather than to curse, hurt, and destroy. Help us to be quick to listen, slow to speak, and slow to get angry. And may we be the kind of women who can gently restore those who are caught in sin.

Father, I pray you would help us all be more aware of the schemes of the devil. May we be quick to see his temptations for what they are, and have the grace to flee from them. Deliver us, too, from the evil of our own flesh. Give us hearts of repentance, that long more and more to be like Christ. In His name we pray, Amen.

Write your own prayer or journal entry in the space below.

_____

_____

_____

_____

_____

_____

_____

_____

_____

_____

_____

_____

Notes

Notes

3

Overcoming Addictions

Leigh hadn't intended to call me that Easter Sunday, but when I answered my parent's phone it was the beginning of a journey with my niece that would show me how God restores life to His children. Even though she is younger than I, the Lord used her as an "older woman" to teach me about addictions. Sadly, she had to learn what she knew the hard way. Although she did not admit it in that first phone conversation, she was, at the time, fighting an addiction to cocaine that left her homeless, deep in debt, guilty of abandoning her son and destroying her relationship with her parents. I will be forever grateful that the Lord allowed me to watch His sovereign work in her life, and to see Him change her from a hopeless addict to a Titus 2 woman.

During her childhood, Christian parents and friends in her church laid for her a foundation of faith, but, in her teen years and through her twenties, she wandered away from the Lord in her desire for acceptance from her peers. Her rebellion led to misery and more need of escape. She used television, movies, books and food to help her avoid the mounting problems. As she became more and more addicted to a lifestyle of escape, she used parties, drinking, sex, and drugs to hide from the realities of life. Her decision to move to Seattle was probably just one more attempt at escape. She hoped that distance from influential friends, a new environment, support from Narcotics Anonymous meetings and some effort on her part might lead to a new life.

Leigh...

...a captive set free

The Lord knew, however, that change of environment and behavior was not enough. Several months after she had moved in with me and landed an enviable job at the Space Needle, I left town for a visit with my grandchildren. I returned two weeks later to discover that Leigh had been missing for three days and that she had stolen my mother's credit card. A call to her boss revealed an old boyfriend had arrived in town, and she was last seen leaving with him and had not returned to work or called since then. We decided we had to call the police.

In his first visit to our home, Officer Hanson explained, "We don't have the time or manpower to go out looking for her, so you will need to wait for Leigh to surface. If she comes around, try to act natural, so she doesn't bolt, but call me immediately."

We began to pray, and after several hours Leigh called to see if she could come by and pick up some clean clothes. When we saw her driving up, my sister-in-law ran next door to call the police, leaving me and my sister to try to detain her long enough for them to get there. While Leigh was making up lies to cover up what had happened, my sister-in-law was trying to remember the officer's name. Meanwhile, my sister-in-law's two-year-old nephew was sitting in his high-chair singing a little song about Officer Hanson. When she reached him, he was just getting off-duty and was free to come immediately. Leigh was shocked to see two policemen walking through our dining room, and we left her with them to join our sister-in-law for an intense prayer meeting.

By God's grace, the officer was a Christian and was able to lead Leigh to confession of the truth. Her boyfriend had broken parole in leaving his home state and was forced to return without seeing Leigh again. She was given the choice of going to jail or voluntarily submitting to the discipline of the church and her family. In the years following her experience of confession and brokenness, she has made Christian friends and has been discipled by older women. She paid all of her debts, is now reunited with her son and her parents, and, most importantly, she has reestablished a connection with God. The path has not been easy or free of pain. Yet, her heart longs to be in a place where she can minister to other hurting women who are in bondage to their addictions, so they can know the freedom she has experienced.

IDOLATRY

In the next phrase of our Titus 2 passage, *"nor enslaved to much wine,"* the important word on which we should focus our attention is "enslaved" (*doulóō*)—not "wine." Paul is not saying wine is evil, or that every would-be mentor must never drink any wine. Wine is not the problem; it is just an agent. Alcohol, which has held people in bondage since the beginnings of civilization, was the first addiction to be identified as such. But we know today there are many other agents of addiction. The pattern is the same no matter what a person uses to try to escape the realities of life.

The essence of any addiction is idolatry. Addictions begin when we seek relief from the trials of life by looking to some other god to meet our needs. We may not consciously think of whatever we turn to as a god, but because

Overcoming Addictions

DAY ONE

Word Study
ADDICTION

The Greek word *doulóō* means "to make a slave of, to bring . . . to be brought under . . . to be held in bondage . . . [rather than] obedience to God."[1] In today's study, we will look at how addictions can enslave us.

we are refusing to go to God or to wait on Him, we begin to look to the counterfeit as our refuge. Eventually the patterns of our behavior become so ingrained they become bondage. As the bondage grows, little by little, we become more and more slaves of the false god and less able to serve and obey the true God. The counterfeit pleasure and satisfaction the idol gives steal from us the true joy God offers. This joy comes from a deeply fulfilling relationship with Him and ministry for Him. The reality is—those who are addicted do not have the time, energy or freedom to minister to other women, which is one obvious reason they are excluded from ministry.

📖 Read Exodus 20:3–6 and Matthew 6:24. Why is it impossible to love God while we are serving our idols? What is worship according to these verses?

_____

_____

_____

_____

Worship, according to verse 6, is loving God and keeping His commandments. We show our love in praise and the acknowledgment of all He is, and we worship Him by serving and obeying Him. This particular commandment and Jesus' words in Matthew 6 make it clear we cannot worship Him and our idols. They are mutually exclusive.

Think about the different attributes of God and how our worship is defined by our response to and acknowledgment of those attributes. For example: God is trustworthy, so our worship is our trust; God is loving, so our worship is receiving that love; God is wise, so we worship by seeking His wisdom and living by it; God is forgiving, so we worship by repentance and confession. Have a brainstorming session that not only comes up with all the attributes and ways we worship that you can think of, but also how idolatry keeps us from that worship. An example of that would be: God is compassionate; we worship by going to Him for comfort, but when we choose to find our comfort in food, we are worshiping a false god.

Why do we make idols for ourselves? Why are tangible gods easier to worship? How do Satan's counterfeits lure us away from the worship and service of God?

_____

_____

_____

_____

_____

📖 Read 1 Corinthians 10:6–14. Notice how this passage is framed by warnings about idolatry. These warnings tell us the entire passage is dealing with idols. Identify the six idols Israel struggled with and compare them to addictions common in our culture. The first one is done for you. (You may need to refer to Numbers 21:4 to give a name to the fifth one.)

"Older women likewise are to live priestly lifestyles, not to be malicious gossips, **nor should they have any addictions,** but should be teachers of beauty, so that they can train the younger women to love husbands, to love children, to be of sound mind, to be pure, to be keepers of the home, to be good and to be submissive to their own husbands that the word of God may not be dishonored."

Titus 2:3–5 (AUTHOR'S PARAPHRASE)

1 <u>Eating</u> : <u>overeating, anorexia, bulimia, chocolate, etc.</u>

2 _____

3 _____

4 _____

5 _____

6 _____

Read verses 11–14 again. How do we flee from idolatry?

_____
_____
_____
_____

Did You Know?
IDENTIFYING IDOLATRY

In I Corinthians 10:6–14, Paul uses a Greek literary form called a *chiastic perikopé*. This is similar to our use of parentheses, where brackets hold a thought together. You can also think of it as a heading that identifies the topic of a section. The Greeks would have recognized the *parichopy*—starting and ending the passage with the same warning—and they would have understood that everything sandwiched between the warnings dealt with the same subject (i.e., idolatry).

The Church has made the mistake in the past of believing that fleeing means having nothing to do with any of these pleasures. Such an interpretation is certainly an overreaction and can't reflect what Paul had in mind, for there are many passages in Scripture that teach us that God gives us the pleasures of life to enjoy. We are not told to flee from pleasure, but to flee from idolatry. All of us must identify for ourselves when we have crossed the line into dependency and then find the way of escape that God will provide. The woman who is "fleeing" acknowledges her struggle and seeks God's grace. She is no longer in bondage, but is on the road to freedom. Being on the road to freedom may be as good as it gets this side of heaven! The woman who is honest about her addictions will be far more effective in ministry than one who pretends she has no addictions or denies in her heart that she is an idolater.

📖 Read Ezekiel 11:18-21 and Luke 15:16-19. Compare these two passages and list the steps that are needed to overcome addictions and know your identity as part of God's family.

_____
_____
_____
_____

All of us need to see our addictions as idolatry and realize how they keep us from full enjoyment and participation in worship and service in our own community of believers. Throughout this chapter we will seek to identify not only the possible idols that abound, but also the Scriptural paths to freedom. The verses above indicate we will need both intervention by God and soul searching and humility on our part.

APPLY What are the idols in your life?

_____
_____

How do they get in the way of worship and ministry?

_____

_____

_____

What do they offer you?

_____

_____

How can you flee from them?

_____

_____

_____

MIND BATTLES

O nce we have identified our addictions and begun to hate how they keep us from obedience to God's will, we need to do battle in our minds. This is done by identifying the lies the enemy has told us and replacing them with the truth of God's Word. It will also be important to understand the difference between the provisions God makes and the responsibilities He gives to us. Too often, we get confused and overwhelmed because we are trying to do what God has already done or promises to do for us. We want to do it ourselves, but the very nature of the beast—a stronghold—makes this impossible.

📖 Read Romans 6:5–23. Make one list of all the verbs used to describe what God has done or promises to do for us, and a second list of the verbs that describe our part.

_____ _____

_____ _____

_____ _____

_____ _____

_____ _____

_____ _____

What does the phrase *"made us obedient"* imply in verse 17? Does this phrase put our obedience under our part or God's?

_____

_____

It is not a matter of trying hard to change our behavior; it is one of believing that Christ's grace can change us through our union with Him.

Is what He requires from us something we do or something we believe? Why is the battle in our minds?

_____

_____

_____

_____

Choice is the key word. We are tempted to think of words like "struggle," "effort," "perseverance," and "self-denial" when we reflect on what it means to overcome sin. But Paul says, "No"—it is simply a matter of choosing to believe that Christ has already done the hard work of gaining victory for us. It is through faith that we claim the victory as our own. We choose to see ourselves as under the control of grace rather than under the control of sin. It is a choice of whom we worship and serve. We can let sin and idols reign, or we can let God reign. The battle is in the mind because it is there that we make our choices. When we choose to let sin reign, we become slaves to sin. When we choose to see ourselves under grace we are made slaves of righteousness. When we don't make these intentional choices, our default settings take us back under the control of our idols.

📖 Read Psalm 62:1, 5, 8 in the New American Standard Bible. Why is it so hard to wait *"in silence for God only"*? What does the word "only" rule out for you?

_____

_____

_____

_____

📖 Why do you think God makes us wait? Also read Deuteronomy 13:1–4 to assist in finding an answer to this question.

_____

_____

_____

_____

BENEFITS OF WAITING

An unwillingness to wait will inevitably lead to addictions and other destructive behavior . . . . Waiting keeps me from hurrying into the next moment, so I don't have to stay in this one. . . . Waiting cultivates aching hope.[2]

—SHARON HERSH

God is after our hearts. He created us for love. David, like the rest of us, is trying to deal with all the disappointments of life and the difficulty of living with other sinners. He keeps coming back to his only real hope—God. God allows our trials to cause us to come back to Him.

How did David deal with waiting according to Psalm 62? What has to happen in our minds to convince us to wait?

_____

_____

_____

_____

David preaches to himself, telling his soul to wait. He pours out his heart before God. He reminds himself of God's power and love. He contrasts his other options and finds trust in God to be the best way. We need to do the same kind of battle in our minds. This will create in us a need to find and use the weapons God has provided for the battle.

APPLY Are you prone to trying too hard to overcome your addictions, or have you learned to rest in Christ's work?

_____

_____

_____

How can you consider yourself dead to sin when you know the sin is still within you?

_____

_____

_____

Are you tempted to think that Romans 6 is merely a mind game?

_____

_____

Is waiting difficult for you?

_____

_____

_____

Where are you today: trying to do what God has done? unwilling to wait? preaching to yourself? battling in your mind? waiting with hope? resting in His promises?

_____

_____

_____

_____

Are you eager to find out what weapons God has given to help in this battle?

_____

WEAPONS THAT DESTROY STRONGHOLDS

Overcoming Addictions
DAY THREE

Scripture refers to addictions as "strongholds." It uses the language of warfare and talks about the weapons we need for the battle that goes on in our minds. In our search for these weapons, we can ask the Holy Spirit to reveal them to us and depend on His strength and wisdom to use them effectively. We are fighting a spiritual battle, and we need to use divine power, divine wisdom, and divine timing to implement our battle strategy.

📖 Read 2 Corinthians 10:3–6. Paul refers to weapons in these verses but does not identify any of them. What can we learn about the warfare apart from naming weapons? What do you think he means by *"taking thoughts captive"*?

_____

_____

_____

_____

The fact that the weapons are "not of the flesh" emphasizes our inability to deal with our addictions on our own.

The fact that the weapons are *"not of the flesh"* emphasizes our inability to deal with our addictions on our own. The warfare is primarily in our minds where *"speculations," "knowledge,"* and *"thoughts"* take place (see 2 Corinthians 10:5). If we would be free from the strongholds of our addictions we must first deal with faulty thinking. Taking every thought captive to the obedience of Christ requires the pursuit of truth and obedience. It would be well worth our time to try to imagine what this would look like in practical living as well as in spiritual warfare.

What responsibility of leaders is implied by Paul's statement that *he* is *"ready to punish all disobedience"*?

_____

_____

_____

This passage implies that some of us have responsibility for others. Paul says he is ready to punish all disobedience, and he can't be referring to self-discipline, because he clearly says *"your obedience."* Like Paul, our goal should be to help younger women to "complete" their obedience. Because Paul does not describe the punishment, we cannot be sure what he means. Too often, we think of punishment in terms of parents grounding their children, vigilantes inflicting bodily harm, or judges handing down prison sentences, but I think what Paul had in mind may be similar to the accountability we offer to one another. The important thing to notice is Paul's readiness to be involved.

Natural consequences of addictions usually develop much later in time and are sometimes irreversible. If we can use punishment to "raise the bottom," it won't take so long for us to hit bottom. If we initiate some kind of accountability or punishment for ourselves (and others) for addictive behaviors, we can better ensure we experience negative consequences and not just the short-term positive reinforcement many of our addictions offer. Any kind of negative consequences for addictive behaviors is a helpful incentive to seek God's weapons and power to destroy the strongholds.

📖 Read Ephesians 6:10–18. What is the one offensive weapon God gives with our armor? How did Jesus use it in the wilderness (Matthew 4:1–11)? What parts do the Holy Spirit and prayer have in the battle?

_____

_____

_____

_____

The pieces of armor listed in verses 14–17 are all defensive; they protect us from the attacks of the enemy. Notice they only protect our front, so we need to "stand firm" facing him. But the one weapon that can do him harm is "the sword of the Spirit," and we are told that is "the word of God." Verse 18 adds "with all prayer." We need to use the Word of God against the lies of the enemy, to depend on the Holy Spirit to enable us to wield that sword, and to know the power of prayer. Think of times you have experienced victories by following Christ's example as He was tempted by Satan in the wilderness. Obviously, Christ knew Scripture and could quote it from memory. Memorizing verses of Scripture is one way to take up the sword.

📖 Read James 4:6–10. How might poverty of spirit and humility be used as spiritual weapons? How does true mourning of sins overcome some of Satan's lies?

_____

_____

_____

When we give up on our own ability to accomplish victory, we are ready to look to God's provision. As long as we are depending on our own abilities we cannot receive grace. Submission is impossible when we rely on ourselves, and we become sitting ducks for the enemy. But when we see our sin, our need, and our misery, we are in a place where God can meet us, deliver us, and exalt us.

APPLY How effective have you found the weapons God provides in your own battle against the idols in your life?

_____

_____

_____

Have you come to a place of true repentance and deep mourning over time and opportunity lost because of your service to false gods?

_____

_____

_____

Have you experienced the kind of suffering God allows in order to help us identify our idols?

_____

_____

_____

Are you willing to face the sacrifice it will take to do battle?

_____

_____

Reread the quote by Mrs. Cowman (side margin of this page) and ask yourself how you measure your life.

"Measure thy life by loss and not by gain, not by the wine drunk, but by the wine poured forth. For love's strength standeth in love's sacrifice and he who suffers most has most to give."[3]

—Mrs. Charles Cowman

ATTITUDES THAT LEAD TO FREEDOM

In this section, we will study the Beatitudes as they apply to our struggle against addictions. Millions of people have been helped to freedom by working through the "Twelve Steps" of Alcoholics Anonymous. I believe their effectiveness stems from their application of the principles Christ taught in the Beatitudes. In many ways, we in the Church should have an even more effective ministry to people caught in addictions—we have the truth that frees; we have the love that cares; we have the Spirit who gives power; and we have the fellowship that offers true accountability and support.

📖 Read Matthew 5:3–9. Examine each attitude conveyed in this passage and seek to understand how adopting that attitude might help you find freedom from your addictions.

"Blessed are the poor in spirit"

What is spiritual poverty? How does admitting our poverty help us see our need for Christ? What does this do to our self-reliance and pride?

_____

_____

_____

_____

_____

True blessing is experienced by those who come to realize their spiritual resources are bankrupt without Christ. They see their total inability to conquer their spiritual enemies and overcome the desires of their own flesh.

"Blessed are those who mourn"

What is the primary thing we have to mourn about? How does being honest about our sin and its effects on us and others prepare our hearts to mourn?

_____

_____

_____

_____

_____

_____

Unless and until we identify our sin and our idols, they have power over us, and we remain in bondage to them. But we often want to avoid the discomfort and embarrassment of seeing our own sin—few believe mourning is really a path to blessing. Yet, as David points out in Psalm 32, when we stop lying to ourselves and others about the existence of our sins and addictions, and begin confessing with real sorrow, we move towards the blessing of forgiveness.

> **True blessing is experienced by those who come to realize their spiritual resources are bankrupt without Christ.**

"Blessed are the meek"

What is meekness? How did Christ exemplify meekness? Why would turning our lives over to God be the most important step of meekness?

_____

_____

_____

_____

_____

Meekness is an inward attitude of patient submission without resentment. A truly meek person feels no need to control. She can allow God to be the one in control of her life. Jesus is our primary example of meekness and the words He said in the Garden of Gethsemane describe it best, "_Not my will but Thine be done._" Meekness is one of the most powerful weapons because it gets us out of the way, and allows God to do His work in us and through us.

"Blessed are those who hunger and thirst for righteousness"

How is righteousness attained? Why does seeing our sin, admitting it, confessing it, repenting of it, and receiving forgiveness for it lead to righteousness far sooner than our efforts to "do it right"?

_____

_____

_____

_____

_____

The first steps to righteousness are described in A.A.'s "Twelve Steps" (Steps 4–7). We are to identify our sin, confess it, be willing to have God change us, and to ask God to remove the sin. Those in churches who hide their sin and put all their efforts into "obeying the rules" are going in the wrong direction in their pursuit of righteousness. Anyone who has sought the help of Alcoholics Anonymous has made a good start toward recovery. However, the "Twelve Steps" technique, though it is replete with references to God and the necessity of confessing to God, is flawed because the foundation of Christ's atonement for all sin is missing. Without the blood of Christ, alcoholics in the "twelve-step" program can only make peace with others—they cannot find peace with God. Without the righteousness of Christ, there is only an empty void once the sin is removed. And the desire alone to have the "defects" removed is not basis enough for God to grant the request. He requires blood.

"Blessed are the merciful"

Committed A.A. members often sacrifice time and energy to help others find freedom. Do they sometimes show more mercy than the Church offers? What kind of mercy do we extend to others in bondage to addictions?

_____

_____

_____

_____

Those in churches who hide their sin and put all their efforts into "obeying the rules" are going in the wrong direction in their pursuit of righteousness.

Too often we are like the priest or the Levite in Jesus' parable of the Good Samaritan—we pass by those in need. We practice judgment rather than mercy. Both the great commission (Matthew 28:19–20) and our call to train younger women (Titus 2) require mercy. We are to extend Christ's compassion to others in need of His help. When we extend mercy to others, we find the mercy we need to overcome our own addictions.

"Blessed are the pure in heart"

What is the focus and goal of a pure heart, according to the promise given after this beatitude? How do you think our hearts are purified?

_____

_____

_____

_____

Jesus promised the pure in heart would see God. We all long to see God and would love to improve our contact with Him. But trying to know and do God's will apart from Christ will not make our hearts pure. Confessing our sins apart from Christ's forgiveness and cleansing will not wash them away. Nothing we can do on our own can make our hearts pure before God. The person and work of Christ is our only way out of spiritual poverty and helplessness. He alone can purify our hearts making them free of addictions.

"Blessed are the peacemakers"

Remember the command to "go" that we studied in Lesson 2? How does the making of amends fall short of that command? If repentance and confession cover half the peacemaking process (dealing with our sin), how do we cover the other half (dealing with the sin of others)?

_____

_____

_____

_____

Christ's forgiveness is the basis for our forgiveness of others.

A necessary requirement for peacemaking is that both parties agree to submit to the authorities governing the process. We are blessed in the body of Christ to know and experience a more complete peace, both with one another and with God, because of the work of Christ. Christ's forgiveness is the basis for our forgiveness of others. His righteousness is the hope for change in our own hearts as well as in others. His authority is the basis for church discipline—when both parties agree to submit to Christ and the authorities governing the process of peacemaking, it is then possible to deal with all the sin that led to the conflict or disagreement. Making amends implies we somehow pay for our own mistakes. True peace is found when we look to Christ's atonement to pay for our sin and the sins of others and when we look to His grace to change us all.

 Which of the beatitudes bring you the most freedom from your addictions?

_____

_____

Is the Holy Spirit convicting you about your need to change any of your attitudes?

_____

_____

Does your church have a Christian "Twelve-Step" group?

_____

_____

Do you think such a group could be an effective tool for evangelism? For discipleship?

_____

_____

WALKING IN FREEDOM

Becoming free is more a venture of faith than one of human effort. Even though the "Twelve Steps" of A.A. contain the idea of dependence on God to effect the change, the implication is if *we* follow the steps *we* can find freedom. There is too much focus on our own ability to do it ourselves, or to depend on others. Some in A.A. have exchanged their addiction to alcohol for an addiction to A.A. meetings. True freedom from bondage to false gods can only be obtained by loving and worshiping the true God. Walking in freedom is not trying hard to change our behavior; it is believing that Christ's grace can change us through our union with Him.

📖 Read Deuteronomy 13:1–4. What is really going on when we are tempted to follow after other gods? How could this fact help us in the midst of ongoing temptation?

_____

_____

_____

_____

God tells the Israelites what's happening when others tempt them to follow after other gods. He is testing them to find out if they love Him with all their hearts. That is really the issue. If we do truly love Him, we will follow, fear, keep, listen, serve, and cling to Him. If only we could see clearly in the midst of temptation that the choice to continue to pursue our idols arises from heart issues that measure our love for God. If we can see it this way every time we are tempted, our choice to love God might come more easily. Satan knows our love for God is what is at stake, but he tries to convince us that our choices are far less significant. He suggests the primary choice is between two almost equal values and that there are no consequences to such insignificant choices. But when we realize that God is asking us if we truly love Him, our answer is far more significant, and that makes it easier to say "No," to the temptation.

FULL LOVE FOR GOD

Full love for God means we must turn to God <u>over and against</u> other things. If our choice of God is to be made with integrity, we must first have felt other attractions and chosen, painfully, not to make them our gods. True love, then, is not only born of freedom; it is also born of difficult choice. A mature and meaningful love must say something like, "I have experienced other goodnesses, and they are beautiful, but it is You, my true heart's desire, whom I choose above all."[4]

—GERALD MAY

THOUGHTS ON REPENTANCE

Our Lord Jesus Christ came to break our hard-heartedness and self-righteousness and to make our hearts humble and soft, so that we can weep over our sin . . . we really have no excuse when we do not have repentance. Jesus won it for us on the cross, and God has shown us that we can obtain it by the prayer of faith, trusting in the victory of Jesus. It is precisely when we become aware of the hardness of our hearts and our complete inability to repent by virtue of our own strength that we should pray all the more earnestly for this gift [of repentance.][5]

—BASILEA SCHLINK

📖 Read Hebrews 6:1; 9:14; and 10:19–23. Recognizing repentance and faith as a way of life, how do we walk on? Do we ever come to a place where we no longer have to repent and believe? How do we draw near?

_____

_____

_____

_____

_____

Entering the Holy Place, drawing near to God, abiding in the vine, walking in the Spirit, knowing God, living in the love of Christ—all these are similar phrases that describe the kind of intimate relationship God desires to have with us. If our desire is to walk in freedom from our addictions, we need to keep two facts constantly before us: our great sinfulness (and need for repentance and forgiveness) and His great love (and provision in Christ). Coming to Him apart from those two basic truths is impossible. There are no steps to true freedom without them.

📖 Read Isaiah 57:15; Micah 6:8; 2 Corinthians 5:7; and Galatians 5:16. What does it mean to walk with God? How do we do that?

_____

_____

_____

_____

_____

Each of these verses gives us a slightly different description of walking with God, but taken together they reinforce the truth of our need for continual humility, repentance, and faith.

Idolatry, addictions, or favorite sins, call them what you may, keep us from loving and serving God and ministering to others. If we really want to overcome addictions, then we must be willing to die to them. It will take humility to admit we cannot overcome them without Christ. It will take repentance to bring us to the point of hating them enough to see them put to death. And it will take faith to believe God's grace will be sufficient without them.

APPLY Think of the dialogue that goes on in your mind just before you choose to turn to one of your idols. What would happen if you introduced the question of your love for God in the midst of that debate?

_____

_____

Have you ever thought of your addictions as diseases or psychological disorders?

_____

_____

If that is what they are, is there any hope for change?

_____

_____

Think about the promise in 1 John 1:9. Could God have made it any easier?

_____

_____

_____

Why is it so hard to confess and repent?

_____

_____

_____

Why is repentance such an important part of worship?

_____

_____

_____

_____

Spend some time with the Lord in prayer.

 Heavenly Father, I praise You for Your jealous love, that will have no other gods before You. You are holy and unique. There is none like You. You are worthy of my complete trust, and I have no need for any other comfort or provision other than what Your hand so graciously gives. I praise You because Your timing is always perfect, even though in my impatience I hate to wait. Thank You for what You teach me in the process. Thank You for every weapon You have given to me to destroy the strongholds in my life. Thank You for changing my heart.

Father, I confess the many idols I allow in my life. They distract me from You and pull my heart away from worship. I long to be free of them. And yet, I fail to use the weapons You have given to me to destroy them. Please forgive me. Help me, Lord, to detest them as You do. I pray that You would increase my faith, and fill me with Your Spirit that I might walk in Your freedom and say no to temptation.

I pray, also, for the women You have put in my life. I pray that Your love would abound more and more in knowledge and depth of insight in each of them. May they be able to discern Your best from Satan's counterfeits. Fill them with the fruit of righteousness and make them pure and blameless as they turn from their idols and serve you wholeheartedly. Deliver us all from evil. Thine be the kingdom, the power and the glory forever, Amen.

Notes

4

Teaching Beauty

She has been my "teacher of beauty," even though she is my daughter. God put within B.J. a gift of beauty that challenged my patterns of thought and priorities right from the start. She is *music* and *poetry* and *dance;* I was *logic* and *clarity* and *hurry.* She loves to grow flowers; I grew vegetables. Her tender heart is often moved to tears; I seldom cried. In our years together, tension was inevitable as our priorities clashed. There were times when my emphasis on the practical and my need to economize inhibited her pursuit of beauty. It wasn't until I realized she had something to teach me that our relationship improved.

I really blew it on B.J.'s sixteenth birthday. When I asked her what she wanted, she said, "Just surprise me!" Secretly she hoped for a special piece of jewelry or beautiful object of art that would somehow commemorate her entrance into womanhood. But at the time I had no idea that was what she had in mind.

Later that week I was visiting my friend Brenda, who asked if I knew anyone who might be interested in buying her old organ. "That might be just the thing!" I thought. Now you should understand this was not an antique but a rather ugly organ. I wrapped up several old organ instruction manuals to represent this "exciting" gift. There was great anticipation, with all her teenage girlfriends gathered around, as she unwrapped her special gift. Her face fell. She tried to cover her disappointment, but her look said, "What do these old books have to do with beauty?"

B. J.

. . . *teacher of beauty*

Teaching Beauty

DAY ONE

Word Study
TEACHERS OF BEAUTY

Kalodidáskalos, the Greek word in Titus 2:3 that is translated, *"teaching what is good"* (NASB), is not found anywhere else in Scripture. It is a combination of *didaska,* which means "teacher," and *kalos,* which means "beautiful, pleasing, good."[1] *Kalós* is usually translated as good, but it is also the common word for beauty. So it is possible that "teachers of beauty" is what Paul had in mind.

"You can learn to play hymns for church," I said, trying to convince her of the great opportunity I was giving her. Not only was I clueless about the change in direction church music was about to take, I simply did not understand B.J.'s need for beauty. I had hardened my heart to my own need for beauty. That hardness had injured the tender heart of my daughter.

But things have changed since that awkward day. Her sensitivity and longing for beauty began to melt my heart and lead me to an understanding of my need to change. The tension and disharmony has diminished because she has taught me to love and pursue beauty as she does.

For my fiftieth birthday, B.J. gave me a picture to hang in my living room. The central focus of the picture is a beautiful woman leading two other women down a flower filled path. There are so many flowers that they spill out onto the matting of the picture. It symbolizes for us the Titus 2 concept.

"Mom, I see you in this picture. You are leading me and Sara down the path of life," she said. "Oh, no," I said, "You are the one in front. You have been my teacher of beauty."

In the King James Version of the Bible, the final phrase of Titus 2:3 says that older women are to be *"teachers of good things."* This final phrase is translated from one Greek word, *kalodidáskalos.* If it hadn't been for B.J., I probably would not have been so excited to discover that the first part of *kalodidáskalos (kalós)* can mean beauty. Even though most translators choose to translate *kalodidáskalos* as "teachers of good" (NASB—*"teaching what is good"*), there is a distinct possibility that Paul had "teachers of *beauty*" in mind. In this week's lesson, we will entertain the possibility that Paul may have intentionally used a form of the most common Greek word for "beauty" and that we, as women, need to consider that possibility. We need to take a closer look at our deep, inner longing for beauty and be sure we teach it rather than squelch it.

THE BEAUTY OF THE LORD

In their choice to translate it as "good," most translators overlook the possibility that Paul intentionally used a form of the most common word for beauty, but as women, we need to consider it. If Paul or the Holy Spirit had beauty in mind, it behooves us to discover why. We all have a deep inner longing for beauty, but, for some of us, it has been squelched rather than fostered. According to C. S. Lewis, beauty is an image of our deepest desires.[2] The dictionary defines beauty as "the quality in anything that gives pleasure to the senses, or pleasurably exalts the mind or spirit."[3] We enjoy beauty because it somehow begins to fill our deep longings. There is a mystery in beauty that defies logic or quantification. We don't always know why we find something beautiful, but we experience an inner stirring of pleasure that longs for more.

What if all beauty is ultimately a reflection of God? We could say beauty is the visible symbol of the unseen glory of God. Henry Drummond says of God's glory, "Of all unseen things, it is the most radiant, the most beautiful, the most divine. On earth, in heaven, there is nothing so great, so glorious, as this. . . . Stripped of its physical wrapping [glory] is beauty, moral and spiritual beauty, beauty infinitely real, infinitely exalted, yet infinitely near."[4] Therefore, our training in beauty will begin with a study of the beauty of God.

📖 Read Psalm 27:4. What can we learn from this verse about the beauty and glory of the Lord? How do we gaze on His beauty?

_____

_____

_____

_____

Consider this quote from John Piper:

> The enemy of worship is not that our desire for pleasure is too strong but too weak! We have settled for a home, a family, a few friends, a job, a television, a microwave oven, an occasional night out, a yearly vacation, and perhaps a new personal computer. We have accustomed ourselves to such meager, short-lived pleasures that our capacity for joy has shriveled. And so our worship has shriveled. . . . The scenery and poetry and music of the majesty of God have dried up like a forgotten peach at the back of the refrigerator.[5]

Discuss how our desire for beauty can also shrivel up. How can we encourage one another to appreciate beauty more, especially the beauty of the Lord?

📖 Read Psalm 29:1–2. What does it mean to worship the Lord in the beauty of holiness?

_____

_____

_____

_____

God's holiness demands we come to Him only in the robes He provides. Think about why God refused to accept Cain's sacrifice (Genesis 4:3–7), and why the guest not wearing wedding clothes was cast into outer darkness in Jesus' parable (Matthew 22:11–14).

📖 Read 1 Chronicles 16:10–11, 27–29. How do these verses describe God's beauty and our worship? What does it mean to *ascribe Him glory*?

_____

_____

_____

_____

Remember the definition for worship in Day 1 of chapter three: worship is the direct acknowledgment to God of His nature and attributes, in praise, thanksgiving, and deeds done in such acknowledgment. We are acknowledging His beauty when we ascribe Him glory. Our worship includes praise for His beauty and the creation of more beauty to acknowledge it.

Beauty is the visible symbol of the unseen glory of God.

📖 Read Luke 10:38–42, John 11:31–36, and John 12:1–7. How did Mary *"ascribe glory"* to Jesus? Notice particularly the position she always took. What did she learn about beauty there?

_____

_____

_____

_____

When we ascribe to the Lord the glory due His name, we are at His feet, not looking Him eye to eye. Notice the progression in Mary's understanding of Christ's beauty and purpose. She sat at His feet drinking in the beauty of His words. She was prostrate before His feet when she expressed her belief in His awesome power over death. And she anointed His feet and wiped them with her hair when she realized He was about to die for her. She was one of the first of Christ's followers to truly comprehend the significance of His coming sacrifice, and she expressed her love and thankfulness by her own sacrifice of love.

APPLY Is your capacity for beauty diminished in any way?

_____

_____

If so, what do you think caused it to diminish?

_____

_____

_____

How could a teacher of beauty help your capacity for beauty to increase?

_____

_____

_____

What would gazing at the beauty of the Lord look like for you?

_____

_____

_____

Meditate on the words of this seventeenth-century German hymn, "Fairest Lord Jesus":

> *Fairest Lord Jesus!*
> *Ruler of all nature,*
> *O Thou of God and man the Son!*
> *Thee will I cherish, Thee will I honor,*
> *Thou my soul's Glory, Joy, and Crown.*
>
> *Fair are the meadows, Fairer still the woodlands,*
> *Robed in the blooming garb of spring:*
> *Jesus is fairer, Jesus is purer,*
> *Who makes the woeful heart to sing.*

Fair is the sunshine, fairer still the moonlight,
And all the twinkling starry host:
Jesus shines brighter, Jesus shines purer,
Than all the angels heaven can boast.

Beautiful Savior! Lord of the nations!
Son of God and Son of Man!
Glory and honor, praise, adoration,
Now and forevermore be Thine!

THE BEAUTY OF CREATION

Why did God create a world of such beauty? Was it primarily for His enjoyment or for ours? John Piper, in a sermon on *The Pleasures of God*, talks about the intricate beauty of the fish that live so deep in the ocean that, for thousands of years, man never knew of or saw, much less enjoyed, their beauty. God obviously created these particular fish for His own pleasure.

Our love and enjoyment of beauty is part of God's image in us. What if women have been given a special calling to not only reflect God's beauty as women, but to teach beauty in such a way that others around us can understand and respond to it in godly ways? Notice that being a teacher of beauty is a description of the older woman, and also that beauty is not one of the specific topics for training younger women. This implies we teach beauty not only to the younger women, but to others as well. There may be some men in our lives who could benefit from what we know and feel about beauty, and certainly children, both boys and girls, need to be taught about beauty.

📖 Read Genesis 1 and notice verses 4, 10, 12, 18, 21, 25, and 31. What do you think the word "good" means in these verses?

_____

_____

_____

_____

📖 Read Psalm 29:9. What should be our response to the beauty God has created?

_____

_____

_____

_____

Why does the soul of a woman hunger for beauty? Is it only a luxury, or is it a basic human need? The true story of a group of women who were detained in a concentration camp during World War II is told in the movie *Paradise Road*. One by one, women died in the cruel, stark, inhumane surroundings.

Beauty calls us to attention. It slows us down. This, in itself is the beginning of contemplation. It is difficult to hurry through beauty. If you are in a hurry, you probably won't stop to be present to "the beautiful." Beauty has the ability to heal life's wounds. It can make us receptive to grace.[6]

—MACRINA WIEDERKEHR

All seemed hopeless until a couple of them envisioned a vocal orchestra that would perform some of the great symphonies they could remember. The main character, played by Glenn Close, was a visionary who knew that the beauty of the music would bring healing and hope to their souls. The other woman was an older missionary, who, as a teacher of beauty, somehow blended her love for music with her love for the younger women in the camp and brought them together. She wrote the music from memory and then trained the younger women to use their voices to imitate the sounds of the instruments. The painstaking effort did more than provide an interesting diversion for the women; it knit their hearts together in the creation and enjoyment of beauty.

📖 Read Psalm 19:1–6. How does God's creation reveal His glory?

_____

_____

_____

_____

📖 Read Revelation 21:1–2, 10–11, 18–23. How did John describe the beauty he saw in his vision of heaven? Do you think the new heaven and new earth will be even more beautiful than the present ones?

_____

_____

_____

_____

The new heaven will be even more glorious than we can imagine. John was limited by both his readers' ability to imagine what he described and his ability to describe what he saw. We just know that our deepest longings for beauty will be fulfilled in the new heaven and earth.

📖 Read Exodus 31:2–6. Why do you think God was so particular about the beauty of the Tabernacle? How do artists join God in the creation of beauty?

_____

_____

_____

_____

Whether or not Bezalel and Oholiab were aware of their artistics gifts, they needed Moses to recognize, encourage, and commission them to use those gifts for the Lord. God is rarely so specific in the revelation of His will, but we can infer from this passage that great works of art are part of His sovereign plan. His creation of beauty did not end on the sixth day. Thomas Kinkade states in his book, _Lightposts for Living_: "Beauty is food for the soul, balm to the spirit, inspiration for anything worthwhile we do with our lives."[7] Edith Schaeffer, in her book entitled _Hidden Art,_ challenges us to discover and use the "leftover beauty in the creation of God."[8] She explains this concept of leftover beauty by saying:

Since [God] created man as a creative creature, by creating him in His own image, these 'creative creatures' have, through the ages, retained fragments of the perfection which He made in the first place—though spoiled, of course, by sin. Every single one of us has been spoiled by sin. But as we look back over history and see artists, musicians and creative people in various fields, we can recognize the 'image of God.'[9]

Schaeffer goes on to define art:

Whatever it is, surely art involves creativity and originality. Whatever form art takes, it gives outward expression to what otherwise would remain locked in the mind, unshared. . . . Art in various forms expresses and gives opportunity to others to share in, and respond to, things which would otherwise remain vague, empty yearnings. . . . One area of art inspires another area of art, but also one person's expression of art stimulates another person and brings about growth in understanding, sensitivity, and appreciation.[10]

A primary function of a teacher of beauty would be to encourage the use of artistic gifts in younger women. Our creativity is part of the image of God hidden within each of us, and one way we can "teach" is by inspiring and stimulating one another to be more expressive.

APPLY What are some of the ways you enjoy the beauty of creation?

_____

_____

_____

_____

For those of you who have seen the film, *Enchanted April* (1992), starring Josie Lawrence and Miranda Richardson, how did the beauty of creation affect the women in this story? If you haven't seen this film, I recommend you rent it some time.

How do the beauty of God's creation and the beauty of art compare and relate?

_____

_____

_____

_____

Edith Schaeffer taught that our art comes from the leftovers of creation. Can you recognize the image of God in some of the creative people you know?

THE BEAUTY OF REDEMPTION

Teaching Beauty

DAY THREE

One of my teachers once commented that the cross of Christ was the most beautiful thing on earth. I have often reflected on this statement, and it has challenged my thinking about beauty. Beauty is not simply what we see, for the visual picture of the cross is grotesque. The agony and the shame of the cross, from the crown of thorns to the blood flowing from Christ's feet, seem anything but beautiful. Yet, as a picture of redemption, the cross represents all that God did to remove the ugliness of our sin and to dress us in the righteousness of Christ. He gave us beauty for ashes.

📖 Read Ezekiel 16:4–14. How do these verses describe what Christ did for us?

_____

_____

_____

This clearly illustrates the lengths to which God will go in order to change us into beautiful people. Isaiah 61:3 tells us that He gives us *"beauty for ashes."* Yet when we forget God, or consciously blot out any remembrance of Him, we turn our beauty back into ashes. Think about the Communists and what happened in Russia when it became an atheistic state. My daughter spent a year in St. Petersburg as part of the Co-mission Project that responded to Russia's invitation to bring biblical teaching back into their public schools. I went to visit her and was appalled by the ugliness and despair that was everywhere. The only beauty I saw was in the art museums. I couldn't help but wonder how different it might have been if the people had been allowed to freely worship God and encouraged to express the beauty buried deep within.

📖 Now read Ezekiel 16:15–18. What did the Israelites do? When and how do we do similar things with the beauty Christ gives us?

_____

_____

_____

_____

📖 Read Isaiah 61:10. What should be our response?

_____

_____

_____

If we really understood all that Christ has done for us, and realized the provision He makes for us, our joy would be unbounded.

📖 Read 2 Corinthians 3:18. Where does true beauty (glory) come from? How do we get it?

_____

_____

_____

_____

Karen Lee-Thorp and Cynthia Hicks have written an interesting book entitled *Why Beauty Matters.* In it they contrast the superficial beauty sought in our culture with the true beauty offered by Christ. Commenting on this verse they write:

> *"The Spirit of the LORD God is upon me, because the LORD has anointed me to bring.... Beauty for ashes; Joy instead of mourning; Praise instead of heaviness."*
>
> Isaiah 61:1, 3 (TLB)

Pride tells us to exploit our beauty to get what we want, or feel ashamed of our ugliness as the proof of our worthlessness. Fear tells us to veil our beauty so we don't draw the envy of other women or the lust of men. But when we choose to become aware of and grieve over our pride, shame and fear, they lose their grip on us. When we allow ourselves to be loved and invest our energy in loving others, we genuinely grow more beautiful, even as being beautiful becomes less of an obsession. . . . Like the moon, whose beauty is seen only when it reflects light from the invisible sun, we begin to radiate another's light. . . . It's as though we look into a mirror, and by the power of the Holy Spirit we cease to see the stressed, aging, bulging body we usually see. Instead, we see the glory of the Lord. And as we continue to focus on that image, we change, more and more resembling it in its glory. The glorious image becomes a truer vision of ourselves than the one we see every day in our clouded mirrors.[11]

📖 Read Ephesians 5:25–27. We usually look at these verses to understand how husbands are to love their wives, but what does it teach us about how Christ beautifies His church?

_____

_____

_____

_____

Christ's promise to make His church *"glorious"* (verse 27 [KJV]) by sanctifying, cleansing, removing all spots and wrinkles, and making us holy and blameless is beautiful. C. S. Lewis' description of our longing for such beauty which is quoted in the side margin of this page is classic.

APPLY Can you identify with C. S. Lewis's description of the longing for beauty?

_____

_____

How would you explain the process of beautification to a new believer?

_____

_____

_____

_____

_____

What did you think when reading the description of the Israelites' adultery (Ezekiel 6:15–18)? Do you ever think of what you do in such gross terms?

_____

_____

_____

_____

EXPERIENCING BEAUTY

Ah, but we want so much more. . . . We do not want merely to see beauty, though, God knows, even that is bounty enough. We want something else which can hardly be put into words—to be united with the beauty we see, to pass into it, to receive it into ourselves, to bathe in it, to become part of it.[12]

—C. S. LEWIS

THE BEAUTY OF WOMEN

My daughter Sara introduced an early manuscript of this study to her church, and some women agreed to discuss it together. I was visiting her the week they were to study this particular lesson. The night before, as I discussed it with her husband, he challenged my use of a word none of the translators had used. He told me that if *kalós* really meant beauty, I wouldn't have been the first to discover it. He suggested I talk to his neighbor, who taught Greek at a nearby college. When I called his neighbor the next morning and explained what I had found, I told him I felt like I was out on a limb. He promised to check into it and get back with me. It wasn't long before he called back to tell me I was safe on that limb. He had found that the Greek scholars who translated the Hebrew Old Testament into the Greek Septuagint chose the Greek word *kalós* to describe Esther's beauty. He felt this was a good indication that *kalós* was the usual and accepted word for beauty. By using it, Paul may have intended to challenge us to develop our natural inclination towards beauty and to teach others what God has revealed to us about beauty.

📖 Read Esther 2:2–4, 7–9, 12, 17. Why do you think men are so attracted to beauty in women? What kind of power and influence can beauty bring?

_____

_____

_____

_____

Much is being written and discussed about beauty in our culture today. As Christian women, we need to be part of the discussion. And as Titus 2 women, we need to be teaching younger women the importance and power of the beauty God has given them.

📖 Read 1 Peter 3:3–5 and 1 Timothy 2:9–10. Is there any place for outward beauty? What is it? When does adorning yourself become sin?

_____

_____

_____

_____

Why do you think Ezekiel, Genesis, and Esther describe beauty in terms of form, clothes, jewels, and makeup, but Peter and Paul tell us to look elsewhere?

_____

_____

_____

_____

Color, design, and sparkle are all created by God and are not evil. It is the extremes we must be wary of. Our priorities can guide our decisions and moderation and modesty are our best boundaries. The quote from Karen Lee-Thorp in the side margin on the next page says it well.

📖 Read Matthew 26:6–13 (NIV). How did Jesus respond to the *"beautiful thing"* the woman did to him?

_____

_____

_____

_____

The New International Version translators chose to use the word "beautiful" in translating *kalós* in verse 10. The disciples complained about the extravagance of beauty, but Jesus loved it. He prophesied fame for this woman who dared to express her worship in a beautiful way.

🛑 APPLY Is a desire to look beautiful ever not good?

_____

_____

_____

_____

_____

Why do you think jewelry, clothes, makeup, and a good figure are so important to some women?

_____

_____

_____

_____

_____

Can you think of a woman you know whose beauty is revealed not just in the way she looks outwardly? What is it that makes her beautiful?

_____

_____

_____

_____

_____

_____

_____

_____

_____

_____

MASTERING THE POWER OF BEAUTY

Theologians have told women that to display our beauty is a sin....Women know that beauty would have been our birthright if sin had not defaced us....We were made to reflect an unstained glory, and our longing for that state won't be silenced by force....Disrespecting human beauty is tragic because it leads us to disrespect women's bodies and our sexuality. . . . To cheapen beauty is to encourage ugly art and abuse of women's bodies....Beauty is not trivial or dangerous; it is powerful and important....Men and women need to be taught how to master the power of beauty for godly ends....Every girl must see herself as beautiful and offer her beauty to those around her in appropriate ways....Beauty deserves to be on the agenda for any faith community wrestling with the big spiritual issues of our time.[13]

—KAREN LEE-THORP

FINDING BEAUTY IN OTHERS

Part of teaching beauty must include helping others see the beauty God has put in them and encouraging them to develop and fully express it to others. Like precious stones buried deep below the surface of the earth, beauty is often hidden and needs to be mined. As we take the time to really get to know others, we should watch for indications of buried treasure, depending on the Holy Spirit to reveal the glory God has implanted in each woman.

📖 Read Ephesians 1:18. What do you think are *"the riches of the glory"* that Paul refers to?

_____

_____

_____

_____

In order to understand this prayer request, we need to define *"His inheritance"* and *"glory."* Revelation 21:2 makes it clear that we are Christ's inheritance. It describes *"the new Jerusalem coming down out of heaven from God, prepared as a bride beautifully dressed for her husband."* All the saints together make up the bride of Christ. **We** are the New Jerusalem. **We** are His inheritance. He referred to Himself as the bridegroom (Matthew 9:15); He gave Himself up for his bride (Ephesians 5:25); He bought her with His own blood (Acts 20:28); and the promise of the joy of being with her helped Him to endure the cross (Hebrews 12:2). If *"glory"* in Ephesians 1:18 means beauty, as Henry Drummond suggests (see his definition of "glory" in the introduction to this lesson), Paul in his prayer equates finding and knowing the riches and beauty that are in each of us with knowing our calling and God's power.

Does Colossians 1:26–27 make it clearer for you?

_____

_____

If *"Christ in me"* and *"Christ in you"* make us rich and gives us glory (making us beautiful), how do we get to know these riches?

_____

_____

_____

_____

The more I get to know the *"Christ in you"* and allow you to know the *"Christ in me,"* the closer we both come to knowing Christ. We are the body of Christ, but if we follow the world's pattern of independence and isolation, we cannot do all this "knowing." There is even an aspect of not knowing ourselves that comes from being isolated. The part of me that is *"Christ in me"* can never be known in isolation. If spiritual gifts are given for ministry to others, but I seldom interact with others, the gifts are not manifested. I won't even know I have them.

BEAUTY AMONG FRIENDS

Special friends strike a resonant chord in your heart; there is something about them, some aspect of beauty or goodness that reminds you of God. I have an inkling that when you see the face of God in heaven, you will say, "Yes, I always knew You!" It was Him all along that you loved whenever you were with that treasured person. In friendship, God opens your eyes to the glories of Himself, and the greater the number of friends with whom you share deep and selfless love, the better and more clear the picture of God you will have.[14]

—JONI EARECKSON TADA

📖 Read Ruth 1:14–18 and 3:1–4. What beauty did each of these women see in the other? In what ways do you think Naomi was a teacher of beauty? How do you think we can teach beauty to younger women?

_____

_____

_____

_____

_____

_____

It must have been the beauty of Naomi's God that compelled Ruth to cling to her, for most of Naomi's other attractions had been stripped from her. Naomi's faith in God and the reflection of His beauty must have shown through the bitterness that accompanied her grief. It is easy to see Ruth's meekness and loyalty revealed repeatedly in this story, but it is also interesting to note the reference to physical beauty. There is no doubt that Naomi taught Ruth to use her feminine beauty to attract Boaz. These few verses touch on a variety of ways beauty can be taught. Both example and words are important. But if we remember that beauty is first and foremost a symbol of the unseen glory of God, we teach it best by seeking His face and encouraging others to join us. As we behold the glory of the Lord, we are transformed into His image (2 Corinthians 3:18). The inner beauty He creates within us will be reflected in our behavior and outward appearance. When women are free to reflect the feminine image of God the world will see true beauty.

APPLY Do you regularly pray that God would open your eyes to see the riches of the glory He has put in the saints in your church?

_____

Who was the most significant teacher of beauty in your life? How did she teach it?

_____

_____

_____

Do you think God's Word has been dishonored in our failure to recognize beauty as an important topic for the Church?

_____

_____

Watch the films _Babette's Feast_ or _Chocolat_ (2001 release starring Juliet Binoche and Alfred Molina) and identify the teachers of beauty in these movies. How did they teach it? Why do you think religion is often seen as the nemesis of beauty?

_____

_____

_____

Close this week's study with a time of prayer.

 Dear Father in heaven, I praise You for Your infinite beauty and excellence. The heavens proclaim Your glory, and I want to join the refrain. How lovely are Your dwelling places. My soul longs and yearns for Your courts. My heart and my flesh sing Your praises. How blessed are those who see Your beauty. Thank You for every reflection of beauty I see here on earth. You satisfy my longing soul and fill my hungry heart with beauty.

Oh, Lord, please forgive me for my failure to worship You more. Deepen my desire for beauty and enhance my appreciation for it. I confess my concept of beauty has been severely lacking, and I have been too concerned with outward beauty and failed to seek You for a meek and quiet spirit. I have trusted in my own beauty and not acknowledged Yours. Please forgive me for wrong priorities. Cleanse my heart, oh God.

I thank You for the glory You have given to all the special women in my life. May I continue to explore and see the riches You have hidden in their hearts. Thank You for their beauty, and I pray I will be an encouragement to each of them to shine. Help me to be a teacher of beauty. And may all of the evil plans of the enemy to deface and mar my beauty be overcome by Your grace and power. In Jesus name I pray, Amen.

Notes

Notes

Part Two

Topics for Training

Loving Husbands

The choice to love is not always easy. Love is putting the needs of someone else before our own. In those times when our choice to love becomes difficult, we must remember that God always chooses love and He commands us to do the same—*"A new commandment I give to you that you love one another, even as I have loved you"* (John 13:34).

When I first met Ann Marie in Denver, she was content as a single woman, and though she longed to be married some day, she was moving forward toward a life of ministry among the Muslims. But after Ann Marie returned from visiting a group of single believers on the East Coast, where she had been discipled and had first learned the significance of community, I noticed something quite different about her. That morning, after church, I asked one of her friends what was going on.

"Ann Marie has just met a man who has swept her off her feet!" she explained.

"That is wonderful news," I said, hiding my envy.

A couple months later, when she returned from a second visit to the East Coast, her circle of friends seemed more subdued. The news was not all good. "Ann Marie is engaged, but her fiancé just found out he is HIV positive."

Ann Marie...

...risking love

Later, Ann Marie told me the whole story. Ron was a former homosexual, and even though they both felt God was leading them toward marriage, when he tested positive for the HIV virus he insisted he could never ask her to expose herself to that kind of pain and danger. She believes God gave her the words that convinced Ron to move toward marriage. She said, "What if I had cancer, wouldn't you still want to marry me?"

Because her parents could not understand why she would take such a risk, and did not approve of the marriage or attend the wedding, Ann Marie walked down the aisle alone. Halfway there, she stopped, hesitating, and the tension in the room was palpable. Then Ron rushed to her side and walked the rest of the way to the altar with her. Although it was prearranged, the little drama clearly told the story of their romance and commitment to one another.

Friends of mine who were in the wedding described it as the most exciting and fun-filled celebration of love and redemption they had ever experienced. Ron said it was the best day of his life. Ann Marie said, "The cloud of doubt and heartache lifted and the stress I felt in the weeks prior was completely gone. The day was so incredible and the love I felt for Ron was indescribable."

Although Ron carries the virus, he has never contracted AIDS, and the doctors now predict that he may be one of the few who never does. Ron says, "What God has done and continues to do in my life is beyond imagination." Together, Ron and Ann Marie have established a ministry in Raleigh, North Carolina, for those struggling with homosexuality called Beyond Imagination. Its name is based on Ephesians 3:20, "*Now to Him who is able to do immeasurably more than all we ask or imagine, according to His power that is at work within us, to Him be glory in the church*" (NIV). Ron's ministry took them to Canada two years after they were married, and there they found out Ann Marie did have cancer. The Canadian health care system completely paid for a life-saving bone marrow transplant for her, and Ron lovingly cared for her through the whole ordeal. Her willingness to marry the man she loved and her decision to go with him to another country was used by God to bring healing and wholeness to them both.

A DIFFERENT KIND OF LOVE

Titus 2:4 is the only place in Scripture where women are encouraged or commanded to love husbands, and it is significant that Paul chooses a form of the Greek word *phileo* for love (*phílandros*). *Phileo* has a different meaning than another Greek word for love, *agapē,* which is most often used for love in the New Testament.

Consider the possibility that God tells us as women to *phileo* because He made men with the kind of needs *phileo* could meet and that He commanded men to *agapē* their wives because He knew that was what women needed. Many popular books written in our day point out the differences between men and women—we will find Scripture indicates some as well.

Read Ephesians 5:22, 25, 29, and 33. Why do you think God gives different commands for husbands and wives? What might be the significance of Paul's using two different words for love? If you are married, how does your husband need *phileo* love? How do you need *agapē* love?

---

*"Older women likewise are to live priestly lifestyles, not to be malicious gossips, nor should they have any addictions, but should be teachers of beauty, so that they can **train the younger women to love husbands,** to love children, to be of sound mind, to be pure, to be keepers of the home, to be good and to be submissive to their own husbands that the word of God may not be dishonored."*

Titus 2:3–5 (AUTHOR'S PARAPHRASE)

Loving Husbands

DAY ONE

_____

_____

_____

Your *philéo* love offers respect and "the highest veneration" to meet a man's need for significance. His need to be trusted and depended on is met by your submission. Your need for security is met by unconditional *agapē* love, which provides you with a trustworthy assurance that you will be cared for even at the sacrifice of the one who loves you. To the weaker sex, *agapē* offers strength and support.

📖 Read 1 Peter 3:1–4. What needs of men are implied by this call for wives to offer them submission, respect, beauty, and a meek and quiet spirit?

_____

_____

_____

Beyond their need for significance, men have a need to see beauty in their wives, which is displayed *both* inwardly and outwardly. Maybe it fills the inner void caused by the missing rib. Or, maybe that is the part of the image of God the feminine side reflects and the masculine side needs. Some answers will remain in the realm of mystery, but God's commands are clear even if His reasons are unclear.

📖 Read 1 Corinthians 7:3–5. What do these verses state about a husband's needs?

_____

_____

_____

According to this passage, a goal in every marriage is to enjoy and delight in sexual intimacy. If this is not the case, a younger woman should not suffer alone, or be in battle with Satan without needed reinforcements just because the older women are too inhibited to talk or pray about such things. Sexual repression, frigidity, and perversion all indicate deeper issues that need to be addressed. Inhibitions and sinful behavior will multiply in an atmosphere of silence. A woman who is bound by fear, guilt, or repression needs to know there are loving, understanding women in her church ready to talk and pray with her about anything that keeps her from loving her husband. Satan has great success in using sexual sins and ignorance to destroy marriages in churches that avoid addressing topics related to sexuality.

📖 Read 1 Peter 3:1–2, 8–9. Is the command to show affection and respect conditional? List the ways we are to love husbands who may not deserve it.

_____

_____

_____

Word Study
LOVE

There are two primary Greek words for love (*philéo* and *agapē*). Paul chooses different words for men and women. Women are to *philéo* their husbands; men are to *agapē* their wives.

Philéo means: "tender affection . . . cherishing the object above all else . . . manifesting an affection characterized by constancy, from the motive of the highest veneration."[1]

Agapē means: "self-sacrificing . . . unselfish love, ready to serve."[2]

Philéo is used 22 times as love, 3 times as kiss. *Agapē* is more common, as it is used 319 times as love.

Extra Mile
LOVE LANGUAGES

If you have never read *The Five Love Languages* by Gary Chapman, and you are intrigued by the idea of loving differently, you will enjoy reading it. It explores individual differences in the way we show and receive love. Chapman identifies five major love languages: Words of Affirmation, Quality Time, Gifts, Acts of Service, and Physical Touch.[3]

We will come back to the verses in 1 Peter, for they have many things to teach us, but today we want to focus on the point that our obedience to God's command to love our husbands is not dependent on their love or obedience. Respect can be given, and love can be shown no matter what they do. However, as we will see in subsequent studies, their behavior will sometimes change the expression of our love.

📖 Read Romans 1:18, 25–26 and 2 Peter 2:6–10, 17–19. Do you think training women to love husbands would include some kind of warning against lesbianism? How do these verses help us understand homosexuality and respond to the sinful behavior in a godly way?

_____

_____

_____

_____

The literal translation of *philandros* (Titus 2:4a) is "love husbands." The pronoun *"their"* is not in the original Greek. This gives older women something to say to those who love same-sex partners instead of husbands. Part of our training in loving husbands must include how this particular love is a fulfillment of the essence of our femininity. Lesbian relationships are a counterfeit that merely fill a void left by other failed relationships. They may look less risky to some, but they lead to false dependencies and ultimate disillusionment.

One reason women choose lesbian relationships is the difficulty of loving someone who is different. The fact that men are different and require us to love them differently presents a challenge that some women don't want to take. They think it is easier to find love and security in a same sex relationship. But Romans 1 implies our sexuality has more to do with worship of God than with personal preference. It is a refusal to love and honor Him that leads us into deviant sexual behavior. Loving husbands is part of our worship. Somehow, the union of a man and a woman reveals the image of God in a way that nothing else on earth can. But the unnatural function of loving a same-sex "partner" is anti-worship.

Second Peter 2:8 refers to our natural distaste for (and even *torment* over) sexual deviations but also explains that people in the gay community are enslaved to their corruption. We need to care for those who are "enticed" or *"barely escape"* (see 2 Peter 2:18), and we also must have compassion for those trapped in the homosexual lifestyle, doing what we can to help them to freedom. Training in all of the areas listed in Titus 2, not just in loving husbands, will teach a woman the true essence of femininity. Janelle Hallman's statement in the side margin of this page challenges to us to offer the kind of love lesbians so desperately need. Healthy, protective relationships in the body of Christ should be part of the healing process for these wounded women.

Problems dealing with sexuality will not go away. The gay agenda is prevalent on high school and university campuses. Many young women are raised in homes where both parents have to work and are too busy to meet the basic emotional needs of their children. Even worse, some grow up in an environment that puts them at great risk of falling into a lesbian lifestyle. They are wounded in ways that put them in need of much healing. We have been

LACK OF NURTURING

Often lesbianism is a result of an absence of nurturing and protection in childhood. The lack of an initial warm, safe attachment with mom and/or a dad who was passive, busy, and unavailable can lead to a woman being without a sense of self, unaffirmed and undervalued as a woman. If a mother gives the "initial source of being" and a father protects her femininity, women and men of the church can offer a secondary source for those who failed to receive what they needed at first.[4]

—JANELLE HALLMAN

given this mandate to train young women to love husbands, and it may be more necessary in our day than ever before. If we learn all we can about Satan's destructive plans, we will be better equipped to set his captives free. Information on ministries that seek to reach out to those in sexual bondage can be obtained through Exodus International and Harvest USA. Check out their Web sites at www.exodus-international.org and www.harvestusa.org.

APPLY What are your husband's primary needs? (If you are not married, can you identify any needs of a relative or some man you know well?)

_____

_____

_____

How can you show affection if you do not feel it? Would that be insincere?

_____

_____

_____

_____

Did the Holy Spirit, through any of the verses above, point to some way He wants to change your loving?

_____

_____

How could you become a secondary source of mother love to women who were not nurtured by their own mothers?

_____

_____

_____

_____

What other ways can you think of to help a woman who is drawn to a lesbian lifestyle?

_____

_____

_____

_____

HIDING FROM LOVE AND INTIMACY

Loving Husbands

DAY TWO

Some women might think they can skip this chapter because they are single, but it might be they need this training most of all. There are as many reasons for being single as there are single people. Many of them

> *"Beloved, if God so loved us, we also ought to love one another. . . . if we love one another, God abides in us, and His love is perfected in us."*
>
> *1 John 4:11–12*

may be good reasons. But consider the possibility that one may be that older women have failed to challenge younger women to face their fears of marriage and deal with sin that may be keeping them isolated. If we are to train younger women to love husbands, included in that should be a confrontation of the fear of this kind of love.

It isn't just a few isolated pockets of single women who may be hiding from intimate love. Even married women can be hiding from love. We were all created for loving relationships with one another and with God. Marriage is the most intimate, and therefore the most revealing, about the kind of relationship God desires with us. When we hide from intimacy we also hide from God. We need to see the full effects of our patterns of hiding and then repent.

📖 Read 1 John 4:7–12. What reasons does this passage give for loving one another? How might these reasons be especially powerful in the marriage relationship?

_____

_____

_____

_____

_____

📖 Read Psalm 27:4, 8–10. What was David's deepest longing? What was his greatest fear? How does knowing that God never forsakes us give us the courage to risk intimate relationships?

_____

_____

_____

_____

_____

_____

_____

Because David lived in the days before Christ came, and before Christ made His promise that His Spirit would never leave us (John 14:16–18), he did not have the same assurance we have been given. Knowing that we will never be utterly forsaken, even if our parents or husbands leave (through death or abandonment), gives us the courage to seek intimate relationships. Because of this assurance, we can be open to truly love husbands. There are no guarantees in marriage, but there is this guarantee in life: because God did forsake His Son (Matthew 27:46), He will never forsake us. By taking our sin and its penalty on the cross, He forever took our deepest fears of abandonment. Knowing we are safe in Him, we can risk loving others.

📖 Read Ecclesiastes 4:9–11. What do these verses teach us about our need for companionship?

_____

_____

_____

_____

Many women have been hurt by the rejection of men, or simply because they have never been pursued by men. Because of the pain and fear of more pain, they cut off their longings and harden their hearts. They are therefore hiding from love. Although there may be more immediate pain in the longing and praying for a husband, or in dealing with the issues that keep a couple apart, the long-term loneliness and coldness can only be overcome when we open ourselves up and take some risks.

📖 Read 1 John 1:6–10. What does it mean to walk in darkness? Could that mean hiding? How might this passage apply both to the single woman who refuses to admit she is hiding from love and to wives who refuse to deal with their own sin or the sin of their husbands?

_____

_____

_____

_____

_____

_____

_____

_____

_____

There is an old saying that before marriage we should have our eyes wide open, but after marriage we should close them. This is simply a form of denial. I wonder how much of the denial we use in our marriages is falsely called acceptance or unconditional love. True love will not accept sin in the loved one. Marriage is a special relationship that God created to be a secure place of love and forgiveness, of confrontation and honesty, of gentleness and humility. Having our eyes wide open we can see both the dignity and depravity of our husbands. Our love must bring out the best in them by respect and encouragement. But it must also be honest and gentle in candid confrontation about the sin we see in their lives. The beauty of the gospel is that Christ has made atonement for our sin. He has paid the penalty and made a way for us to be forgiven. Our part is to confess our sin, repent, and ask for forgiveness and cleansing. A husband or wife has the closest vantage point to see most sin, and to deny it in ourselves or in our mates removes us from the reach of the gospel—denial keeps us from confession. The only sins that are forgiven and cleansed are the ones that are confessed. So if we say we love our husbands, but deny or overlook their sin, we do them no good. It is not loving to pretend they have no sin.

📖 Read Isaiah 54. The setting of this chapter is built around the time when the nation of Judah (southern tribes of Israel) was in captivity and many of its people had been exiled to conquering nations. During this time of exile, it can be said that God had abandoned his chosen people for a time. In Isaiah 54, the nation is pictured as a young wife separated from her Husband (the Lord). But through this analogy, God shows that He still loves His chosen people much like a loving husband loves his wife. List all the words or phrases you can find in this passage that could be descriptions of pain you might experience in marriage.

THE NEED FOR ATTACHMENT

Many of us struggle with a need for genuine, deep, warm, personal relationships. This need is manifested in a deep sense of not "belonging".... Disconnectedness is the most destructive result of sin's entrance into the universe. It is the deepest and most fundamental problem we can experience. It is a violation of the very nature of God....Attachment is our greatest need.[5]

—JOHN TOWNSEND

_____

_____

_____

_____

_____

TRUTH ABOUT MARRIAGE

The truth about marriage is that it is a way not of avoiding any of the painful trials of life, but rather of confronting them, of exposing and tackling them most intimately, most humanly. It is a way to meet suffering personally, head on, with the peculiar directness, the reckless candidness characteristic only of love. It is a way of living life with no other strategy or defense or protection than that of love.... Marriage is intended to be an environment in which [a man] will be lovingly yet persistently confronted with the plainest and ugliest evidence of his sinfulness and thus encouraged on a daily basis to repent and to change.[6]

—MIKE MASON
The Mystery of Marriage

Your list above could be overwhelming, but God's promises and His comfort are more than sufficient to meet our needs and heal our wounds. Feel the impact of these words from Isaiah 54 amidst the long list of painful circumstances and find comfort in the promises God gives to those who are suffering:

> *Fear not....*
> *For your husband is your Maker,*
> *Whose name is the LORD of hosts;*
> *And your Redeemer is the Holy One of Israel,*
> *Who is called the God of all the earth.*
> *For the LORD has called you,*
> *Like a wife forsaken and grieved in spirit....*
> *But with everlasting lovingkindness I will have compassion on you....*
> *And My covenant of peace will not be shaken....*
> *And all your sons will be taught of the LORD;*
> *And the well-being of your sons will be great.*
> *In righteousness you will be established....*
> *No weapon that is formed against you will prosper....*
> *This is the heritage of the servants of the LORD.*

What does this passage say to a woman who stays in an abusive marriage because she believes her only security is found in her husband? How might verses 14 and 15 help?

_____

_____

_____

_____

Seeing God as a loving Husband and knowing His compassion and kindness will give courage to a woman who needs to love her abusive husband from a distance. God wants her *"far from oppression and terror."* But such a woman will also need the support and encouragement of the Church. Too many abused women have been advised by a confused church to submit to abuse. We will explore what the Bible teaches about submission in lessons 11 and 12. Suffice it to say, submitting to abuse is wrong. An abused woman is hiding from the true love of God if she refuses to deal honestly with the situation.

The promises in Isaiah 54 are not just for the widow, the divorced, or the abused. They are for us all. No matter what difficulties we face in marriage, even if they are not listed in these verses, we need to remember that God says He is a husband to those He has chosen, and He promises to see us through any trials. Our relationships with God through Christ are sufficient to enable us to love boldly, without hiding, even if our husbands fail to love us.

APPLY How aware are you of God's loving care for you?

_____

_____

_____

Does the security you get from God's promise help you take the risk of loving boldly?

_____

_____

Even though you claim intimacy is your deepest desire, isn't it also your greatest fear?

_____

_____

If you are single, honestly ask God to reveal to you the barriers you have set up against loving a husband.

_____

_____

_____

_____

If you are married, what keeps you from being totally open and vulnerable with your husband? How does that affect your marriage?

_____

_____

_____

_____

FAITHFULNESS

Loving Husbands

Loving a husband in faithfulness is one of the most important things a woman can do to make her marriage strong. Even for a woman not yet married, part of loving a future husband is to save herself for him. Refusing sex before marriage, both with other men and with her future husband, is the best way to build a foundation for a faithful love that will last a lifetime. This is especially hard in a culture like ours, where sex outside of marriage is not only accepted, but is also expected. In contrast, the Bible makes it clear that God's design and purposes for marriage exclude any kind of immorality. Exploring what God says on the subject will give conviction and determination to withstand the pressures of our society and the temptations of the destroyer.

Read 1 Thessalonians 4:1–8. How do we *"walk and please God"* according to these verses? By whose authority did Paul give this command? Why do you think it is the *"will of God"*? Why would He care about it? Isn't He for love, and the free expression of love?

_____

_____

_____

_____

_____

_____

_____

GROUNDWORK OF MARRIAGE

Marriage begins when two people make the clear, unqualified promise to be faithful, each to the other, until the end of their days. . . . A promise made, a promise witnessed, a promise heard, remembered and trusted—this is the groundwork of marriage. . . . We do the thing God does, establishing a covenant with another human being: we ask faith in our faithfulness to that covenant.[7]

—WALTER WANGERIN

God is love. It is the very nature of His being. But immoral love goes against everything God is trying to teach us about love. It is the counterfeit and the despoiler of true love. Marital love was meant to be a picture of God's love (His commitment and faithfulness to us) and to provide a secure place to raise godly children. But counterfeit love is all about love without commitment. It is a place of unfaithfulness and insecurity. Immorality has stripped society of its mores and destroyed the foundations of family life. Among Christians it has made a mockery of God's love.

Having sex before the vows of faithfulness are made undermines the foundation of marriage before it begins. If a man does not respect a woman enough to protect her virginity, why should any woman expect him to protect her marriage from infidelity? How can a man who is so focused on his own physical needs be trusted? After all, such a man will ignore a woman's need for security and commitment, expecting a woman to meet his needs while hers go unmet. What's to keep him from doing the same thing to her years down the road when he "needs" someone new? A man so focused on himself that he will not pay the "bride-price" is not worth pursuing.

For those of you who are single, I implore you—don't sell yourself so cheap! You are worth more than diamonds! Wait until he has made a public vow to you, a promise to be faithful to you until death.

According to 1 Thessalonians 4:8, whom do we reject when we decide to have sex outside of marriage?

_____

I wonder why Paul uses the description of God as the one who gives us the Holy Spirit in this context. Could it be that immorality blocks us from receiving the Spirit's work in our lives? Is that a major way we *"quench the Spirit"*? If you are tempted to infidelity or are involved in immorality, take a look at your priorities. This passage seems to be offering the choice between spiritual growth and illicit pleasures. Although waiting for marriage or for your husband to love you well is hard, it is the place where you will be most open to the Holy Spirit.

Read 1 Corinthians 6:18–20. What makes the sin of immorality different from other sins? How does seeing your body as a temple help you protect it?

_____

_____

_____

_____

_____

_____

_____

When we sin against our bodies by immorality, we are defiling the temple of the Holy Spirit. When we intentionally focus on what is at stake by our choices, we are more prone to make the right ones. Satan distracts us by saying the question only involves the immediate choice between pleasure and no pleasure. God is telling us there are a lot more factors to be considered. Again we see not only marital happiness is compromised, physical risk is taken, and spiritual damage is done.

📖 Read Deuteronomy 22:20–21. Why was God so concerned about purity and *"purg*[ing] *evil from Israel"*?

_____

_____

_____

_____

If one person strays from the ancient path (Jeremiah 6:16) and experiences no consequences, those who follow find little reason to stay on the path. Just as God longed to see His people prosper and find blessing by living according to His ways, one of the best reasons to establish godly practices in our relationships is to preserve purity for our posterity. If, some day, you want your children to save themselves for marriage and your grandchildren to know the blessings of a godly heritage, determine now to swim against the tide and depend on God's grace to enable you to flee immorality, if not for your own sake, at least for theirs.

📖 Read Matthew 5:27–30. If you think the Old Testament was harsh, what do you think of Jesus' command in these verses? Why is He so concerned about a little lust? What should we do when we are tempted?

_____

_____

_____

_____

_____

Jesus saw further than the immediate—He saw the long-term effects, even to eternity. Temptation has to be dealt with quickly and drastically. It is no small thing that can be ignored or handled alone. If you are being pulled towards immorality confess it to a close confidante. You may lose face (or eye or hand) but Christ is saying you are flirting with a fire that can utterly destroy you. Don't worry about what people might think—you must get help. Satan will try to convince you to hide what you are thinking or doing. Jesus wants you to be bold in your fight against temptation.

Temptation has to be dealt with quickly and drastically.

📖 Read Romans 6:12–19. What does Paul say about lust? How do we *"let sin reign"* in our bodies according to these verses? What do we need to do to escape our slavery to sin?

_____

_____

_____

This is not just mind over matter, or tricking ourselves into thinking we are something we are not. Paul is talking about the spiritual power that can be ours by realizing what has already been done in Christ to secure our freedom. When we *"present the members of our body"* to God, we are tapping into His incredible resources to find the strength to overcome our sinful lusts. The battle is real and the pressure intense. But God's grace is greater than our sin. We may lack self-control, but we have the promise of God's provision to make us *"obedient from the heart."*

📖 Read Psalm 51:1–3, 7, and 10–11. What about women who have already lost their virginity or are involved in an affair? Is there any reason for them to *"flee immorality"*? Do you believe in the possibility of "second virginity"?

_____

_____

_____

Women who have already committed acts of immorality should not let Satan convince them that there is no longer any reason to abstain from immorality because they have once, or repeatedly, fallen. There is always forgiveness for those who truly repent. And this promised cleansing makes us *"whiter than snow."* In God's eyes, we are again virgins. There is every reason for those involved in immoral relationships to put an end to such behavior and begin today to love their husbands (or future husbands) by maintaining the purity God gives them.

Those of you who have never had an extramarital affair might feel you are "off the hook." But as Linda Dillow and Lorraine Pintus explain in their book, *Intimate Issues* (WaterBrook Press, 1999):

> Faithfulness to our vows is more than the absence of an affair or the absence of a divorce document. Faithfulness is the presence of love, devotion, honor, loyalty, and encouragement. Faithfulness is positive and dynamic; it means we actively seek the welfare of our spouse. . . . You may not cheat on your husband with another man, but do you cheat on him by withholding yourself sexually and emotionally?[8]

📖 Read Revelation 2:19–23. What did the Son of God have against the church in Thyatira? In what ways does the church today tolerate immorality? What does He find when He *"searches [our] minds and hearts"*? What should we do?

_____

_____

_____

_____

There is every reason for those involved in immoral relationships to put an end to such behavior and begin today to love their husbands (or future husbands) by maintaining the purity God gives them.

I wonder if the Church's tolerance of the pervasive immorality in our culture and the media isn't worse than the problem in Thyatira. Consider what we allow into our homes in the name of entertainment. Think about the sin that is overlooked by those who are called to discipline the members of the Church. What standards do we maintain for those who teach and lead our children? Christ's call to repentance in verse 21 is for us all.

APPLY For those not yet married—how is refusing sex before marriage (both with others and with your future husband) a way to love your husband? What if you have already lost your virginity—what reasons has God given you today to stop having sex before marriage?

_____

_____

_____

_____

_____

What does saying "no" to your flesh do to you?

_____

_____

_____

What resources has He given to help you say "no" to fleshly lusts?

_____

_____

_____

How does your church compare to the one in Thyatira?

_____

_____

_____

LOVING IN ANGER

Loving Husbands

DAY FOUR

One of the hardest times to love a husband is when you are angry with him or he is angry with you. However, since love is a choice and anger is an emotion, loving your husband in the midst of conflict is still possible. Learning to deal with anger is one of the best ways to protect your love. If you suppress your anger rather than talking about it, the suppression can affect your choice to continue to love. Suppression can eat away at your commitment, until none is left. If, on the other hand, you allow your anger to explode into violence, it can destroy the opportunity to handle disputes rationally. Allowing the emotion to control the volition puts the proverbial "cart before the horse." As you study the Scripture passages for today, notice how volitional choices can triumph over angry emotions.

📖 Read Ephesians 4:26. Is anger wrong? How do you sin when you are angry? Are you more prone to silence or violence?

_____

_____

_____

Anger is neither right nor wrong. It simply is. This verse tells us to be angry. Because we live in a fallen world, and sin is everywhere, we will either be angry or in denial. What we do with our anger takes us into sin or towards reconciliation and renewal. This verse tells us we sin in our anger when we don't deal with it before the end of the day.

📖 Read Ephesians 4:22–25. What four ways of dealing with anger do you find listed in these verses? What do you think each one means?

_____

_____

_____

_____

_____

There will be many applications of these four steps, but they should all include repentance, allowing God's truth to change your thinking, putting on the robe of Christ's righteousness, and speaking the truth. The process of dealing with our anger always involves communication. Trying to defuse anger in any other way will prove futile. We need to talk to God, talk to ourselves, and talk to our husbands. Sometimes we need to talk to older women as well. Not talking about it gives Satan the opportunity to spread his lies and destruction.

📖 Read Colossians 3:8–15. What are we to put off? What are we to put on?

_____

_____

_____

_____

"And so, as those who have been chosen of God, holy and beloved, put on a heart of compassion, kindness, humility, gentleness and patience...."

Colossians 3:12

After reading a passage like this, one wonders how we can put on and off such strong emotions. It sounds like a garment that can be easily changed. Yet, in the midst of conflict, especially in a marriage when so much is at stake, it is much more difficult. How do we get rid of the anger? We have already seen that denial or suppression is not the answer. Denying or suppressing a matter is not putting it aside or taking it off, but rather just covering it up.

Before we can make the choice to put off our anger we need to understand it. Anger is sometimes the outer layer of our emotions, covering the more tender emotions of pain or fear. We dare not carry our hurt and anxiety so close to the surface, so we hide them behind our anger. The _"truth"_ we need to speak to our husbands includes these hidden feelings. When we remove the outer layer of anger and deal honestly with what is under it we can eventually get to the place deep within our hearts where we can either repent or forgive, usually both. Then, we are ready to put on love.

We make the choice to put on the robe of righteousness once we have removed the robe of anger. Notice that love is the last description of the robe of righteousness. We don't look for the love somewhere within us. It is part of the wardrobe Christ gives to us. He offers compassion, kindness, humility, gentleness, patience, forgiveness, and love. Couples who memorize Colossians 3:12–15 readily know what is available in the wardrobe God provides for them. (Maybe memorization is what is meant by the phrase in the next verse, *"let the word of Christ richly dwell within you."*)

It would be easier if this putting off and on could be a one-time occurrence, but it needs to be practiced over and over again. With a lot of practice over the years, it does become easier and more natural, but as long as we still live in this fallen world and have to deal with our own imperfection, we will always need to choose. Love is a choice, and this passage helps us to see some of the particular aspects of making that choice.

One final comment on this passage is for the women who are married to non-Christians. Because you have this "wardrobe" available for your use and he does not, you carry more of the responsibility for being the one who can change. As 1 Peter 3:1 and 2 tell us, it will be by your behavior of putting on love as it is described here that you may win your husbands to the Lord. Your anger with their stubborn disobedience will accomplish nothing.

📖 Read 1 Thessalonians 3:12 and Philippians 1:9. What does Paul do to help his disciples to put on love? How can Paul's prayers be models for our prayers?

_____

_____

_____

_____

We should often pray these prayers for ourselves and for others. They remind us that God is not only the source of love—He is the cause. He can cause our love to increase and abound. So, if our love is too small or not growing properly, it needs to become a matter of prayer. I experienced this many years ago, when my husband and I started going to a small church where the pastor was trying to build up the men of the church to become true leaders. One of the first things he needed to do was to transfer control from the women to the men. I don't know if it was the control issue or the pastor's abrupt way of doing things, but I found it very difficult to love him. I knew what he was trying to do was right. I also knew God called me to love him as a brother in Christ and as my pastor. So I persistently prayed Paul's prayer from Thessalonians, asking that God would cause me to love him. In answer to my prayer, something in my heart began to soften towards him, and eventually, I did grow to love him. It was through this supernatural change that I realized how effectual this prayer can be.

APPLY How would you rate the communication in your marriage?

_____

_____

_____

_____

GIVING OUT OF ABUNDANCE

"Until I am aware that my needs are already met in Christ, I will be motivated by emptiness to meet my needs. When by simple faith I accept Christ's shed blood as full payment for my sins, I am brought into a relationship with an infinite Being of love and purpose who fully satisfies my needs for security and significance. Therefore I am freed from self-centered preoccupation with my own needs; they are met. It is now possible for me to give to others out of my fullness rather than needing to receive from others because of my emptiness."[9]

—LARRY CRABB

How do you usually deal with your anger?

_____

_____

_____

_____

How do you put on love?

_____

_____

_____

How often do you pray that God would increase your love?

_____

_____

_____

_____

Do you ever pray that for others?

_____

_____

Loving Husbands

DAY FIVE

Contrary to the famous line from the 1970 film _Love Story_, love does involve saying you're sorry.

LOVING IN FORGIVENESS

A famous line from the 1970 movie _Love Story_ is, "Love means never having to say you're sorry." But Scripture teaches that saying, "I'm sorry," is part of the process of repentance, confession, forgiveness, and reconciliation. By this process we stay in loving relationships with others and with God. Because we are called to love sinners, we must continually forgive them. Love is saying, "I'm sorry," and it is saying, "I forgive you." These two statements should be heard often in our homes. If they are rarely spoken, it indicates the practice of denial and hiding. If we do not apologize or express forgiveness, we are not being honest about our sin or the bitterness that is growing deep within our souls. It may one day explode in destructive ways. Honest love is rare in many homes—some women may have never experienced it.

📖 Read Matthew 18:21–35. Who is the king, who is the forgiven slave, and who is the fellow slave? In what ways are our debts to God always much more than the debts others owe to us?

_____

_____

_____

_____

_____

When I applied this parable to my marriage, at first I felt like my husband had a million dollar debt he owed me after his adulterous affair, and I had maybe a hundred dollars worth of debt. But as the Holy Spirit dealt with my heart, He used James 4:4–5 to convince me that I was the one with the ten million dollar debt that had been forgiven, and He was asking me to forgive my husband's hundred dollar debt. I was reminded of the innumerable times I had chosen friendship with the world over worship of God and real-ized the pain and jealousy it brought to the heart of God. (James was correct in addressing me as the "adulteress.") The pain and jealousy God feels is far greater than any pain that is felt when our husbands hurt us or when we hurt them. No matter what our husbands do to us, we can always translate their offenses into some similar offense against God of which we are guilty. God forgives us and requires that we forgive others.

📖 Compare Luke 24:47 and 2 Peter 3:9 with Matthew 6:14–15, 18:21–22 and Luke 17:3–4. We are required to forgive unconditionally, even for repeated offenses when it is obvious the repentance is not real, yet God requires repentance before He will forgive. Why the double standard?

_____

_____

_____

God is the only judge, and He alone knows if we are truly repentant. His forgiveness is the ultimate forgiveness; ours only represents our personal relinquishment of anger and bitterness. Our forgiveness is as much for our own sake as for the sake of the offender.

📖 Read Matthew 7:1. Why are we tempted to judge? What happens if we do?

_____

_____

_____

The act of forgiveness is a relinquishing of any right to judgment. We some-times hold on to unforgiveness because we want to be sure offenders suffer for what they have done. When we fear God will be too merciful, we seek our own revenge. We want to be sure the guilty one pays. We may not be this forthright in our thinking, but, subconsciously, this is how we live out our anger and bitterness. The only antidote is forgiveness. It is trusting God to be the judge.

📖 Read 1 Peter 2:21–23. What five steps of forgiveness did Christ exem-plify for us? What might they look like in a past, present, or future con-flict with your husband?

1)_____

2)_____

3)_____

4)_____

5)_____

TRUE FORGIVENESS

Real reconciliation is possible if one is willing to trust.

Real negotiations are possible if one is willing to risk.

Both steps invite repenting and rebuild-ing of the relationship in return.

Care enough to trust again.

Care enough to risk again.

Care enough to turn and invite change in return.[10]

—DAVID AUGSBURGER

First Peter 2:22 states that no deceit was found to come out of the mouth of Christ. When my husband first admitted his adultery, I told him immediately that I forgave him. I knew that Christ's blood had paid for his sin, and I wanted the pain I felt and the separation between us to be over right away. I also knew forgiveness was the key. But it was a false forgiveness. It was an attempt to deny what had happened, to deny the pain and destruction it had caused, to deny the problems that had led to his fall, and to deny my part in those problems. The deceit found in my mouth was the deceit of denial. It was many months before I began to understand all that was involved in true forgiveness, and many years before I could say in all honesty that I had forgiven him.

Do you think forgiveness is a process or a pronouncement?

_____

_____

APPLY What areas of your marriage (or other relationships if you are single) need reconciliation?

_____

_____

_____

Are you willing to talk about them with an older woman?

_____

_____

How do you measure your own debt to God? How does it compare to the debt your husband (or someone else) owes you?

_____

_____

_____

_____

How can the thought that God continues to forgive you—even for the sins you keep repeating—help you to forgive repetitive sins committed by your husband or by others?

_____

_____

_____

Do you tend to offer forgiveness too soon, thereby offering pseudo-forgiveness? Or do you wait too long to forgive others?

_____

_____

What kind of training does your church have in this area of forgiveness? What improvements can be made in this area in your church?

_____

_____

Loving husbands is a life-long calling for those women who have them and a challenge to those who don't. It takes faith, fortitude, and forgiveness. **Faith**—because our ability to love comes from God. **Fortitude**—because love takes courage and commitment. **Forgiveness**—because we live in a fallen world and perfect love is only found in heaven.

Spend some time with the Lord in prayer.

 I praise you my Father for sending Your Son, Jesus Christ, to reveal to me Your sacrificial love. I praise You, Christ, for longing for my love so much that You would die to redeem me and make me beautiful in Your sight. I praise You, Holy Spirit, for filling my heart with Your love and enabling me to love others.

Father, I confess I have not received and responded to Your love as I should. I fail to come to You each day to be filled with Your love. I look to other sources of love or deny my need for love. I have failed to love my husband by faith with the supply of love You grant to me. I have offered a fleshly love in the hopes that a man will meet my needs. I have held on to my resentments when my husband has failed to love me well. Please forgive me and cleanse my heart and renew a right spirit within me.

I pray for single women I know and ask that You would protect them from temptation and all that Satan does to discourage and destroy them. I pray that they might see You as a loving husband, and that You would show them Your everlasting kindness. May they know Your peace, provision, and protection.

Deliver my study group from evil, from the world around us, from the forces in the heavenlies and from the enemy within. There is so much to keep us from loving our husbands well. We need Your power and strength to persevere in our love. May the way we love them bring honor and glory to You and to Your kingdom. For Jesus' sake, Amen.

Write your own personal prayer in the space provided below.

_____

_____

_____

_____

_____

_____

_____

_____

_____

_____

_____

_____

_____

Notes

6

Loving Children

As I listen to the stories of those who come to me for counseling, I am often reminded to be thankful for my godly parents. Few have been as blessed as I. The protection and trust I was given throughout my childhood shielded me from much of the pain and shame others must struggle through. The consistency of my parents' discipline and training gave me a foundation that prepared me to offer stability and soundness of mind to a younger generation.

When I reflect on how my mother loves her children, I think of the phrase "love always hopes." Not only did she believe in us and give us the freedom to be who we were, she accepted us even in our sin and rebellion. More significantly, she always hoped in God for us. Her faith in His grace and faithfulness in our lives enabled her to trust in His sovereignty even when we made wrong choices. Today, at over eighty years of age, she perseveres when so many of the other members her age in our church have left. Some in her generation have found it difficult to handle the changes brought by the younger generation. I believe what enables her to stay active and supportive is the hope she has in God's grace working in the lives of a younger leadership. Even though they don't "do it the way we used to," she hopes and believes God is leading them.

Her life has been one that personifies the words of the old hymn, "Trust and obey for there's no other way to be happy in Jesus,

Betty...

...a loving mother

but to trust and obey." Although her generation may not have expressed their love in ways psychologists today tell us are important, they did learn to trust and obey. Their legacy gave us the important foundation of discipline, faith, and perseverance.

Mother's "love language" is serving, and her life manifests that love in a myriad of ways. She has served the Lord both in the church and in para-church organizations for years. She served her four children "twenty-four/seven" all the years we lived in her home. She was always there for us; the home was well kept; the food lovingly prepared and delicious; and the doors were always open for our friends. She modeled loving service for others by sewing like Dorcas, practicing hospitality, and being available for conversations with friends and neighbors. She broke all the records by loving and caring for young children in the church nursery for over fifty years. Her obedience to what she understood was faithful and consistent. It is a benchmark for many who follow after her.

WITH WIDE OPEN HEARTS

I n the midst of a culture that shows its disdain for children by abortion, abuse, and materialistic priorities that limit the size of families and how children are to be raised, Christians are to love children. Specifically, older women in the church are called to train younger women to love children. We are to open our hearts and our arms to each precious child and do all we can to protect children from the enemy's design to destroy them.

📖 Read 2 Corinthians 6:11–13. What can we learn from the way Paul spoke to his *"children"* and the way he related to them? What do you think it means to "open wide our hearts"?

_____

_____

_____

_____

_____

I remember a movement years ago that tried to get parents to hug their children more often. They distributed bumper stickers that said, "Have you hugged your child today?" The symbolism of a hug speaks volumes. First our arms are open wide. Then we pull the other into our own personal space. In the end, we open our arms again, releasing the other to be himself or herself. A hug can be an expression of a wide-open heart.

Following Paul's example of speaking freely, how can we make our communication more free and open?

_____

_____

_____

"Older women likewise are to live priestly lifestyles, not to be malicious gossips, nor should they have any addictions, but should be teachers of beauty, so that they can **train the younger women** to love husbands, **to love children,** to be of sound mind, to be pure, to be keepers of the home, to be good and to be submissive to their own husbands that the word of God may not be dishonored."

Titus 2:3–5 (AUTHOR'S PARAPHRASE)

Honest communication—both listening and speaking freely—is the first duty of love. Children know they are loved by the way we listen and speak to them. We reveal the love that is in our hearts by our tone of voice, our gestures, and our body language as well as by our words.

Why do we sometimes "withhold our affection"?

_____

_____

_____

_____

Too often we withhold our affection simply because we get distracted by less important things or angered by circumstances. Also, subconscious barriers can cut us off from one another and from our children.

How does Paul use his own example of open communication and affection to encourage the Corinthians? What does this teach us about training others?

_____

_____

_____

_____

_____

Proverbs 15:30 says, *"Bright eyes gladden the heart."* What is the message your children read about themselves in your eyes? Do your eyes light up when you listen to them?

_____

_____

_____

_____

_____

📖 Read Matthew 19:13–15. In what ways do we hinder our children from coming to Jesus? As we are opening our hearts to them and training them to open up with us, should we not also help them open up to Christ? How do we do this?

_____

_____

_____

_____

_____

We need to learn to open our hearts to one another and to God and then teach our children to do the same. John Ryle talks about the importance of training children to pray. You can read his comments in the side margin of this page.

Word Study
LOVE CHILDREN

Younger women also need to be trained to love (*philéō*) children. Again, *philéō* is synonymous with tender affection, cherishing and respect. It is interesting to note that Paul uses the Greek word *philóteknos* (literally, "love children"), which does not include any form of the English word, "their," implying we are to love all children, not just our own.

ADVICE FOR PARENTS

Parents, if you love your children, do all that lies in your power to train them up to a habit of prayer. Show them how to begin. Tell them what to say. Encourage them to persevere.

Remind them if they become careless and slack about it. Let it not be your fault, at any rate, if they never call on the name of the Lord.[1]

—JOHN RYLE

> *"And whoever welcomes a little child like this in my name welcomes me."*
>
> **—Jesus Christ Matthew 5:18 (NIV)**

📖 Read Matthew 18:5–6 in the New International Version. In what ways does our society not welcome children? What can we do to change that, at least in the church? How can your particular church become one that is known for *"loving children"*?

_____

_____

_____

_____

_____

_____

Miriam Adeney, a Christian anthropologist, compares American child-rearing with the way Filipinos care for their children. In the Philippines, ". . . small children are prized. . . . Caring for them is a joy. . . . A whole cadre of committed caregivers circle each child. The major concern is to surround their children with good people. . . . No one is left lonely. Everyone has a place and a people." In contrast, "American children are raised to achieve independently . . . . Privacy is valued. . . . [There is] compartmentalization between childless and child-blessed people . . . . We surround our children with good toys and learning activities . . . and keep them home on a rigid schedule." She suggests,

> We need to develop slightly different models of childsharing . . . models whereby the responsibilities—and the rights—to be significant role models, disciplinarians, and trainers for the children can be more broadly shared. The child himself needs to know who his parents are, who has ultimate responsibility and authority. But he also needs other adults to play a significant role in his life. Recognizing that, we can network those relationships for our children . . . . Our own ancestors did not huddle in isolated nuclear families, but shared many childraising hours with kin, neighbors, and helpers. Sharing children can benefit everyone. And it can enable all of us to serve more holistically, with all our hearts and souls and strength and minds.[2]

Because many extended families are scattered across the globe, our churches need to be filled with surrogate sisters, brothers, aunts, uncles, and grandparents. Loving one another and loving children requires an intimate involvement and togetherness that is so different from our culture that others will recognize that we are Christians by our love.

🛑 **APPLY** Do you have a wide-open heart?

_____

_____

Why is it sometimes difficult for you to open up?

_____

_____

_____

_____

Do you ever withhold your affection? Why?

_____

_____

_____

_____

How and what do your eyes speak?

_____

_____

_____

_____

LOVE ALWAYS PROTECTS

For most of us the desire to nurture our little ones is so much a part of us, we give it little thought. Yet because our culture no longer sees this as one of the highest priorities in life, we need to proclaim its importance. In 1 Corinthians 13:7, we are given four descriptions of love that can help us encourage young mothers to love their children as God does. The first description is that love always protects.

Psalm 71 describes four ways God protects his children. The key phrase David uses to describe this protection is *"a rock of habitation."* The phrase paints a picture of a secure dwelling place, a welcoming embrace, a stable environment, and the availability of "round the clock" nurturing. My heart was grieved when I read the following quotation from a secular feminist:

> We have turned society on its head in the past twenty years; we choose to think our confusion is all about jobs, money, politics, when, in fact, we are hungry for the nurturing that women once embodied. We have all lost our mommies, including we women, which is why so many turn to other women instead of men. Give me a breast to lie on![3]

The call to older women in the Church is to turn the tide and train younger women, who may not have known what it was like to have a *"rock of habitation,"* to be that for their own children. Some of you have good memories, as I do, of a mother who was always there and always available. Others may need to look to God's example or to stories of better mothers.

📖 Read Psalm 71:1-4. Describe how God protects His children, then describe how our love can offer the same kind of protection:

Protection from Shame
(*"let me never be ashamed"*)

_____

_____

_____

_____

David's request that the Lord would "let [him] never be ashamed" implies that God protects His children from shame. This not only rules out using shame as a form of discipline, but also includes protecting children from any kind of shame others would try to put on them.

One of my sons had a learning disability, and we were always careful to keep him from feeling shame about it. Thankfully, we were in a school system (a Christian school) that understood learning disabilities, and not only provided excellent therapy for him, but also protected the LD children from the ignorance that puts them down or expects less from them. From the beginning, we told him that God had designed his brain in a different way, because He was calling him to some very special tasks. He has always had to work harder and longer to accomplish his goals, but he has learned determination and perseverance that enable him to use all of his creative and intellectual abilities. We often pointed out to our son that geniuses like Einstein had learning disabilities, and we reminded him that there was no shame in being different.

Protection from Indifference
("incline Thine ear to me")

_____

_____

_____

_____

_____

In the midst of David's requests for God to deliver, rescue, and save him, he inserts the phrase, "incline Thine ear to me." This not only reinforces all that has already been said about showing our love by listening to our children, but it also reminds me of how important it is to be sure our children know they can tell us everything. Many younger women are found in counseling offices because their mothers failed to protect them from the emotional, verbal, and physical abuse of men in their lives. The fact that their mothers were indifferent toward abuse or did not believe the child's accusations is sometimes one of the hardest things for these young women to deal with. We, as older women, not only need to incline our ears to the younger women, but also train them to listen to and believe their children.

Protection from Isolation
("Deliver me. . . . Be a rock of habitation, to which I may continually come. . . .")

_____

_____

_____

_____

_____

We need to become a rock of habitation for our children even if we may not have experienced such parental fortitude during our own childhood years. We must resist conforming to the world's patterns. Because we are swimming upstream, we will need to join forces and make a concerted effort to be countercultural.

> **We, as older women, not only need to incline our ears to the younger women, but also train them to listen to and believe their children.**

_____

_____

_____

The last area of protection referred to in these verses is God's rescuing us from the oppression of the wicked. The loving protection we offer as mothers involves establishing a sense of security and safety under God's care. We do this not only through praying with and for our children but also through intervening and rescuing them when they fall into temptation.

For example, soon after my husband left the home for the last time, I was reminded of the chorus "Mighty Warrior."[4] This song helped me establish a safe refuge for my children. We probably sang it together every evening for about a month, both to tell Satan that he had to clear out and to assure the children (and me) that even though Daddy was gone, the Lord was with us, and He was the authority now. The words of the chorus continually reassured us that Jesus had "all authority" in our home while Satan had "no authority."

Several years later one of my sons was being pursued by a youth worker in our church, which normally would have encouraged me, since I knew he needed more male influence in his life. But somehow I had a check in my spirit about the man. I shared this with my prayer partner and we decided to pray specifically that if there was any danger present, it would be revealed before the trip to Disney World that they had planned together. The day before the trip I got a call from the pastor's wife to inform us that the man was in jail for molesting another young man. God had rescued my son from the hand of the wicked.

Read 2 John. This brief letter to a mother and her children speaks not only of the importance of love, but also of protection from evil influence in the home. What kind of teachers do we receive into our homes (verse 10) who do not *"abide in the teaching of Christ"*? (See verse 9.) What about those who teach our children outside the boundaries of our homes (in our schools, churches, etc.)? How can we protect our children from deceivers?

_____

_____

_____

_____

_____

Love protects children from deception. The primary way to do this is to teach them the truth. It is fascinating to see how many times John mentions love and truth in this letter. They are inextricably tied together, for all the grace, mercy, and peace we have from God come to us in truth and love (verse 3). But the warning John gives to this mother (and all of us) is to be aware of all the deceivers out in the world, and to be careful not to allow them into our homes or let them influence our children. We often do far more than give greetings to all the deceivers in our culture today. We sit our children down in front of a picture tube and let lies permeate their minds. We send them to schools whose stated goals and philosophy are clearly anti-Christian. What are we thinking?

📖 Read Proverbs 23:13–14; 29:15. How can we protect children from their own sinful nature?

_____

_____

_____

_____

These verses must not be interpreted as an excuse for abuse. Our discipline is never to be an outlet for our anger, but only another way we love our children. Just as God disciplines those He loves (Hebrews 12:6), we must, in love, protect them from their own sin.

📖 Read Proverbs 31:8–9. What can we do to help protect the smallest children, those who are yet unborn?

_____

_____

_____

_____

Our love for children should motivate us to be active in speaking out against abortion. Whether God leads you to become active in the pro-life movement, to volunteer at your local women's center, or to write letters to your senator when legislation concerning abortion is imminent, you need to let your voice be heard.

APPLY Are you a rock of habitation for children?

_____

_____

How did your mother nurture and protect you?

_____

_____

_____

_____

_____

What kind of training would you like to see in your church that might help you better understand your role as a protector of children?

_____

_____

_____

How involved are you in the pro-life movement?

_____

_____

LOVE ALWAYS TRUSTS

One primary means of respecting children is trusting them. This does not mean that we don't expect that they will at times seek to deceive us. We know that because of their sinful natures they will lie occasionally, but they must know that we have no tolerance for lying. Because love rejoices in the truth, there needs to be such a celebration of truth that our children would rather confess and accept the consequences of their failures than live in deception.

When there is not allowance for or expectation of sin, deception is inevitable. But a family that is honest with its struggle with sin, and has the grace and mercy to forgive, can live in an atmosphere of trust where each member is free to speak the truth. In legalistic families, where the **appearance** of keeping the rules is most important, children are forced into a lifestyle of deception. In order to be who they are while still maintaining the persona they are expected to project, children in such homes learn to deceive others and even themselves. If love is conditional based upon their attitudes and performance, children soon learn to hide their true feelings and activities. This can quickly degenerate to total mistrust and the destruction of an open relationship. God as our Father allows us to make our own choices, even when they are wrong, because His love always trusts. He knows we are sinners, and He knows we are not trustworthy, yet He chooses to give us a free will because He wants our love to be freely given back to Him.

📖 Read Galatians 5:1, 5, 13–16. When there is no trust, we turn to legalism. How can we avoid being legalistic? How can we be sure our children know what it means to walk in freedom and grace?

_____

_____

_____

_____

> **God as our Father allows us to make our own choices, even when they are wrong, because His love always trusts.**

For some, trust is leaving a breakable vase within reach of toddlers' hands so they can learn obedience and self-control. For others, it is allowing them to make choices when there is less risk involved. It is valuing our children for who they are and affirming that value by believing in them and respecting them. That value is not only based on what they do but also on the potential and dignity that is theirs because of who they are and to Whom they belong. Trust is building up their personal self-confidence by giving them freedom of choice. Of course that includes allowing natural consequences and parental discipline to follow the wrong choices that are inevitable.

Trust is the opposite of control. It is easier for us to be authoritarian parents, to have strict rules, and to build solid boundaries so we don't have to deal with all the messiness freedom can bring. But if we truly love our children, we should give them increasing amounts of freedom as they mature. We will not allow our fears to enslave them. I have known parents who, because of their fear, severely limit their children's opportunities to do anything without direct parental involvement. Their need for control and lack of trust hamper their children's development of inner strength and personal dependence on God.

> *"Trust is the intangible glue that cements relationships."*[5]
>
> **—Pat Springle**

Legalism is dependence on rules and discipline to create boundaries that will keep children in line. Don't get me wrong. I am not saying there should be no rules or discipline. Both are necessary in training the young child and in guiding the adolescent. But our dependence cannot be on rules and discipline. Love is dependence on the Holy Spirit to give the gift of faith and waiting for the hope of righteousness in our children. Legalism controls. *Love always trusts.*

📖 Read Luke 15:11-13, 20. What kind of trust was necessary for this father to give his son the wealth and then wait expectantly for his return? In what way is trust in God and in our children linked?

_____

_____

_____

_____

_____

_____

Would you be willing to give a prodigal son money, allow him to leave, and be waiting and watching for him to return? It would take a lot of trust. I am sure the father was trusting God to watch over his son and work through the circumstances and in his son's heart, more than he was trusting his son to make good choices. Proverbs 22:6 states, *"Train up a child in the way he should go, even when he is old he will not depart from it."* Our application of this proverb should not focus primarily on our ability to train, or a child's ability to stay on the right path, but rather on the trustworthiness of the principles of God and the power of the Holy Spirit.

📖 Read Matthew 6:25–34. I want to change the direction of our thinking here in this last Scripture reading. Think about how we trust God for and with our children. If love always trusts and we are called to love children, how does this passage help us understand God's promises to supply all we need to raise all of the children He gives to us?

_____

_____

_____

_____

The enemy brings fear into Christian's hearts as well as those in the world by the lie that there is not enough to go around or that the times we live in are too bleak to raise children; therefore, we need to stop multiplying. But God has not told us to stop. He needs our children to accomplish His purposes in these last days. We should not let fear dictate the size of our families. God wants us to trust and obey.

APPLY Are the relationships in your family built on trust or legalism?

_____

_____

Why do you think trust is such an important part of love?

_____

_____

_____

Do your children know you trust them?

_____

_____

Do you love children enough to have lots of them if God leads you and your husband in that direction?

_____

_____

If God is leading or has led you to have several children, do you trust Him enough to provide for your family?

_____

_____

LOVE ALWAYS HOPES

In an age of despair, hope has become a primary need. Our children learn to hope by watching us cope with the trials of life. If we could remember God is always involved in the process and His goal is to make us like Christ, we would be better equipped to encourage our children by our hope-filled love. When we worry and fret, we need to confess it as sin to our children so they will know it is not acceptable. Ross Campbell describes the need for hope:

> As your children grow into adolescence, they need optimism and hope. . . . You are in the best position to give this precious gift, but it takes work. You shouldn't listen to the proclaimers of gloom and doom or pass along their message. Teenagers are so sensitive to pessimism, especially from their parents. . . . Encourage means to "inspire courage"; your words will give them courage to face the future. . . . It is so important that they come to understand and deeply believe that Christian hope does not depend on what the world does to them. It depends only on what they do in the world as they live in response to God's great love for us. As parents we can be encouragers, dispensers of the hope that our children and teenagers so desperately need—even in the best of times and certainly in the worst.[6]

📖 Read Romans 5:1–8. Think about the significance of hope in a troubled world. What do these verses tell us about hope? How does the love of God always hope? How does His love give us hope? What is the purpose of suffering?

_____

_____

_____

_____

According to these verses all of our troubles have one ultimate purpose—to teach us to hope. Hope will never disappoint us because it is founded on the love of God. His love is the bedrock of all hope. And the cross of Christ is the ultimate expression of that love. Our *exult*[ing] *in hope of the glory of God"* may not be obvious to our children in their younger years, but they easily pick up on fears and anxieties when our hope fails. As they grow older they will learn how and why we respond to tribulation with hope.

Thinking about the significance of hope reminds me of Lucille, whose story is told in Lesson 1. She used to tell me repeatedly, "The Lord is with you and He is for you." The constant reminder of that simple statement gave me hope. It convinced me that though my world seemed to be falling apart, He would never leave me, so things would be all right. By His grace, I was able to take that hope home with me and give it to my kids. My optimistic attitude and faith in God's protection and provision set the tone of our home. I can't say that I never worried, but I can say in hindsight that there was never a real cause for worry. All things work out for good (see Romans 8:28). When I did worry and stew and fret, I confessed it as sin to my children. Now they are the ones who tell me not to worry. Many times, their hope is stronger than mine. My prayer for them is that God would strengthen their inner being so they would know more and more the love of Christ (Ephesians 3:16–19), thus giving them the only true foundation for hope.

📖 Read Hebrews 6:9–20. What do you think it means to hope in our children? As we found in the case of trust, how is our hope in them linked to our hope in God?

_____
_____
_____
_____
_____
_____
_____
_____

All of our hope is based on God's grace and faithfulness. The more our souls are anchored in hope the greater our faith and patience can be both for our own lives and the lives of our children. If our love always hopes we can be confident the choices they make, right or wrong, will in the end be made right. At times we must flee for refuge to Jesus—but our hope can always be sure and steadfast. Fear and despair have no place in our hearts when we hold on to hope.

An excellent example of love that always hoped is given in the book *Come Back, Barbara* by C. John Miller and Barbara Juliani. It is the story of Christian parents who had to watch a prodigal daughter leave them and her faith and of how God gave them hope in the midst of waiting. I definitely recommend it for parents of teenagers and for any women who fear what might happen to their children. We need to encourage each other to *"realize the full assurance of hope until the end"* (Hebrews 6:11).

"Love in a woman's heart comes from her level of responsiveness to the hope within her. Hope remembers things lost and envisions things not yet known."[7]

—Jan Myers

Read Jeremiah 29:11-14. How does the sovereignty of God in the lives of your children give you hope for them?

_____

_____

_____

_____

Even though this is a message given to the Israelites in exile, God's Spirit can speak it to our hearts when we need hope. We know without a doubt that our ultimate hope for heaven will be good, and we also have His promise in Romans 8:28. Our prayers that our children would call upon Him, come to Him, pray to Him, and seek Him with their whole hearts are the kind of prayers He loves to answer. Sometimes their waywardness is the thing He uses to draw us to Him in ever deeper dependence. It certainly keeps us on our knees, and that is where He wants us.

APPLY Why is worry so destructive? What do you do to keep from worry?

_____

_____

_____

_____

_____

How does our clamoring for control reveal a lack of hope?

_____

_____

_____

_____

What kind of hope do you have for your children? How does that reveal your love for them?

_____

_____

_____

_____

_____

How does the truth that "God is with you and He is for you" give you hope?

_____

_____

_____

_____

_____

LOVE ALWAYS PERSEVERES

When a little baby is so cute and innocent, love is easy. The difficulty in loving grows as the innate sinfulness of a child is more and more revealed. Perseverance in loving is needed most when sin is most apparent. Our sinful natures want to take the easy road and turn to legalism when loving becomes difficult. Because I am a recovering Pharisee myself, my first thought about perseverance was in regard to discipline and consistency. Somehow, I equated perseverance with toughness and the need for control. But as I have studied and prayed and thought about love persevering, I have come to the conclusion that it is the affection and respect, the acceptance and forgiveness, and the dependence on grace that must persevere. We are tempted to revert to legalism because a legalistic approach keeps things tidy and under control. We think we are persevering when we hold tight to the rules and don't bend. But God's call to persevere in our love has more to do with relational consistency. We persevere in affection and respect even when a child misbehaves. We persevere in forgiving *"seventy times seven"* (see Matthew 18:22). We persevere in our dependence on the Holy Spirit. *Love always perseveres.*

📖 Read Psalm 136; Isaiah 49:15, 16; 54:7, 8. How would you describe God's persevering love? What does a younger woman need to hear when she is at the end of her rope with a child and admits she is having great difficulty in loving him? How can she find the grace to love him?

_____

_____

_____

_____

_____

_____

One thing is for sure in this business of loving children and seeking to train others to love children—we are not adequate in ourselves. Both the younger woman who seeks to love and the older woman who ministers to her can only find adequacy in God's grace, in His overflowing supply of love and wisdom. We must always return to God's everlasting loving-kindness.

📖 Read Romans 2:4. Why is God patient? For what is He waiting? How does God's patience give direction and purpose to our persevering love?

_____

_____

_____

_____

_____

_____

_____

_____

This verse indicates God's patience comes from His deep desire to see us repent. We must always remember that the goal is repentance—both our repentance for failing to love and the repentance of our children. Because repentance is a work of the Holy Spirit, it brings us back to prayer and dependence on Him.

APPLY Is your working goal with your children a desire for you to see them get their lives in order or is it a desire for you to love them in a way that draws them to the love of God?

_____

_____

_____

_____

How would these goals counteract one another? How could they dovetail?

_____

_____

_____

_____

Do you think of perseverance in terms of discipline or love?

_____

_____

_____

Where do you turn when you are at the end of your rope with your children?

_____

_____

_____

_____

Has your love matured enough to be called "enduring love"?

_____

_____

_____

Close your study time with a word of prayer.

 Loving Father, how I praise You for the perfect example You give to me of a loving parent. Thank You that Your love endures forever. I praise You for being a rock of habitation that I can come to; You are always there for me. Thank You for trusting me and giving me freedom—even though I fail so often. Father God, You are reliable, wise, steadfast, generous, and kind. Thank You for Your love.

Father, I confess I fall so short of Your calling for me to love children. Please forgive me for closing my heart and withholding my affection from the children in my life. I also confess my indifference to the plight of suffering children and that I don't do enough to fight against abortion. Please forgive me and change my heart. Fill me with Your compassion and enable me to love with perseverance.

ENDURING LOVE

As Christians we have a job to do with each of our lives. To get it done, we must endure. As we do, we deepen in our maturity, and see how much we once thought of as love was just sentimental feelings. . . . Ultimately, allowing God to love you is the only way you will succeed in showing love—tender love, tough love, patient love, seeking love, forgiving love, and "doing" love. Such love eventually triumphs. . . . It is enduring love. When your love is ignored or rejected, you keep right on showing love . . . enduring love is God's weapon for defeating sin.

—C. JOHN MILLER
AND BARBARA JULIANI
Come Back, Barbara

Lord, I pray for all the mothers I know who are in the midst of loving and raising the future generations of Your servants. Please fill their hearts with Your love and enable them to instill faith and hope in their children. Give them patience and endurance. Make them like trees planted by streams of water that they may yield the fruit of godly children. I pray that their leaves will not wither and whatever they do will prosper. Make their delight be in Your Word. May it sustain them, daily. May they trust in You and depend on You to be better mothers.

Please deliver those in my study group from Satan's temptations to indifference, fear, shame, isolation, oppression, legalism, hopelessness, and impatience. Lord, we need Your power and glory in our lives. May Your kingdom come and Your will be done, Amen.

Take some time to write your own prayer in the space provided.

_____

_____

_____

_____

_____

_____

_____

_____

_____

_____

_____

_____

_____

_____

_____

_____

_____

Notes

Notes

7

Sound Minds

More than any other friend, Carla has challenged my thinking and helped me become more aware of the battle of the mind. She entices me with her poetry to think more deeply, and has always, by example, called me to live my life more fully. She was one of the first friends I turned to when I found out about my husband's affair.

On that very night, after a dispassionate interchange, my husband left the room, and I dialed Carla's number. In a matter-of-fact way, I reported to her the details of what I had discovered, and described my conversation with him.

"I am sure he is going to straighten out now, and things will soon be back to normal." I told her.

"How are you doing, Barbara?" she asked.

"I am fine," I said, totally convinced that I was. My highly developed denial system helped me believe the news of the affair had little effect on me.

"You don't have to be strong!" she wisely said to me. Her words cut through my walls, and I began to cry.

A few minutes later, my husband came back into our room. He was also weeping. I will always remember that night of weakness and need, of sorrow and hope, of honesty and vulnerability.

Carla...

...speaking love

"Older women likewise are to live priestly lifestyles, not to be malicious gossips, nor should they have any addictions, but should be teachers of beauty, so that they can **train the younger women** to love husbands, to love children, **to be of sound mind,** to be pure, to be keepers of the home, to be good and to be submissive to their own husbands that the word of God may not be dishonored."

Titus 2:3–5 (AUTHOR'S PARAPHRASE)

Sound Minds

DAY ONE

Occasionally, I wonder that if I had been able to continue to be vulnerable with my husband, whether he might not have chosen to leave me. But by morning I had regained the cold indifference that I thought was strength. I wouldn't realize until years later how unsound my thinking was and how wise Carla's advice had been.

A few months later, I conveyed to Carla my conviction that if I had enough faith, God would have to do something to change my husband and cause him to return to me. I had taken some verses out of context and convinced myself they were God's promise to me that my husband would come back. Sometimes, our minds confuse faith with presumption, and it takes friends like Carla to clarify things for us. "As I read Scripture," Carla said, "I find that there are only a few guaranteed promises like, 'I will be with you always' and 'I'll wipe away your tears in heaven.' How long are you going to continue to torture yourself with false expectations? It is like hitting your head against a brick wall." Those were hard words, but God used them to change the way I was thinking.

It was Carla that got me hooked on the truth of Galatians 5:6. She once said this verse might be the most significant statement Scripture makes about living our lives. It says, *"The only thing that counts is faith expressing itself through love"* (NIV). She was also the friend who told me to put Lucille in my back pocket. (See the introductory story in Lesson 1.) She saw something in an "older woman" that would be of great help to me further down the road. If she had not had the soundness of mind to recognize it and the wisdom to say it, I may never have pursued Lucille. It was Carla's faith working through love that got me started on the Titus 2 path.

While preparing this lesson, I asked Carla to send one of her poems that would illustrate movement towards a sound mind. She sent the following:

No Longer an Orphan

I have always kept something back,
A reserve in case of danger, disaster, famine, or loneliness.
I have not trusted Him completely.
I have worried, manipulated, prayed, hoped, fretted, cried—
Died a thousand deaths at the hand of terror rather than give over, surrender;
Fall into the arms of Jesus with complete abandon.
I have lived like an orphan.
And so, have made my abode with danger, disaster, famine, and loneliness.
It is enough! I'm home.

OVERCOMING FUTILITY

Notice a form of the same Greek word is used twice in our passage, once in verse 4 and again in verse 5. It is the word *sōphrōn*. In its first usage, Paul is calling older women to **train the minds** (*sōphronízo*) of younger women by talking about the list of topics that follow. The second time he identifies *sōphrōn* as one of the topics that needs to be addressed. There is no other Greek word for "training" used in Scripture, and *sōphronízo* is only used this one time. On the other hand, *sōphrōn* is used many times and is translated in many different ways.

Paul often used various forms of the word *sōphrōn* in his letters to the early churches. Since he thought it was so important to train others to have sound minds, it would follow that he would have done some training through his letters. In my search for Pauline passages with a training emphasis, I found Ephesians 4, which we will study today. The key to having a sound mind is revealed in what he calls *"learning Christ"* (verse 20), and our part is simply to *"speak truth"* to one another. The *"renewal in the spirit of our minds"* is accomplished by the Holy Spirit, but He always works in tandem with the truth. The more truth we speak to one another, the more darkness is dispelled. The more truth we articulate, the more ignorance is changed to knowledge. The more truth we believe, the sooner we lay aside a former manner of life and embrace a life of holiness.

Read Ephesians 4:17–25. How does Paul contrast those who are deceived and those who know the truth?

_____

_____

_____

_____

Paul identifies those who are *"corrupted by deceit"* with words like *"futility,"* *"darkness,"* and *"ignorance."* He ties in the behaviors that this corruption naturally leads to: *"sensuality, impurity and greediness."* In contrast, he identifies those who know the truth as people who have *"learned Christ."* They are *"renewed in the spirit of [their] minds,"* have *"put on a new self,"* and are *"created in righteousness and holiness."*

What is futility? What results of futility do you see in women today?

_____

_____

_____

_____

Dictionary definitions of "futility" use words like "uselessness," "occupied with trifles," "serving no useful purpose." How many younger women do we know who seem to be occupied with trifles? How much time is spent in doing things that serve no useful purpose? Paul says it is going to take training to move them from futility to having sound minds. But he talks in this passage about a specific kind of training.

Read Ephesians 4:20–21 again. What do you think it means to *"learn Christ"*(verse 20, NASB)? What ways of learning Christ does Paul mention in this passage?

_____

_____

_____

_____

_____

_____

 *Word Study*
SOUND MIND

Sōphronízō is the Greek word translated *"train"* or *"encourage"* in Titus 2:4. It means "to cause to be of sound mind by training . . . [that] would involve the cultivation of sound judgment and prudence."[1]

Sōphrōn, translated "self-controlled" in Titus 2:5a, "denotes [a person] of sound mind; hence, self-controlled, sober minded, and discreet."[2]

Sōphrōn is translated using many different English words, including "self-controlled," "temperate," "sober minded," "prudent," "discreet," "wise," "disciplined," "thoughtful," and more recently, "cool, calm, and collected."

"But you did not learn Christ in this way, if indeed you have heard Him and have been taught in Him, just as truth is in Jesus."

—Ephesians 4:20–21

SHARING KNOWLEDGE OF CHRIST

Whatever they think I may have in the way of comfort and healing, and I, who in the old days would have shrunk with fear from any such charged encounter, try to find something wise and hopeful to say to them, only little by little coming to understand that the most precious thing I have to give them is not whatever words I find to say—but simply whatever, spoken or unspoken, I have in me of Christ, which is also the most precious thing they have to give me.[3]

—FREDERIC BUECHNER

"*Learning Christ*" must refer to more than learning facts about Him. Wisdom is given to us through an intimate relationship with Him. Being taught in Him is being taught the truth by Him, by His Spirit, by His people. "*Learning Christ*" is the best way to gain a sound mind.

📖 Read Ephesians 4:25–27. What is falsehood? How do we lay it aside? What kind of opportunities does our silence give to the devil?

_____

_____

_____

_____

The thing that keeps us from speaking the truth is that which must be laid aside: "*falsehood.*" Our first interpretation might be that Paul is referring to lies, and most of us think we really don't have that much trouble with lying, so we have no struggle in laying it aside. But the next two verses help us to understand what he is really talking about:

> *Be angry, and yet do not sin; do not let the sun go down on your anger, and do not give the devil an opportunity.*

According to these verses, the way we sin with our anger is to let the day end without dealing with it. And the primary way to deal with anger is to talk about it. I believe the "*falsehood*" that we need to lay aside is denial or the refusal to speak truth. When we don't get our anger out in the open and talk about it, Satan is given the opportunity to deceive us. He is ready to fill our minds with all kinds of lies and accusations that fuel the fires of our anger and let it grow out of proportion. He does this in all of our relationships and is constantly taking every opportunity we give him. The way to combat it is with loving connection, loving communication of the truth, and a lot of grace.

These verses explain why Satan has worked so hard to build barriers between the generations in order to cut off communication. If he can keep us from speaking the truth to one another, he can continue to deceive. If we do not take advantage of opportunities to speak the truth, or even create opportunities, Satan gets more opportunity to deceive. Communication is vital. Satan knows this and has developed elaborate means to communicate his deceit. He has so filled our environment with his lies that we in the Church need to find that many more ways to speak the truth. Yet the current trends in lifestyle create fewer opportunities for communication among Christian women rather than more. We get so busy with our own lives and become so stressed with the overload that when we find any extra time, we simply want to be entertained—which often becomes an opportunity for Satan to feed us more lies.

📖 Read Titus 2:11–14. The Greek word translated "*sensibly*" in the New American Standard Bible (NASB) and "*self-controlled*" in the New International Version (NIV) is a form of the word *sōphrōn*. According to these verses, what teaches us to live according to a sound mind? What else does the grace of God teach us?

_____

_____

_____

We need to be totally dependent on the grace of God to be taught and to teach others.

APPLY Do you have a friend like Carla?

_____

_____

Do you spend enough time with her?

_____

_____

_____

How did you "*learn Christ*"?

_____

_____

_____

_____

_____

What keeps you from speaking the truth?

_____

_____

_____

_____

When do you need to lay aside the falsehood of denial?

_____

_____

_____

_____

GAINING WISDOM

Wisdom is found primarily in knowing God and relating to Him and secondarily in knowing and relating to others. Knowing others is important to wisdom because we learn Christ from one another. It is the "Christ in you" that makes Christ more tangible to me. Wisdom is mysteriously tied to relationships. Our training for sound minds must always begin and end in relationships—it cannot be only the passing on of information. The more we learn about God, the more He changes us into His image. The more we know Him intimately and begin to fear and reverence all that He is, the wiser we are and the more sound our minds become. The more we relate openly and honestly with one another, the more Christ in us is revealed to others.

Read Proverbs 9:10 and 1 Corinthians 1:30. How do these verses point to the relational aspect of giving and gaining wisdom?

_____

_____

_____

_____

Our relationship with the Lord is what we think and believe about Him and how He communicates with us and we with Him. Wisdom and a sound mind are produced through a relationship with Christ and growth in the knowledge of God.

Read Philippians 3:8 and Colossians 2:1–3. How does the fact that the treasures of wisdom are hidden point to the necessity of digging and searching for them?

_____

_____

_____

_____

The verse from Philippians indicates how Paul invested everything in his search for wisdom. His desire to learn Christ was all consuming. But it did not stop there. The verses from the letter to the Colossians indicate he struggled on their behalf as well. This is what Titus 2 is calling us to do for younger women. When wisdom is incarnate in us ("_Christ in us_") we reveal it to others through relationships. As Paul did, we can live out the value of knowing Him before them. It is in our nature to want wisdom to come easy—to have it imparted to us without struggle. Yet Paul's example shows us that to really know Christ, we often must suffer the loss of all else. It is hard work to get our priorities straight. It often takes sharing in the fellowship of His sufferings (see Colossians 1:24).

Read 1 Corinthians 2:7–16; 4:1, 16. What do these verses teach us about wisdom? What do they say about speaking to one another? What does it mean to be "_stewards of the mysteries of God_"?

_____

_____

_____

_____

THE WISDOM OF GOD

We speak God's wisdom in a mystery, the hidden wisdom. . . . For to us God revealed it through the Spirit. . . . Now we have received . . . the Spirit who is from God, that we might know the things freely given to us by God, which things we also speak, not in words taught by human wisdom, but in those taught by the Spirit, combining spiritual thoughts with spiritual words. . . . we have the mind of Christ.

I CORINTHIANS 2:7–16

Revealing hidden wisdom is the work of the Holy Spirit. So we need to trust and depend on the Spirit's work in us and in those we are seeking to help. Paul's statement that "_we have the mind of Christ_" is one of the most exciting facts of this whole mysterious subject—and the most promising. The mind of Christ must certainly be a sound mind. If such a mind is available to us and to the younger women we are seeking to train, there is a sure hope for us all. Like Paul, we need to "_speak God's wisdom,_" and trust that the Holy Spirit will use our words to develop sound minds in those to whom we speak.

APPLY What do you need to do to gain more wisdom?

_____

_____

_____

_____

How can you better share wisdom with others?

_____

_____

_____

Are you willing and even eager to suffer in order to gain wisdom?

_____

_____

Do you see yourself as a steward of the mysteries of God?

_____

_____

Sound Minds

DAY THREE

HOPE FOR THOSE IN DESPAIR

One of the most common enemies of a sound mind is depression. It debilitates the mind's capacity to function and to maintain an equilibrium that allows for everyday living. Sometimes depression is caused by a chemical imbalance that can be helped by proper medication. Often it is the body's defense mechanism to handle severe loss and is a necessary part of the grieving process. Other times it has its origin in the spiritual realm.

One spiritual cause of depression is hopelessness. In those situations where there is nothing we can do to change things, there are two primary attitudes our hearts can take. The first heart attitude embraces hope, exercises our faith in future grace, and waits for God to reveal how He will make it all work together for good. The second attitude refuses to live with hope or bear the pain of waiting.

There are times when women are depressed even though they still hope in God. Depression is not always sinful. It is sometimes a courageous willingness to face the reality of living in a fallen world. Jesus said, _"Blessed are those who mourn."_ There is plenty to be sad about, and those who reflect deeply will feel it deeply. People who are shallow in their thinking or who depend on denial to cope may never struggle with depression. But their sin of denial is worse than the honest attempt to deal with reality. We need to be wary of those who say all depression is a sign of weakness or lack of faith. A sound mind is one that can face reality with both heartbreak and hope.

📖 Read 1 Corinthians 10:13; 2 Corinthians 12:9 and Galatians 6:2. How do these verses help provide some answers to those who claim they have been given more than they can bear?

_____

_____

_____

_____

Our minds can yield to depression when things look impossible. But three promises found in these verses are a sure provision. God gives us a way of escape; He gives us grace; and He gives us one another. Think of examples from your own life of how God kept these promises for you.

"Why are you in despair, O my soul? . . . Hope in God."

Psalms 42:5

📖 Read Psalm 42. Though David is not clearly identified as the author, C. H. Spurgeon states in his *Treasury of David* that "this psalm must be the offspring of [David's] pen . . . [as] it bears the marks of his style and experience in every letter." How did David deal with depression? How could we use his example to help ourselves and others out of depression?

_____

_____

_____

_____

_____

David is willing to both embrace his sorrow (verse 3) and hope for restoration of joy and praise (verse 11).

Think about what happens when our hearts refuse to embrace sorrow in times of crisis. Do you agree that a measure of depression is at times unavoidable and is better than denial? Notice how honest David is when he pours out his soul before God.

_____

_____

_____

_____

_____

A mind in denial can be just as unstable as one in depression. An excellent resource in dealing with this question is Jan Meyers's book, *The Allure of Hope*. She identifies the following results of refusing to embrace sorrow:

✓ loss of a winsome spirit and passion
✓ gnawing emptiness of heart
✓ loss of childlike innocence
✓ temptation to check out of life
✓ lack of vulnerability
✓ dulling of our senses[5]

Discuss what happens when we refuse to hope. Even in the face of mocking enemies David reminds himself to hope in God. He remembers God's faithfulness and better days.

_____

_____

_____

_____

Refusing to hope is the opposite extreme of refusing to embrace sorrow. Jan Meyers describes the results of refusing to hope as:

- ✓ resignation to misery
- ✓ self-contempt
- ✓ clamor for control
- ✓ sheltered or closed hearts
- ✓ killing of desire
- ✓ forgetting Eden and heaven
- ✓ loss of femininity and beauty[6]

A mind that either refuses to embrace the sorrows of life or to hope for a better tomorrow is not a sound mind and needs the help and encouragement of others in the body of Christ.

APPLY Why might it be important to learn more about depression even if you don't struggle with it?

_____

_____

_____

_____

_____

How do you respond to others' depression?

_____

_____

_____

_____

Why is it important to discern the cause of depression?

_____

_____

_____

_____

Are you willing to live with hope and bear the pain of waiting?

_____

_____

HARSH WINDS

Hope uncovers the heart so that it is exposed to the harsh winds of desert beauty. Sheltering the heart (refusing to hope) keeps the harsh winds from penetrating but also precludes the chiseled beauty that harsh winds can craft in the hardest of volcanic stone.[7]

—JAN MEYERS

What kind of beauty is created by the harsh winds of trying times?

_____

_____

_____

_____

WORRY OR ANXIETY

Worry or anxiety is another common enemy of a sound mind. Like depression, anxiety has many causes and it is not easy to untangle its complexity. Sometimes, fear is simply a lack of faith. Other times, it can come from a variety of factors—childhood experiences, unmanaged floodgates of adrenaline, hormones, spiritual attacks, and illogical fears can all be part of anxiety disorders or panic attacks. When we recognize anxiety in others that comes from faulty thinking or a deceived mind we can speak truth to one another. When the anxiety stems from a medical condition, we can help others see and accept the provision God gives through doctors and medication. When the perceived anxiety comes from isolation and painful relationships, our presence and care and direction can help. When it comes from spiritual oppression, we should pray for one another. At least we can walk with one another in the midst of our fears and wait together for God's supply of truth and grace.

📖 Read 2 Timothy 1:7 and Romans 8:15. Contrast a sound mind with a spirit of fear. What are the origins of your worry and fear?

_____

_____

_____

_____

_____

_____

_____

_____

It is important to identify the origins of fear, because we should treat each of our fears differently, depending on the origins of each fear. For example, there are women who have medical or emotional roots to their anxiety who need to be protected from unnecessary guilt. The church has a reputation of judging those with anxiety disorders as faithless Christians, when in fact, in order to live with their disorders, some of them need and have far more faith than many Christians who appear to be emotionally stable. On the other hand, if our fear comes from a lack of faith or an attack from the enemy we should talk about it with other Christians and pray together for God's wisdom and power. Talking about these things can help, and certainly praying together for God's wisdom and power is indispensable.

📖 Read Matthew 6:25–31; 10:29–31 and Psalm 37:1–9. What are some antidotes to anxiety according to these verses?

_____

_____

_____

_____

Knowing that God faithfully cares for all His creation, but especially for His own children, is the primary antidote for anxiety. Psalm 37 lists many things we should seek to do when we are tempted to worry. Being disciplined enough to trust, rest, and wait is often far beyond our capabilities. We need God's grace most of all, but we also need the support and encouragement of our sisters and older women. Talk about all the different suggestions David gives in this psalm and how we can help one another follow them.

📖 Read Psalm 34:4–8; Isaiah 26:3 and Matthew 14:27–31. Why is focus important in combating our fears?

_____

_____

_____

_____

These three passages are similar in that they emphasize the importance of having minds fixed on Christ rather than having minds focused on our problems or fears. Think of ways to seek the Lord, to look at Him, and to keep your mind steadfast.

📖 Read Psalm 91:4–5; Isaiah 51:12–15, 52:12; 54:10, 14. What can we expect from God?

_____

_____

_____

_____

Let the list you compiled from all these verses feed your soul.

📖 Read Ephesians 3:16–19 and 1 John 4:18. How can we encourage and pray for women who struggle with anxiety?

_____

_____

_____

_____

The knowledge of Christ's love for us is the key to overcoming fear and anxiety. Once we are convinced of His love and are rooted and grounded in it, fear is cast out. Those who are filled with fear need to be filled with the fullness of God. Of course, we cannot fill ourselves with God's fullness, but we can talk of being filled, pray for it, encourage each other to seek it above all else, and challenge any thoughts that would doubt it or take us in another

> *"Do not fret. . . .*
> *Trust in the Lord. . . .*
> *Feed on His faithfulness. . . .*
> *Delight yourself in the Lord. . . .*
> *Rest in the Lord. . . .*
> *Wait patiently for Him. . . .*
> *Do not fret. . . ."*
>
> ### Psalm 37

direction. We need to continually bring the anxious and fearful back to the love of Christ.

APPLY What helps you most in the midst of panic?

_____

_____

_____

_____

Do you ever call God "Abba"? What would it take to get you there? Do you feel rooted and grounded in His love?

_____

_____

_____

_____

What do you worry and fret about most? How can you make your mind steadfast?

_____

_____

_____

_____

_____

Which promise gives you most faith? What can you do to increase your faith?

_____

_____

_____

_____

Sound Minds

DAY FIVE

VIGILANCE IN SPIRITUAL WARFARE

Since our struggle is against spiritual forces of wickedness (see Ephesians 6:12) and the battle is waged primarily in the mind, having a sound mind necessarily includes a resistance to the enemy's lies and the bondage he uses to keep us trapped in his control. There is controversy in the Church concerning exactly how Satan tempts us and to what extent he can control a Christian's mind. If we put aside the debate and simply agree that Scripture tells us to resist him, no harm can come from praying against him, especially if we use the kinds of prayers that we find in Scripture. Considerable harm can come when we choose either of two extremes: ignoring Satan's power or fearing Satan and thus doing no battle. We know only God can give us a sound mind, and Satan is out to deceive and enslave our minds. We need to be vigilant in spiritual warfare if we would have sound minds.

📖 Read 1 Peter 4:7. Which comes first—praying for a sound mind or having a sound mind in order to pray? How are these two mutually dependent?

_____

_____

_____

_____

This verse indicates that we not only need to pray for sound minds, but we need sound minds in order to pray. We have already seen that having a sound mind is totally dependent on a personal relationship with Christ. A life of prayer, of study and meditation in His Word, of walking in His grace, and moving in the power of His Spirit is our only hope to produce sound minds and our only resource to train others to have sound minds as well.

Read 2 Timothy 2:24-26. How do these verses direct us in our desire to help others escape the *"snare of the devil"*? Notice the dual themes of truth and repentance.

_____

_____

_____

_____

Once we have received the grace to walk in kindness, patience, and gentleness, we move toward the goal of helping the one who needs more "soundness" of mind to repentance and the knowledge of the truth. Remember what we discovered about overcoming futility and the importance of speaking truth to one another. Also, no change occurs without true repentance. The power of the enemy is broken when we repent, for it will always open the door for the work of Christ in our hearts.

Share examples of experiences you have had when Satan deceived you with his lies and someone helped you to see the truth.

_____

_____

_____

_____

APPLY How open are you to thinking about spiritual oppression and warfare?

_____

_____

How do you think we can help others be freed from the *"snare of the devil"*?

_____

_____

_____

_____

What part does prayer play in your efforts to obtain a sound mind and help other women have sound minds?

_____

_____

_____

_____

_____

The following poem will serve as the closing prayer for this week:

Father I know that all my life
Is portioned out for me;
The changes that are sure to come,
I do not fear to see;
I ask thee for a present mind,
Intent on pleasing thee.

I would not have the restless will
That hurries to and fro,
Seeking for some great thing to do,
Or secret thing to know;
I would be treated as a child,
And guided where I go.

I ask thee for the daily strength,
To none that ask denied,
A mind to blend with outward life,
While keeping at thy side,
Content to fill a little space,
If thou be glorified.

In service which thy will appoints
There are no bonds for me;
My secret heart is taught the truth
That makes thy children free;
A life of self-renouncing love
Is one of liberty.

—Anna L. Waring, 1850

Feel free to write your own prayer in the space provided below.

_____

_____

_____

_____

_____

_____

_____

Notes

Notes

8

Purity

As far back as I can remember, my sister Becky was one of the quiet ones. It was difficult to know what was going on with her because she always kept things in. To me, she was a mystery until she was forty-one years old and the walls began to crumble. The phone rang, and I was shocked to hear my sister's voice. She and her husband were on the mission field in Africa and rarely had access to a phone.

"We need to find the cause of David's headaches and fatigue so we have decided to come home on medical leave," she said. "Please be praying for us."

Three weeks later, they called again, this time from Seattle. "The medical tests are getting us nowhere, but something else has come up, and we need you to come as soon as possible."

Becky was alone when she picked me up at the airport and said there was something she had to confess. We went to a favorite spot by the lake and sat on a bench under a cherry tree.

"I need to tell you about something I have been hiding for seventeen years." She went on to tell me about an affair she had while David was in medical school and sexual abuse she was beginning to remember from her childhood. God had convinced her it could no longer stay hidden. That was the beginning of nine months of labor to bring forth the most amazing rebirth I have ever witnessed.

Rebecca . . .

. . . a purified saint

" 'Though your sins are as scarlet, they will be as white as snow. . . .' "

—Isaiah 1:18

Up to that point, Satan had convinced her that the truth must never be told. She was the daughter of a well-respected Christian family; she couldn't bring shame to them. She was the wife of a prominent Christian leader; what if he couldn't forgive her? She and her husband were missionaries representing Christ, and many churches back home; their ministry would be destroyed. She was the mother of two impressionable young boys; this would be too difficult for them to handle. No one must ever know the truth. She thought she had successfully covered her sin and shame; confession to God and belief in His forgiveness was enough.

God used sleepless nights, pointed sermons, questions from her husband that were no less than inspired "words of knowledge," wise counselors, persistent intercessors, memorization of God's Word, tears, pain, prayer, praise, and more prayer. He would unlock memories, melt frozen emotions, dismantle walls, open doors to intimacy, and give Becky a new clean heart. He effected so many changes in her life and personality, by the time it was over she decided to change her name to Rebecca. He enabled her to not only confess to her family but to all who knew her and supported their ministry. Her confession led many to similar repentance and renewal. Rebecca not only experienced personal purification—she has since taught many others to find purity.

The following is a poem written by David while in the midst of recovery and the rebuilding of their marriage.

> *Never was a wound felt so deeply*
> *As when you tore our one flesh in two*
> *That it was your hand and not another*
> *Made that wound a yawning abyss*
> *That could not be filled again.*
>
> *Who could restore what never was,*
> *What surgeon could repair such death?*
> *By what hope could such treachery be forgiven,*
> *Or such despair be overcome?*
>
> *There is a Healer, Restorer, Redeemer,*
> *Who takes all bondage, grief, and brokenness*
> *And by His glorious sacrifice,*
> *Creates anew what ne'er was dreamed.*
>
> *So as I lie with you beside me*
> *And feel your loving warmth around me;*
> *Gazing on your beauty within and without,*
> *I cry to the One who has done what could not be done,*
> *Alleluia!*

*"Older women likewise are to live priestly lifestyles, not to be malicious gossips, nor should they have any addictions, but should be teachers of beauty, so that they can **train the younger women** to love husbands, to love children, to be of sound mind, **to be pure,** to be keepers of the home, to be good and to be submissive to their own husbands that the word of God may not be dishonored."*

Titus 2:3–5 (AUTHOR'S PARAPHRASE)

Purity

DAY ONE

THE PATH TO PURITY

Although training younger women to be pure is usually thought of in terms of helping them "stay pure," we will focus on an effort to help those who have been affected by sin to find the purity that Christ offers and to avail themselves of His cleansing blood. In many ways this is the larger task. We are all affected by sin. We were all born in sin. King David said, *"I was brought forth in iniquity, and in sin my mother conceived me"*

(Psalms 51:5). So even a newborn baby is not pure. In that sense it is impossible to "stay pure," since no one is pure to begin with. The process of becoming pure is ongoing and never ending until it is completed in glory. We are all involved in this process, to some degree, every moment of our lives. The more involved we are willing to become, the more effective the cleansing.

Arguably the best promise in all of Scripture is found in Isaiah 1:18: *"though your sins are as scarlet, they will be as white as snow."* This is also a major theme of Scripture. Both the Old and New Testaments are full of references to the fact that God has made a way for our sins to be forgiven. We will look at three of these references to discover the path to purity.

📖 Read Leviticus 5:5–10. Discuss the picture of the process of forgiveness and cleansing given to the Israelites in this book of the Old Testament. What would you say are the primary components of the process?

_____

_____

_____

_____

These verses introduce the two primary components in the process of purification: confession and atonement. Confession is what we do and atonement is what is done on our behalf. In the Old Testament, the sinner had to bring a spotless lamb to the priest, but the blood of the lamb was only representative of the blood of Christ. The lamb in itself could not pay for the sinner's guilt.

Atonement is God's idea. It is the only way men and women have ever had to be reconciled to God. It was first symbolized in the garden when God killed an animal so Adam and Eve could cover their shame because the fig leaves could not suffice. Then it was reinforced by God's acceptance of Abel's blood sacrifice and His refusal to accept Cain's offering of the fruit of his own labor. If we are not willing to accept the atonement, or payment, God has provided in the blood of Christ, we are left with a debt that will require our own death. Death is the penalty for sin. Atonement is the gracious gift of God that allows the death of a sacrificial victim as a substitute for ours.

📖 Read Hebrews 9:11–16, 22. How is Christ's atonement the fulfillment of the Old Testament sacrifices? How do we avail ourselves of this cleansing?

_____

_____

_____

_____

The atonement is and always has been a blood sacrifice that pays the penalty for sin. In the Old Testament, the blood had to be sprinkled on the altar. In the New Testament, Christ fulfilled all that God required when His own blood was sprinkled on the altar in heaven. Under the Old Covenant, believers regularly exercised their faith by bringing a blood sacrifice to the Temple; this sacrifice was a foreshadowing of Christ's sacrifice. Under the New Covenant, we regularly exercise our faith by symbolically partaking of Christ's flesh and blood (see John 6:53). This sacrament is a picture of our

Word Study
PURE

The Greek word, *hagnós*, translated *"pure,"* "signifies pure from every fault, or pure from carnality."[1]

Doctrine
ATONEMENT

Atonement is the gracious gift of God that allows the death of a sacrificial victim to substitute for the death of a sinner. It is the only reparation God will accept for the payment of the debt we owe for our sins. Without the shedding of blood, there is no forgiveness of sin (see Hebrews 9:22).

becoming partakers in Christ's atonement by faith. Participating in the Lord's Supper is a way to not only remember Christ's sacrifice, but also to partake of it for ourselves.

📖 Read Romans 3:22–25. How do these verses sum this all up for us?

_____

_____

_____

_____

We will always fall short of God's glory—anything we have to offer him is like filthy rags.

As much as we would love to offer our own righteousness, or at least be able to clean up the mess we have made of our lives, these verses tell us that righteousness must come from God. We will always fall short of God's glory—anything we have to offer him is like *"filthy rags."* Paul calls his own righteousness rubbish or dung in Philippians 3:8 and 9, and Isaiah 64:6 says *"our righteous deeds are like filthy rags."* Some have said Isaiah's mention of filthy rags was in reference to menstrual rags. Imagine how far short of glory it would be for us to try to offer a soiled tampon to God. All we can bring is our humble repentance and the belief that only Christ's blood can make us pure.

🛑 APPLY How would you explain the path to purity to a younger woman who is feeling impure? What verses would you use?

_____

_____

_____

_____

Do you walk the path to purity enough that you could guide someone else along the path?

_____

_____

Do you have any unconfessed sins that keep you feeling impure?

_____

_____

_____

What fears keep you from confessing them?

_____

_____

To whom do you need to confess them? Who has been hurt or deceived by your silence?

_____

_____

_____

_____

THE ALLURE OF DENIAL

So many Christians live in denial; they are focused on works, trying to be good enough to attain some level of purity. We need to help them see they are on the wrong path. Just as Becky believed that hiding her sin was her only choice, many women are convinced they must present an acceptable persona to the rest of us. Rather than feeling they should pretend to have their lives all together, it is better that they bring themselves to admit they are still struggling with sin. We must develop safe places where we can talk about things (in the present or the past) that keep us in fear and bondage. Together we can confess and be cleansed on a regular basis.

There is a group of women in Seattle who have met for prayer weekly for over nine years. It is their practice to divide their time of prayer into three sections: adoration, confession, and intercession. Their regular times of confession have brought the experience of personal purity to a deeper level for each of the women who participate. James 5:16 promises healing to those who confess their sins to one another and pray for one another. When I have the opportunity to join with this group, I not only experience a deep sense of forgiveness, I am often convicted of the same sins I hear my sisters confess. Sometimes, they are sins I have been blinded to, and the Lord uses their confession to bring my sin to light. What better way to train younger women to be pure than to let them see God take us through the process together?

📖 Read Genesis 3:7–8. What were the first two things Adam and Eve did after they sinned? How are we like them?

_____

_____

_____

_____

Since Adam and Eve first hid in the garden, we have all attempted to hide our sin and shame. We must uncover all the lies the enemy tells us which keep us in hiding. Confession breaks the power of secrets. Talking about our sin breaks the power of silence. Bringing it all to the light breaks the power of darkness. We must speak the truth about our sin, because it is truth that sets us free (see John 8:32).

📖 Read 1 John 1:5–10. Note how many times the phrase *"if we say"* is used in these verses. Would you agree that *"walking in the light"* is more about honesty than particular behavior patterns? What is John really asking of us here? What is our part in the cleansing process?

_____

_____

_____

Our part is to confess our sins, to be honest—not self-deceiving. Denial is self-deceit, the lie that everything is fine. It is presuming we have no sin, or our sin isn't all that bad. Denial is a Pollyanna smile that refuses to look at

> **"If we say we have no sin we are deceiving ourselves."**
>
> **I John 1:8**

reality. It leaves us walking in the darkness—cut off from true fellowship. It makes us comfortable in a church that has no time for confession of sins, or leaves us at a loss for what to say to God when opportunity is given in a church that practices confession.

Read Philippians 3:13. Discuss how this verse is taken out of context by those who use it to deny what has happened in the past. (Read verses 3–14.) Was Paul forgetting former abuse, or his own "works" of righteousness? Why would there be a significant difference?

_____

_____

_____

_____

Satan is behind every lie that keeps sin in the dark. He knows the power of confession and the cleansing that is available. His only hope is that he can convince us to keep things hidden. This enables him to stay in power and continue to keep us down and out of kingdom work. There is no *"pressing on"* when we are held back by sin and its effects. We must find and walk the path to purity.

APPLY Do you know some people who use denial to hide from their problems? Have you ever thought you can see it in them because it is also in you?

_____

_____

_____

_____

What are your chosen methods for managing the difficult problems you face?

_____

_____

_____

_____

What are some things in your past you have tried to forget? Is there a better way to deal with them?

_____

_____

_____

_____

How much of the time are you walking in the darkness of denial rather than in the light of confession?

_____

_____

IGNORING SPIRITUAL CONCERNS

Often in the church we look for convenient methods, formulas, or structures that will help us manage difficult problems. . . . this hope is based on finding solutions rather than on grappling with the issues of sin and repentance. . . . it discounts or ignores spiritual issues by assuming that God's deliverance, healing, and provision will free us from the difficult circumstances of life that so often beset us.[2]

—HENRY SCHAMBURG

THE POWER OF SHAME

Often the thing that keeps us from the pursuit of purity and honesty is our shame. Like Adam and Eve, we try to hide from God and the truth because we are ashamed of our sinfulness or of the effects of others' sin upon us. Shame is what makes us want to hide or pretend. We are embarrassed that we are not what we should be or want to be, so we fear to move into the light. The power of shame is that it immobilizes us. It keeps us from one another. It keeps us from admitting or speaking the truth. It becomes a prison that isolates and incapacitates.

We need to look at the effects of past sexual abuse in women who are still suffering from the pain, confusion, and shame that hang on for years. They need to experience the reality of the purity that Christ offers, and they often need help from other women to get there. Remember that the process can be painful, like the fire that purifies metal. Expect "training in purity" to require a willingness on our part to travel a path strewn with sorrow and pain. Shame not only keeps younger women in hiding, it keeps older women distant and silent because they fear it. To get to purity we all must overcome shame.

📖 Read Hebrews 12:1–2. How did Christ deal with shame? If He had not hated and scorned the power shame had to keep Him from the cross, where would we be? If shame is an *"encumbrance"* or *"the sin which so easily entangles us,"* what are we to do with it?

_____

_____

_____

_____

_____

_____

_____

Imagine what went on in the Garden of Gethsemene. Jesus was struggling through the process of accepting what lay before Him. The shame of the cross—not only the disgrace of the physical nakedness, but the spiritual reality of taking on the sin of the whole world—would have been a powerful force, one from which He would naturally recoil. When we remember Christ was fully human, we know the shame He faced was real, and the description of Him sweating drops of blood indicates the intensity of His battle. But this verse tells us the way He dealt with the shame was to despise it. In other words, He hated and scorned its power to keep Him from following what the Father had planned for Him. Since we know Christ was sinless, this tells us that experiencing shame is not wrong; it is simply part of living in a fallen world. The sin is allowing shame to keep us captive or incapacitated. We sin when we choose to dwell in the shame, making it our identity. Jesus despised shame, and so must we. His active response refused to accept what shame tried to put on Him. To despise our shame, we first need to recognize it and see the power it has over us. As we identify shame as a hindrance, we can throw it off as Hebrews 12:1 states. We do this by identifying what is not true, letting it go, and then honestly dealing with true guilt by taking it to the Cross.

📖 Read Psalm 34:4–5. Shame tries to keep our focus on our guilt or the consequences of someone else's guilt. Where do these verses tell us to keep our focus? How is that similar to Hebrews 12:2?

_____

_____

_____

_____

Both Psalm 34:5 and Hebrews 12:2 tell us to focus on Jesus. Shame focuses on guilt. The pervading guilt that overcomes us separates us from God. As Dan Allender states in his book, *The Healing Path* (WaterBrook, 1999), "Shame shuts us down. . . .It blocks us from receiving and giving and leaves the soul hungry but too ashamed to admit its condition."[3] The guilt may be our own or someone else's. For example, a young girl who is raped often feels shame even though she has done nothing wrong. With our focus on Christ, we won't deny guilt, but we also won't dwell on it. Christ's work on the cross dealt with guilt and made a way for forgiveness and purification.

📖 Read Philippians 3:18–19. What do you think it means to make shame your glory?

_____

_____

_____

_____

There are women who flaunt their sinful practices or their victimization, finding in them their identity or their excuse for not becoming all that God is calling them to be. They see themselves as sinners more than saints, which is a false humility that focuses more on sin than on the cross of Christ.

📖 Read Isaiah 54:4–5. What does God do with our shame when we bring it to Him?

_____

_____

_____

_____

Though we are filled with fear, shame, humiliation, and disgrace, God has chosen to be a Husband, Lord, and Redeemer.

Redemption is the result of atonement. God is our Redeemer because He sent Christ to atone for our sins. Though we are filled with fear, shame, humiliation, and disgrace, He has chosen to be a Husband, Lord, and Redeemer. He promises the shame will be forgotten when we are covered by His grace.

APPLY What have you done in the past with your shame?

_____

_____

_____

_____

Do you see the difference between clinging to it and despising it?

_____

_____

_____

How has Satan deceived you in this area?

_____

_____

_____

_____

_____

Does your church have effective ways of dealing with sexual immorality in the lives of its people? How does it deal with shame?

_____

_____

_____

_____

THE CONNECTION BETWEEN SEXUAL PURITY AND SPIRITUAL PURITY

When we talk about purity, we need to address not only physical purity but the far deeper reality of our need for spiritual purity and the mysterious connection between the two. In 2 Corinthians 11:2–3, Paul speaks of purity of devotion to Christ and states his desire to present the Christians in Corinth as pure virgins to Christ as their husband. His choice of words such as *"jealousy"* and *"betrothal"* clearly indicate that a loving marriage relationship is analogous to a Christian's relationship with Christ. Paul also intertwines marriage relationships with the Church's relationship to Christ in Ephesians 5:32, where, in the middle of his discourse on marriage, he says, *"This is a profound mystery, but I am talking about Christ and the church."*

This mystery Paul speaks of in Ephesians begs many questions. For starters, do we experience jealousy in our marriage relationships because God wants us to know how He feels when we stray from Him? Does the guilt felt over adultery actually point to a deeper guilt of spiritual adultery? Why did adultery carry a death penalty in the Old Testament? Do God's swift judgments against adulterers in the Old Testament teach the importance of marriage, or do they teach the importance of purity as well? Could it point to the importance of a faithful relationship with God? Did God put the desire for intimacy in our souls to simply meet our physical and emotional needs, or to shadow deeper spiritual needs?

📖 Review and discuss the book of Hosea. (Read the following verses together as an overview: 1:2; 2:18–20; 3:1; 4:6–7, 10–12; 6:1–3; 10:1–2; 14:1–3, 8–9.) How did God teach Hosea about His love, patience, and forgiveness? Why do you think God chose that instructional method?

_____

_____

_____

_____

God not only taught Hosea about the pain He endures because of our spiritual adultery; He also teaches us about His longings through the pain of our own marriages or state of being single.

Marriage teaches all of us more about our relationship with Him. Suppose God set up love, passion, faithfulness, sacrifice, submission, and all that marriage entails and promotes as the most significant illustration of the kind of relationship He desires with us. This can give meaning to our sorrows and understanding of why the pain is so deep when either or both spouses fail to get it right. It might also explain why God commanded the death penalty for adultery in Old Testament law.

📖 Read Genesis 17:9–14 and Romans 2:28–29. Why do you think God chose to use circumcision to signify the cutting of covenant?

_____

_____

_____

_____

So much of what God teaches us in the physical (and sexual) realm is meant to help us understand the spiritual. In His plan of circumcision God chose to use the male sexual organ as the place designated for cutting flesh—picturing God's covenant with His people. The significance of the connection between the sexual and spiritual symbols is important. In the New Testament, Paul clarifies that the whole point of circumcision is for God's chosen people to have circumcised or consecrated hearts, leading to undivided devotion to Him (see also 1 Corinthians 7:35 NIV).

📖 Read 1 Corinthians 6:13–20. Discuss the meaning of verse 13: *"the body is . . . for the Lord and the Lord is for the body."*

_____

_____

_____

This passage teaches that our bodies are *"for the Lord"* in that His Spirit dwells within them, He has bought us, and we have been joined to Him in some mystical way. But it does not tell us what is meant by *"the Lord is for the body."* Each of us needs to seek God's wisdom to understand what it might mean. I sometimes suspect that God intentionally leaves it mysterious so we have to pursue intimacy with Him to find the answer. If He spelled it out in His Word, we would accept the intellectual answer and never seek to know Him.

According to verse 18, why is sexual immorality different from other sins? What do you think it means to sin against your own body? (verse 18)?

_____

_____

_____

_____

Again, I am not sure of the answer to my own question, but I suspect it has to do with the parallel facts that sexual intimacy results in "one body" and spiritual intimacy results in "one spirit," which implies that the one can interfere with the other in some way. Charles Kraft explains in his book, *Deep Wounds*, that when people have become one in a sinful relationship, that bonding will have emotional, relational, and spiritual effects. These bonding effects will not dissipate until there is complete confession, repentance, and a renouncing of the bond. Kraft's point helps us understand why God is so insistent on sexual purity. It also explains why Satan can use immorality to destroy lives and relationships, and why, when the sin is never dealt with, it can have such long-lasting results.

Read Ephesians 5:25–27, 32 and James 4:4–10. Think about how Christ not only loves the Church, but how He loves you personally and compare that to how you love Him.

_____

_____

_____

_____

_____

APPLY Meditate on James 4:4–10. Ask yourself, *What do lust, adultery, and jealousy have to do with my relationship with God?*

_____

_____

_____

Remember the idol of "play" mentioned in 1 Corinthians 10:7 which we discussed in Lesson 4? In what ways are you tempted to impurity by some of your leisure activities?

_____

_____

_____

_____

Would you call your pursuit of Christ passionate?

_____

_____

SEXUAL SINS

The satanic strategy of making sexual sin a prime goal has steadily become more apparent in biblical and cultural history. . . . Sexual sin enslaves us to the "gods" to whom we unwittingly yield ourselves. Every time we sin by misusing the sexual parts of our bodies . . . their power over our behavior increases. . . . Sexual sin always involves the presentation of one's body to the dark powers that wish to control it.[4]

—JOHN WHITE

"Sexual intimacy bonds people to each other. And such bonding is more than a physical thing. It is spiritual."[5]

—Charles Kraft

Can the gap between the passion we long for and the reality we experience be somehow filled by our relationship with Christ rather than by the immorality we are tempted to use to fill it?

_____

_____

_____

THE BEAUTY OF MARRIAGE

For good reasons, God has implanted a passion within our hearts to be totally known and loved. Purity finds the reasons and pursues them rather than the mere physical enjoyment that accompanies passion. Sexual purity is not an ice-cold denial of our sexuality. It is the expression of the deepest possible intimacy two people can have with one another. Part of what we need to explore is why sexual intercourse is only pure within the lifelong covenantal faithfulness of a loving marriage.

God gives the gift of marriage to bring fulfillment of our passions, yet Satan uses these same passions to take us to what Mike Mason, in *The Mystery of Marriage*, calls "some of the most abysmal levels of human degredation."[6] The degradation women experience can range from abominable abuse to seemingly innocent vicarious exposure through explicit and demeaning movies and television. Sex outside of marriage can damage us, but marital sex can bring healing. The beauty of marriage is found in its mysterious connection to the love, holiness, and power of God. Because man and woman are created in the image of God, man and woman together reveal that image in a way that cannot be seen otherwise. Purity can only be obtained at the Cross, but it can be experienced in marriage.

📖 Read 1 Thessalonians 4:3–7. How is sanctification (or becoming holy) defined in these verses? What is its opposite? What does that imply about marriage?

_____

_____

_____

_____

Sanctification is not only about changes God makes in our souls but also how we use our bodies and how we relate to others. Defining sanctification or holiness in terms of our sexuality underlines the importance of sexual purity in our salvation as well as in our marriages. Impurity and lustful passions are identified in this passage as the opposite of holiness. Paul may be implying that marriage is one of the tools God uses to bring about our sanctification. Those who never marry are obviously sanctified by God in other ways, but I believe the sanctification process is often facilitated through the significant relationship between husband and wife. A good marriage will teach us how to control our bodies in a way that is holy and honorable. A marriage destroyed by sexual immorality will teach us the pain of unfaithfulness.

📖 Read 1 Corinthians 4:1–5. What reason does Paul give for marriage in this passage? What is implied about our need for sexual intimacy? What reasons do you think God had for creating those needs? How does the side margin quote on this page from *The Mystery of Marriage* by Mike Mason help?

_____

_____

_____

_____

_____

_____

If sexuality in our culture has been degraded to simply getting pleasure from another person, we need to teach the truths of Scripture in a way that presents the sanctifying nature of marriage. Without the ministry of older women, younger women who have experienced past abuse and never dealt with it can enter into marriage and not know its healing power because they see the sexual act in marriage as more of the same kind of degradation. They simply learn to endure sex. We need to break through the barriers that keep people silent about these kinds of things and seek God's wisdom and healing together.

📖 Read Song of Solomon 8:6–7. What do these verses teach us about love and marriage? What do you think the seal is? What is the purpose of jealousy?

_____

_____

_____

_____

Commentaries agree that the seal was a symbol not unlike our wedding bands, indicating both private and public commitment. These verses express the power of love and the lasting nature of marriage. To say love is as strong as death and when it is threatened the reaction is as severe as Hell, teaches us how very important faithfulness is. No matter how ardently our culture tries to convince people that it really doesn't matter whom you sleep with, we in the church must express the same passion for the truth that these verses exhibit. Faithful love is worth far more than all the material wealth of the richest home in town. And there is nothing wrong with godly jealousy. Jealousy protects our marriages and should be highly regarded as *"the flame of the LORD."*

🛑 APPLY Think of ways and opportunities to train younger women in your church about how purity can be exemplified. Is it enough to live model marriages before them? Should premarital counseling as we know it today be supplemented by having older women train new brides?

_____

_____

_____

SEX: WHAT GOD INTENDED

Surely it was God's full intention for the physical joining together of a man and a woman to be one of the mountaintop experiences of life, one of those summit points of both physical and mystical rapture in which He Himself might overshadow His people in love, might come down among them and be most intimately and powerfully revealed. How horribly tragic, therefore, that it is here at this very point, here at this precious male-female encounter which ought to be overflowing with holiness, here that godless people have succeeded in descending to some of the most abysmal levels of human degradation.[7]

—MIKE MASON
The Mystery of Marriage

If you are married, how has intimacy with your husband cleansed and healed past shame?

_____

_____

_____

_____

In what ways has your marriage not fulfilled some of your passions? Why not?

_____

_____

_____

_____

If you are not married, how does the beauty and promise of marriage give you hope and perseverance to wait for your longings to be fulfilled in God's time and in His ways?

_____

_____

_____

_____

HOLY MATRIMONY

One of the most fundamental and important tasks that has been entrusted to marriage is the work of reclaiming the body for the Lord, of making pure and clean and holy again that which has been trampled in the mud of shame. . . . The free and loving exchange of nakedness that takes place between a husband and wife is just one of the spectacular ways in which the divine ordinance of holy matrimony actually sets about to reverse the curses of original sin. Marriage attacks original sin, in effect, at its visible root, in the shame of nakedness, and defeats and heals this shame by directly confronting it on the safe and holy ground of a covenant relationship.[8]

—MIKE MASON
The Mystery of Marriage

Close your study time in prayer.

 Father in heaven, I praise You for Your purity. You are spotless and holy. You are the same yesterday, today, and forever. Thank You for all You have done to make me pure. Praise You for Your provision of atonement in the blood of Your Son. Thank You for Your merciful forgiveness.

Lord, I confess I allow my shame to keep me in hiding. I live in denial and pretend everything is fine when it isn't. I love darkness when my thoughts and actions are evil. Please forgive me and continue to bring my sin into the light. Please give me the gift of repentance and make me pure.

I pray for my friends who have not found the path to purity. Please give me words and attitudes that will help me guide them to the Way. I pray for Your mercy and grace on their behalf. I pray that they may be strengthened with power through the Spirit in their inner being so Christ may dwell in their hearts through faith to grasp and know His deep love for them and be filled with His fullness.

Please deliver those in my study group (including myself) from the temptation to commit immorality. Although we do not completely understand the connection between sexual purity and spiritual purity, we know Your word reveals one, so make us especially fearful of sexual sins and guard us from the inundation of temptation in our culture. We pray that Your kingdom, power, and glory will be made known in us as we resist the evil around us. Amen.

Notes

Notes

9

Keepers of the Home

I have always thought of my friend Susan as one of the best examples of a keeper of the home. She has a wonderful way of maintaining a safe and comfortable environment for her three children and has an amazing gift of hospitality—of which my son often took advantage. When Susan told me her story of what happened on the day of the Columbine massacre, I knew I wanted to include it in this chapter. I had already come to the conclusion that intercession for the members of my family was a key factor in my *"keeping the home."* The way God used Susan's prayers before, during, and after that terrible day clearly illustrates what God is asking when He calls us to be keepers of our families.

For several years before the day of the shooting at Columbine High School, Susan was part of a mother's prayer group that prayed for the school's students and faculty. They had been praying for general and specific needs that had come to their attention, but in January, Susan felt much more intensity in her intercession and a burden to pray for revival at the school.

The night before the shooting, Susan had a dream that her oldest son, Stephen, had died. Remembering the dream, she prayed a short prayer for her children's safety that day as they entered the doors of Columbine. At 11:25 a.m. she received a call at work from a co-worker's son telling her the school was under gunfire. She was one of the first parents on the scene. The police would not let her pull into the parking lot but sent her to the park nearby, where she could watch, wait, and pray.

Susan...

...keeper of her family

There were many tears and prayers as Susan told people about her dream and of the short, gentle prayer she had prayed that morning.

Inside, two of her children, Stephen and Diana, were in the cafeteria with some of their friends from the Bible club. When the two boys, Eric Harris and Dylan Klebold, started shooting, they got under their table and began to pray. Moments later they joined other students in a race away from the cafeteria. Diana was behind Stephen as they hurried down the hall, with the sound of gunfire all around. When Stephen realized Diana had fallen he tried to go back to get her, but a friend grabbed him and urged him on.

Jonathan, Susan's second son, had walked Cassie Bernall to the library, but left her to go to the music room. He was there when the shooting began and ran from the music room into the hall and saw Diana. Jonathan and Diana then successfully escaped the shooting zone and were among the first students to get out of the building. Soon they found Susan in the park. But none of them knew where Stephen was. As they formed a small circle to pray together, more and more students and parents joined them. Eventually, the police came and told them to wait at a near-by elementary school. Soon after they arrived they were joined by relatives and the pastors from their church. There were many tears and prayers as Susan told them about her dream and of the short, gentle prayer she had prayed that morning. One pastor assured her that God heard and answered those prayers.

When Stephen got outside, after losing contact with Diana, the policemen had told him to get away from the building. They feared the bombs that had been set might explode. He and several other students took refuge in a near-by home, where they hid for over two hours. They were watching the media coverage of what was happening across the street and eventually heard that parents and students were being reunited at the elementary school. After hours of intense fear all four members of the very close-knit-family were finally together.

Several months later, after an article was printed in *People* magazine about Diana's experience, a student called Susan to tell her that Diana had not tripped and fallen that day. He had seen Dylan Klebold's rifle pointed straight toward Diana's head. Almost instinctively, this student pushed Diana down and saw bullets hit the wall behind her. Susan was thankful she had not been immediately informed just how close her daughter had been to death. Even today, as she recounts the story, her eyes fill with tears of praise to God, our Keeper.

The Lord had strategically placed Susan in a position as intercessor, and kept her in prayer throughout the day. Because of Susan's availability to the Lord and her watchful eye and careful heart, He was able to use her to be not only a keeper for her own children, but for the thousands of other young people whom Satan wanted to destroy that day. Since then, God has used Susan's family and church in the revival Susan had been praying for. Hundreds of young people in the Denver area have given their lives to the Lord. He also gave Stephen and Jonathan a song that they sang before the nation and around the world to remind us all that, ultimately, God is our Keeper and He can turn tragedy to peace and hope.

"Friend of Mine"

Columbine, flower bloom, tenderly I sing to you.
Columbine, roseblood red, heartbreak overflow my head.
Columbine, flower bloom.
Columbine there's hope for you.
Columbine, friend of mine.
To your gain, on the mark.
With your love, love again.
Comfort peace and sweet release come from you.
Where, it's true, I hide myself in you.
Can you still hear raging guns ending dreams of precious ones.
In God's son, hope will come, his red stain will take our pain.
Columbine, friend of mine.
Peace will come to you in time.
Columbine, friend of mine.
Turn a page, to your gain.
Keep your heart on the mark.
Comfort us with your love.
Love again.
Christ of grace attend this place we look to you.
Honor you.
Fix you in our view.
Columbine, flower bloom.
Tenderly I sing to you.
Columbine, roseblood red, heartbreak
overflows my head.
Columbine, friend of mine.
Peace will come to you in time.
Columbine, friend of mine.

—© 1999, Jonathan and Stephen Cohen

KEEPERS LIKE GOD

Traditionally this phrase has been interpreted to mean housekeeping. Because we don't have doorkeepers or watchmen on the walls, we don't naturally think of what Paul has in mind by his choice of a word that means "to keep or watch." His original readers would have understood his word picture, but the only common use of "keeper" today is one that I believe gives the wrong picture. In our minds, the word "house-keeper" connotes cleaning the house and not much more. Also, our minds limit Paul's word, *oikós* (family, household, or home) to a building, when its deeper meaning includes all inhabitants of a household. If we limit Paul's use of *ourós* (keeper, keeping) to cleaning, we miss the meaning of "keeping" in the Bible that is a rich expression of overall care and protection. Limiting God's Word in this fashion ignores what the rest of Scripture teaches us about the woman's role. Because of this denigration of our God-given role, many women have chosen to forsake it and pursue men's roles, leaving their homes without a keeper and their families in a state of chaos. To get a better understanding of what it means to be a keeper, we will first look at how God is described as our Keeper.

Keepers of the Home

DAY ONE

Word Study
KEEPERS OF THE HOME

The Greek word translated, *"keepers at home"* in Titus 2:5, *oikourós,* is another unique word Paul may have coined for women. It is a combination of *oíkos,* which means family, household, or home,[1] and *ourós,* which means keeper.[2]

If Paul meant to say "housekeeper," he could have used the words *oikía* for house and *katartízō* for cleaning. Some manuscripts use the word *oikourgós,* which is translated *"workers at home."*[3]

"The LORD is your keeper; the LORD is your shade on your right hand. The LORD will protect you from all evil; He will keep your soul. The LORD will guard your going out and your coming in from this time forth and forever."

Psalms 121:3–5, 7–8

📖 Read Numbers 6:24; Psalm 121:3–8; Isaiah 27:3 and John 17:11–12. What do these verses tell us a keeper is and does? How would the particular things God does as our Keeper help us understand our role as keepers of the home?

_____

_____

_____

_____

_____

If we see the Lord as the true Keeper of our homes, our position is more or less one of "assistant keeper." We join Him in what He is doing and participate by prayer and following His lead as the One who "keeps" us.

Read 1 Thessalonians 2:7–12. How was Paul a keeper like God? What *oikos* was he seeking to keep? How did he do it?

_____

_____

_____

_____

Paul talks about caring for the Christians of Thessalonica like a mother and a father would care for their children. He saw them as his family, or *oikós*. He "kept" them by tenderly caring for them, loving them, and imparting the gospel to them. He exhorted, encouraged, and implored them to walk in the Spirit. Verse 13 says he constantly prayed for them. In verse 20, he calls them his *"glory and joy."*

📖 Read 2 John 1:1, 4–8. How was the "chosen lady" a keeper of her family (*oikos*)? Do you think her children were her biological or spiritual offspring? What is she told to *"watch"* in verse 8? (Think of losing as the opposite of keeping.)

_____

_____

_____

_____

_____

If the *"children"* this chosen lady had been given to disciple and oversee were younger women, this letter has even more impact and significance for us. We all have families, whether we are married with children or not. Each of us has a circle of influence that includes those we are called to watch. The fact that John makes his command to *"Watch yourselves"* plural indicates we are to look out for more than just "numero uno." This idea of *watching* and *not losing* is along the same lines as *keeping*. This is another challenge to keep our *oikos* safe and secure in truth and love.

APPLY Name some women you have known who have been keepers in this same sense.

_____

_____

_____

Do you know of homes that have been damaged because the women in these households did not understand this calling?

_____

_____

Do some of your priorities need to be changed in order to be a better keeper?

_____

_____

KEEPING THE HOME IN OUR PRAYERS

I believe our first responsibility in keeping our homes is to pray for those in our families. Our work of intercession is far more vital than we think. We often aren't aware of the spiritual warfare that is going on or how important it is to stay on our knees to keep the enemy of our souls from destroying our homes. When the Lord said to the serpent in the garden, _"I will put enmity between you and the woman, and between your offspring and hers"_ (Genesis 3:15), He was referring to more than just the hatred we women tend to have for snakes. Some women have suggested that we as a gender have a special responsibility to be in Satan's face, especially when it comes to our families. If this is true, it gives us a calling to spiritual warfare that cannot be ignored. We are to be like mother bears, guarding our cubs. I wonder if some of the defeats families are experiencing can be tied to the fact that so many women have lost sight of their vital intercessory role and have decided they can better help their husbands by bringing in a second salary.

📖 Read Ephesians 6:18 and 1 Thessalonians 5:17. What part does prayer play in our spiritual battle? How often do we need to pray?

_____

_____

_____

Think of ways we can manage our time to allow for specific prayer times as well as having an attitude of prayer or an ongoing dialogue with God.

_____

_____

_____

"Pray without ceasing. . . ."

1 Thessalonians 5:17

📖 Read Lamentations 2:18–19. Why do we wait until the situation gets this desperate before we cry out to the Lord for our children? Shouldn't we start *"at the beginning of the night watches"*?

_____

_____

_____

_____

_____

TURN TO THE EXPERT

At every stage of their lives, our children need and will greatly benefit from our prayers. The key is not trying to do it all by ourselves all at once, but rather turning to the expert parent of all time—our Father God—for help. Then, taking one step at a time, we must cover every detail of our child's life in prayer. There is great power in doing that, far beyond what most people imagine. In fact, don't ever underestimate the power of a praying parent.[4]

from *The Power of a Praying Parent*
Copyright ©1995
by Stormie Omartian
Published by Harvest House
Publishers, Eugene, OR
Used by Permission

Doctrine
KEEPING COVENANT

The covenant is God's agreement with His people to be their God and provide for their needs. It is "kept" by our entering into communion with Him and relying on His faithfulness. In the new covenant Christ brings this relationship to its highest level of achievement and enrichment.[5]

—Loosely adapted from
The New Bible Dictionary by
John Murray

📖 Read Psalm 103:17–18. What requirements are given in these verses that precede an expectation of God's loving-kindness and righteousness for our children? What part do you think prayer would have in each of those requirements?

_____

_____

_____

_____

_____

Many years ago, I heard a pastor make the statement, "The best measure of your dependence on God is how much you pray." I have often remembered this statement and been convicted by it in times of prayerlessness. If we say we are depending on Him for our families but never pray for them, we are not really dependent—we are seeking to control things on our own. These verses call us to fear Him, keep His covenant, and remember His precepts. Each of these requirements implies a dependent relationship that submits, obeys, and follows our Lord. The importance of prayer is clear in all of them.

APPLY How often do you pray for the people in your family?

_____

_____

Do you ever see yourself in battle with the enemy?

_____

_____

_____

How can you reprioritize your life to make more room for prayer?

_____

_____

_____

_____

BUILDING OUR HOMES

Next to interceding for our families, edifying its members would be our second most important responsibility as keepers. The Greek word for edify, *oikodoméō*, could be literally translated "home-builder." Part of building our homes involves building self-esteem in the members of our families. There have been many books published in the last two decades about the importance of building self-esteem in both our mates and children. I suspect there is a direct correlation between low self-esteem and our society's loss of the keeper role. We are called to build up our households, to be sure all of its precious members are assured of their value, both in the home and as they leave the home to enter the community. They must be nurtured and cherished in a way that prepares them to stand tall and courageous. Cassie Bernall, the young girl who bravely confessed her belief in God while a gun was pointed at her head, knew who she was and to Whom she belonged. Her mother's story, penned in the book, *She Said Yes: The Unlikely Martyrdom of Cassie Bernall* (New York: Pocket Books, 2000), illustrates the faithfulness of one woman's struggle to build her home.

📖 Read Psalm 127:1–2 and Proverbs 14:1; 24:3–4. What do you think it means to build our homes and how can we do it?

_____

_____

_____

_____

A discussion of these verses may lead to the question of roles in the home. Biblically, the husband has the role of leading, ruling, providing, and protecting, while the wife, according to these verses, is to help by seeking wisdom to understand, know, build up, and beautify the people and the relationships that make up a home. Of course, these roles can overlap and sometimes cross. We are given a broad outline of what our parts are and how we were made, but individual differences in personality and circumstances can change the picture somewhat.

📖 Read Romans 15:1–6 and 1 Thessalonians 5:11. How do these verses help us understand our work of home-building edification? Also, how do we encourage younger women to do this?

_____

_____

_____

_____

Affirmation and encouragement are the building blocks of self-esteem. Everyone needs more of both. Remember your *oikós* or family can include all the people in your circle of life. Our "homes" include not only immediate family members but close friends, as well. Consider how these verses extend home-building to ministry among other women.

Affirmation and encouragement are the building blocks of self-esteem.

Few women realize what great service they are doing for mankind and for the kingdom of Christ when they provide a shelter for the family and good mothering—the foundation on which all else is built.

A mother builds something far more magnificent than any cathedral—the dwelling place for an immortal soul.[6]

—DOROTHY PATTERSON

APPLY What specific things do you try to do to build up the people in your home or circle of friends or family?

_____

_____

_____

How well do you know and understand the people in your home?

_____

_____

_____

In what ways could you let the people in your home know what a treasure they are?

_____

_____

_____

_____

Keepers of the Home

DAY FOUR

KEEPING OUR HOMES OPEN

Whether we realize it or not, we are the doorkeepers of our homes. We are usually the ones who decide who comes in and who goes out and when. We monitor whether the door is opened or closed. We are often the ones who invite guests and prepare the home for hospitality.

While our culture is marked by a desire for privacy, Scripture commands hospitality. As our society becomes more individualistic, our redeemed hearts long for more community. Our command to love one another extends to the "love of strangers," which is the literal meaning of hospitality. But hospitality is becoming extinct in our culture. Our example of openness to those outside the home will do much to train younger women and our own children in the gift of mercy.

A great illustration of hospitality is found in the character of the priest in the classic novel, *Les Miserables* by Victor Hugo. The priest not only opens his home to Jean Valjean, an escaped convict, but knowingly permits him to take some of his silver. When the police bring him and the stolen silver back, he covers up for the accused, and asks him why he did not take the candlesticks that he had offered as well. The priest's hospitality and mercy become a turning point in the life of the convict. He uses what was given to him by the priest to begin building a life of love and mercy toward others.

📖 Read 1 Peter 4:7–11. Do we normally consider hospitality to be as important as the other disciplines listed in these verses? Why do you think Peter expects complaint about his challenge to be hospitable?

_____
_____
_____
_____

Peter is calling us to the four great responsibilities of the Christian life: prayer, love, hospitality, and using our spiritual gifts to serve others and glorify God. How often do we give hospitality such prestigious billing? In some circles of our culture, hospitality has become a lost art. This should not be the case in the Christian home.

Hospitality is an area of great need for grace or Peter would not have included the warning about complaining. It is not something we can do in our own strength. It is not mere entertaining. It takes prayer and love and God's special gifts. It is pouring out grace and love to all God brings to us, in a way that draws them to God.

📖 Read Romans 12:10–16. How do all the commands in these verses define and describe an open home? What makes it open? What should our priorities be? How can we encourage one another to become women who keep our homes open?

_____
_____
_____
_____
_____
_____

I remember a time in my late 30s when I was struggling with the question of how I could _"set my mind on the things above, not on the things that are on earth."_ I knew I was focused on getting my home fixed the way I wanted it, and most of my time was taken up in housekeeping. I had asked myself what were "the things above"; what was destined for heaven, and what was going to be left behind? The answer was that the only two things the Bible tells us will last forever are God's Word and His people. The logical conclusion was I needed to focus more on those than on changing, improving, and caring for the material things in my home. I began to explore ways I could meet my neighbors and develop relationships with them. I eventually opened my home for a neighborhood Bible study where I could focus on both the people and the Word at the same time.

📖 Read 2 John 1:10–11. When do we need to close the door to our homes?

_____
_____
_____
_____

As keepers, we must close the door on anything or anyone who would bring teaching into our homes that does not honor Christ.

> _"Entertaining has little to do with real hospitality. . . . Its source is human pride. . . . it says, 'I want to impress you with my beautiful home. . . . This is mine. . . . Look please and admire.' Hospitality does not try to impress but to serve. . . . It whispers, 'What's mine is yours.'"_[7]
>
> **—Karen Mains**

Is your home open to others outside of your family?

_____

Do you think of hospitality as a discipline or a gift? Or both?

_____

_____

How could an older woman help you become more hospitable?

_____

_____

_____

How are you doing in your role as a doorkeeper?

_____

_____

_____

Keepers of the Home

DAY FIVE

KEEPING OUR HOMES SIMPLE

God's Word teaches us that life is all about loving Him and others, yet we are easily pulled into the lie that it is about making enough money to live comfortably and feel secure. The woman who has a clear understanding of her calling to be a keeper of the home knows that she must not only keep love flowing freely, but she must also keep her demands for material possessions minimal. The discipline of simplicity and contentment, if consistently practiced, can help to free us from the snare of needing more. It will not be true in every case, but "keeping it simple" might free some women from the need to take a second job, thus enabling them to do the job of keeping the home.

As we endeavor to truly keep our homes, it can be a full-time job, especially in the years of raising children. I am encouraged to see an increase in the number of women who understand the critical role of the mother in the lives of preschool children, and am waiting for the day when even more understand how important it is to children of all ages, including and especially teenagers. The hours children are in school can be well spent in "seeking the kingdom" and ministry to others in our "extended family."

📖 Read Matthew 6:25–33 and 1 Timothy 6:9–11. What is Christ saying to you about your worries and priorities? Who are the rich? (Think about this question in global terms.) What temptations, snares, and foolish and harmful desires are out there?

_____

_____

_____

It is easy to read these verses and feel they do not apply to us because we define *"the rich"* as those who are in the millionaire category. Yet, when you compare the American standard of living to the rest of the world, we are a nation of rich people. The *"temptations and snares"* are everywhere. The *"foolish and harmful desires"* are constantly paraded before us. And even though God's Word warns us of the *"destruction"* that comes from it, we continue to long for what money can buy.

📖 Read Psalm 116:5–7 and Philippians 4:11–13. What do these verses teach us about simplicity and contentment? What is Paul's secret of contentment? What is soul-rest?

_____

_____

_____

_____

During my husband's midlife crisis, when his priorities and values changed dramatically, he began to say that it would be necessary for me to find a career and begin to help support our children. In his new way of thinking, support could only be measured in dollars. The courts disagreed with this logic and decided that my children, having lost the father from their home, did not need to lose their mother as well. I am so thankful that my children and I received enough support that I did not need to work full time. It breaks my heart to see the plight of many single mothers who must work outside the home. Many welfare programs now require that anyone receiving aid also work, making it impossible for single mothers to stay at home with their children. How different it would be if there were more who understood the biblical mandate that women be keepers of the home.

In those early years of being a single mother, there were many adjustments to be made. Before the divorce decree secured our financial support, I took a part-time job, convinced that I had to be sure my family would not have to lose our home. I remember how harried I was trying to keep up the home, deal with all the emotional trauma for myself and the kids, and commute to a job that I hated. There was no rest. Even though I knew I had God's promise of grace, it seemed far away and insufficient. Eventually, the Lord convinced me that I could quit the job, trust in Him, and wait on His compassion and salvation. I am not sharing this story to present any kind of prescription for single moms, but to illustrate what God did with one of His children.

He opened the doors for me to move to Denver and go to graduate school. We moved from a large, well-equipped home to a small townhouse, taking only a few necessary things, and leaving everything else for a missionary family on furlough. After a year, we so loved our new simple life in Colorado we all agreed we wanted to stay. When we drove our van back to Virginia, I told the boys that since we had lived comfortably and happily without all our stuff for a year, we could limit what we would take back to what would fit in that van. I expected the experience of getting rid of all our stuff and selling our home to be difficult and terribly sad. And yet, it proved to be one of the most freeing experiences I have ever had. Taking off that weight of responsibility and the accumulation of years of material goods gave me a sense of freedom I had never felt before. Since that time I have reproduced the same experience over and over again, not always willingly, but as God has led me. I continue to be challenged to simplify my life.

> *"De-accumulate. Masses of things that are not needed complicate life. They must be sorted and stored and dusted and re-sorted and restored ad nauseam. Most of us could get rid of half our possessions without any serious sacrifice."*[8]
>
> **—Richard Foster**

A good rule of thumb is to toss anything that does not pass the test of being functional or beautiful.

APPLY Do you consider yourself to be "messy," a "neat-freak," or somewhere in between?

_____
_____

How would simplifying your life help?

_____
_____
_____
_____

Where are you on a scale of 1–10 in the area of contentment?

◄ | 1 | 2 | 3 | 4 | 5 | 6 | 7 | 8 | 9 | 10 | ►

How could an older woman help you find contentment?

_____
_____
_____
_____
_____

What facet of keeping your home challenges you the most?

_____
_____
_____
_____
_____

How has busyness and business outside the home affected the practical, emotional, and spiritual health of your home?

_____
_____
_____
_____

Spend some time with the Lord in prayer.

 Lord, I praise You for being my Keeper, for protecting me from all evil, for keeping my soul and guarding my every step. Thank You for giving me the important position of being Your assistant-keeper of the home You have given to me. Thank You for the grace and power You give me to enable me to manage on Your behalf. Thank You for the gift of prayer, giving me access to Your throne of grace continually.

Father, I confess I fail to come to You. I too often try to do things in my own strength. I say I believe in prayer, but my prayerlessness proves I don't. Please forgive me and make my heart long for Your presence and my soul wait for You. I confess, too, my self-centeredness. I am more concerned for my own comfort and fulfillment than for the people in my family or the friends in my *oikós*. Help me to build them up and protect them from evil. Please forgive my selfishness and reset my priorities. Please fill me with Your Spirit and enable me to walk with You.

Father, I pray for each person in my *oikós,* that they would know You, the only true God, and Jesus Christ whom You have sent. Help me to glorify You by accomplishing the work You have given me to do. Give me grace to manifest Your name to each one You have given me. Holy Father, keep them in Your name. Help me to speak the words of truth You have given through Christ. May we be one with You. Keep us all from the evil one. Sanctify us in the truth. May we all be filled with Your glory and love. For Your name's sake we pray. Amen.

Write your own prayer in the space provided below.

_____

_____

_____

_____

_____

_____

_____

_____

_____

_____

_____

_____

_____

_____

_____

_____

_____

Notes

10

Being Good

*I*was having afternoon tea with Dodie in the commons of her dorm on campus. We were talking about our lives and comparing the different paths that had brought us to the graduate program in counseling. Her life had been one of excitement, travel, dancing, and celebration. She loves life and God passionately and pursues them both with all her heart. Her love for people and the kindness she shows everyone draws everyone she comes into contact with into her wacky, wonderful world. My life, on the other hand, was practical, frugal, plain, and proper. I made all the right decisions, kept all the rules, and never dreamed of coloring outside the lines.

That afternoon, Dodie challenged me: "Why do you choose to live this way, Barbara?" I was stumped. I have always tried hard to be a good Christian and do God's will. What other choice is there? Dodie gently suggested, "Perhaps it is not really God you are serving but your idol of being a good girl."

Things came into a clearer perspective when Dodie took me to see the film *Enchanted April.* The movie opens with two middle-aged women in England, Lottie and Rose, who are enduring the rain, unhappy marriages, and unfulfilled lives. Lottie, who reminded me of Dodie in many ways, sees an advertisement in the newspaper for a vacation villa in Italy and convinces Rose, a lonely, straight-laced good girl, to go with her. San Salvadore turns out to be an enchanted hideaway that Lottie refers to as a "tub of love."

Dodie...

...representing grace

The story chronicles the change that is effected in each guest who spends time there. Somehow, all the strained relationships and dysfunctional patterns of living are mysteriously healed by the atmosphere of love, beauty, and forgiveness.

Watching this transformation in Rose and the others stirred something in me—some longing to be awakened in this same way, to be released from my self-effort at "being good" and open my soul to the kind of mystery and enchantment that a community of true faith and grace offers. Together, Dodie and I realized a new goal of helping our churches become true "tubs of love."

Lottie's character paints a picture of a Titus 2 woman inviting others to enjoy and partake of the mystery of God's grace. Like Dodie, her openness to love and life is contagious, and her freedom is winsome. Afternoon tea and a trip to the movies did more to change my life than years of directions on how to "be good." Her example of joyous celebration of life and vigorous pursuit of God enticed me to a rich, full worship rather than the meager, dutiful, sinful worship of the false god of being a good girl.

Being Good

"Older women likewise are to live priestly lifestyles, not to be malicious gossips, nor should they have any addictions, but should be teachers of beauty, so that they can **train the younger women** to love husbands, to love children, to be of sound mind, to be pure, to be keepers of the home, **to be good** and to be submissive to their own husbands that the word of God may not be dishonored."

Titus 2:3–5 (AUTHOR'S PARAPHRASE)

DEFINING GOODNESS

As we begin our exploration of what Scripture teaches about being good, it is important to realize we will encounter many varied uses of the word "*good*" and even more interpretations and applications of its meaning. The most common admonishment a parent will give a child is to "be good." Some people believe God's message to us is the same. I don't believe it is. For centuries Satan has confused and befuddled many in this regard. As you study and discuss the passages and questions in this lesson, please be open to what the Holy Spirit would teach you. Pray that God's truth will be revealed in clear and precise ways.

📖 Read Luke 10:38–42. How does Jesus define good to Martha? Was He telling her serving was not good? What do you think "*the good part*" was that Mary had chosen?

_____

_____

_____

_____

The effort we put into changing our behavior in order to "be good" could be better spent getting to that place of quietness before God. But it seems we are more prone to "do" rather than to "be." We want to **do** good because it is tangible and measurable. It gives us a sense of worthiness. Doing good can be seen by others, and they will think and speak well of us. We cannot relax in His presence or rest in imputed righteousness because we want to prove that our own righteousness is sufficient. Our evil nature wants to prove that it is good by doing good, so the process develops into our making continual efforts to change our behavior. But Jesus teaches that the one necessary thing is to learn to sit at His feet and listen to Him; it is in that position and during that process He makes us good.

Read Colossians 1:9–12. Below is a list of the steps in the progression Paul expects to see in our spiritual growth. What does each of these phrases imply has to happen before good work is born?

. . . we . . . ask that you may be

_____

_____

_____

filled with the knowledge of His will

_____

_____

_____

all spiritual wisdom and understanding

_____

_____

_____

increasing in the knowledge of God

_____

_____

_____

strengthened with all power, according to His glorious might

_____

_____

_____

for the attaining of all steadfastness and patience

_____

_____

_____

the Father, who has qualified us

_____

_____

_____

Are the things we do (i.e., *walk, please, bear fruit,* and *give thanks*) the cause or the effect of what God provides?

_____

_____

Word Study
GOOD

The Greek word, *agathós*, translated "good" in Titus 2:5 "describes that which, being good in its character or constitution, is beneficial in its effect."[1] It literally means kindheartedness as opposed to legalistic behavior.

OUR HIGHEST PRIORITY

It is a moment of staggering importance for women. No longer relegated to the kitchen, we are encouraged, by none other than Jesus himself, openly and actively to study and learn more about him. . . . Jesus calls Mary, Martha, and the rest of us to make knowing God our highest priority.[2]

—CAROLYN JAMES

If we see *"bearing fruit"* as a result of being *"filled"* by Christ's Spirit, this implies goodness comes from intimacy. It is like the fruit of the womb. We bear children as a result of intimacy with our husbands. Likewise, our good works are the fruit of intimacy with Christ. This verse is not saying that our work bears fruit, but that the good works are the fruit of knowing Him. *"Increasing in the knowledge of God"* is what happens as we live in the cycle of being filled, walking, and bearing fruit. This knowledge is relational knowledge, not head knowledge. It is knowing God like Adam knew Eve. It is intimacy.

📖 Read 2 Thessalonians 1:11. Where do you think *"our every desire for goodness"* comes from? What reason does verse 12 give as Paul's goal in praying this? Why is it important that those desires are fulfilled by God rather than through our own efforts?

_____

_____

_____

_____

_____

_____

Don't overlook the important fact that both our goodness and our faith are according to His grace. That means the ability, the wherewithal, the desire, are all of Him. We can never take any credit for them.

APPLY How were you trained as a child? Did your parents tell you to "be good" or to "have fun"?

_____

_____

_____

What would happen if we made a point of encouraging our children to "enjoy God"?

_____

_____

_____

How do you "sit at His feet" (Luke 10:38–42)?

_____

_____

_____

_____

Where are you in Paul's progression of spiritual growth?

_____

_____

_____

"We pray . . . that our God may . . . fulfill every desire for goodness."

2 Thessalonians 1:11

KNOWING GOOD

Ever since the Garden of Eden and the eating of the fruit of the tree of the *knowledge* of good and evil, mankind has been bent on figuring out what is good. We want to know good as well as to experience the taste of evil. If we can know what is good we can do it in order to try to mend the broken relationship with God. Even as Christians, we spend a great deal of time searching for the "will of God," but we must ask ourselves why. Could it be because we still want to know how to be good in the hope that if we do we will gain some favor with God and earn His blessing? Should "knowing good" be our goal?

📖 Read Romans 12:1–2. According to verse 2, the will of God is good. How and why do we "prove" it? How are our minds renewed? How does this passage compare to Luke 10:38–42?

_____

_____

_____

_____

_____

_____

When you compare Romans 12 with the passage in Luke, you can see some important similarities. The worship of presenting oneself to God as a living sacrifice could be compared to taking our position at the feet of Jesus. And the renewing of our minds can only occur when we listen to what He teaches us. So if we want to find or prove the good will of God, this is where we start. Again, our efforts are in getting to the place of openness to God.

What distracts us, according to the verses in Romans?

_____

_____

_____

Conformity to the world and all its busyness and distractions keep us from knowing the will of God.

📖 Read John 14:16–26. What part does the Holy Spirit play in our knowing good?

_____

_____

_____

_____

_____

_____

> **The renewing of our minds can only occur as we listen to what Christ teaches.**

DIRECTOR OF SPIRITUAL GROWTH

By His self-imparting [the Holy Spirit] is the spiritual life of the believer, causing him to know the indwelling of the risen Christ. He is the Author, Source, and Director of power for the lifelong process of spiritual growth, and it is only as He is the sphere of the believer's walk that victory over sin is possible. Setting the saint free from a stringent, legalistic clinging to the letter of the law, the Spirit is the Spirit of Christ the Liberator and the Transformer of the sinner, bringing him into conformity with the image of Christ.[3]

—G. WALTERS

Knowing good and knowing Christ must be one and the same. Being good cannot happen apart from Christ and His Spirit's work in us. The mystery of His abiding in us and our ability to know Him, to keep His commands, and to love Him are tied together in a way that negates the possibility that one could happen without the other. We cannot know good without the Holy Spirit's teaching us. We cannot be good without His abiding in us. If we truly love Him, we cannot help but keep His word. It is His abiding in us that makes us know that which is good, and gives us the grace to be good.

📖 Read Galatians 5:13–18. What is the difference between walking by the Spirit and walking under the law? Why does our flesh prefer law?

_____

_____

_____

_____

_____

_____

Walking by the Spirit is walking in freedom—freedom to love and serve, freedom from the flesh, freedom from the burden of the law. Walking under the law is bondage—bondage to rules, bondage to the flesh, bondage to what others think of you. We prefer the law because we think it gives us control, credit, status, and independence.

What would you say to a younger woman who told you she was so tired of trying to keep all the rules that she was tempted to give up totally?

_____

_____

_____

_____

_____

_____

_____

Years ago, George Harvey, a counselor in Virginia Beach, showed me a simple diagram that helped me understand the difference between living under the law and living under grace. On the next page is an expanded version of his diagram. The first three columns describe three different ways to live under the law. The arrows point to where the behaviors and attitudes will eventually lead.

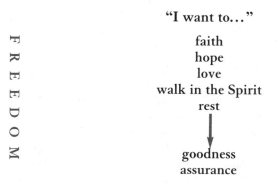

LAW

Pharisee	Failure	Rebel
"I should…"	"I can't…"	"I won't…"
works	burn out	refusal
self-effort	give up	do own thing
pretend	withdrawal	flaunt
keep the rules	fear the rules	forget the rules
pride	discouragement	exhilaration
↓	↓	↓
try harder	depression	consequences
self-righteous	guilt	despair

B O N D A G E

GRACE

Union with Christ

"I want to…"

faith
hope
love
walk in the Spirit
rest
↓
goodness
assurance

F R E E D O M

A NEW WAY TO LIVE

Perhaps, like me, you've been working hard to figure life out, to get it right so things go well. The Bible calls that approach the *old way* of the *written code.*… There's another way to live. The Bible calls it the *new way* of the *Spirit.* Those who take this route find themselves flowing toward the Father in rhythm with the Spirit as He opens their eyes to see the beauty of Christ.[4]

—LARRY CRABB

It is very important to note where "goodness" comes into the diagram. It is not where most people would naturally put it—at the bottom of the list of all their efforts at keeping the rules. Rather it is the result of living in freedom, of walking in the Spirit, of resting in His love. When we meet Christ and He fills us with His Spirit, our hearts are changed, and all those things that used to be such a struggle for us become the things we truly want to do. Yet, because we still have our old natures and will not be completely free of sin until we are in heaven, we fall back into bondage from time to time. It happens every time our focus is taken off of Christ and we begin to look more at ourselves. Our way back into grace is always through Christ.

 I once heard a preacher say the tree of the knowledge of good and evil represented "the Law." He explained that Adam and Eve chose to eat the forbidden fruit because they preferred rigid guidelines over relationship. Think about your own desire to know good and evil—is it a safeguard for you that somehow protects you from your fear of intimacy with God?

_____

_____

_____

_____

_____

Do you like the control of deciding for yourself what is good and what is not good? Larry Crabb says that such an approach, according to the Bible, "is the old way of the written code." But there is a new way to live—the way of the Spirit. According to Crabb, "Those who take this route through life find themselves flowing toward the Father in rhythm with the Spirit as He opens their eyes to see the beauty of Christ."[4]

Is dependence on the Holy Spirit a fearful thing for you? Why?

_____

_____

_____

What is your personal motivation? Are you more motivated by passionate relationship or by getting it right and making life work for you?

_____

_____

_____

Being Good

DAY THREE

Being good does not come from efforts at good behavior but from time spent in getting to know the Lord.

FINDING GOOD

We must relinquish our natural tendency to think good can be accomplished through self-effort. We can't know good and choose to do it; we must find good outside of ourselves. Our goodness depends on our connectedness to the vine and our willingness to receive grace. It is not our own attempts to be good. He creates; He works; He prepares—and we just "walk" in it by faith. This is a difficult thing for us to comprehend. In our day-to-day life we keep coming back to self-effort. There is an innate desire to prove we can be good. So we continue to hide the evil in us from others, and even from ourselves, and try to be good by doing good. Even as Christians who know we are saved by grace, we fall back into the struggle. We don't want to live by faith. We want to do it ourselves, we want to do it our way, and we want to get the credit.

Second Peter 1:3 states that God's divine power has granted to us all we need for life and godliness (being good) through a true knowledge of Christ. Godliness comes from knowing Him. Our responsibility is to go to the places where the Holy Spirit promises to meet us. As we spend time in His Word and with His people we are more and more *"filled . . . with spiritual wisdom and understanding."* So our pursuit of goodness is not an effort to know and keep the law as much as an effort to know Christ and to keep in relationship with Him.

📖 Read 2 Corinthians 9:8–10. Where does righteousness come from according to these verses? Why does it say *"all grace"* and *"all sufficiency"*? What do we try to add?

_____

_____

_____

This makes it clear that the sufficient supply comes from His abundant grace. Our "goodness" or righteousness is a harvest of His work in us. God makes *"all grace abound to"* us, giving us *"an abundance for every good deed."* He supplies and multiplies our seed for sowing and harvesting righteousness. This means it must all come from Him. Our goodness comes from our dependence on Him for both seed and growth. Ephesians 2:8–10 makes the same point:

> *For by grace you have been saved through faith; and that not of yourselves, it is the gift of God; not as a result of works, that no one should boast. For we are His workmanship, created in Christ Jesus for good works, which God prepared beforehand, that we should walk in them.*

It is *"by grace through faith."* It is faith, not effort, that we bring to the equation. God has planned from the beginning that we would bear the fruit of good works, but He knew that because of our sin, He would need to supply everything.

📖 Read Galatians 3:2–3, 21–26. Will we ever find good by keeping the law? What is the purpose of the law?

_____

_____

_____

_____

Paul's point is straightforward in theory but difficult in practice. We are not perfected by the flesh (verse 3); righteousness is not based on the Law (verse 21); and the Law is meant to lead us to Christ, not to provide a way of justification (verse 24.) This means we will never find good by keeping the Law. All our efforts to do it right, to make the right choices, to obey the rules will not make us good. We will come up short every time. Our flesh wants to believe we can do it. But these verses make it clear it is impossible. The purpose of the Law is to prove we need Christ. He is the only one who did everything right. He is the only one good enough.

📖 Read Galatians 4:9, 21. Why are we as Christians still tempted to find a sense of goodness in our efforts at law keeping?

_____

_____

_____

_____

The Galatians wanted to be under the Law again. They were turning back to the *"weak, worthless, elemental things"* of the Law. In other words, even though they had found Christ, they wanted to add to what He had given them—a sense of their own goodness by voluntary slavery to the Law. In the same way, rather than living in broken humility knowing we can do nothing but accept what Christ has done, we try to be like Him. Our flesh wants pride, not humility.

CHRIST THE TRANSFORMER

Christ is the end of the struggle for righteousness [being good] since He not only fulfilled the law for us, but was cursed for us as well. He has not only attained our perfection but atoned for our imperfection. There is nothing more to struggle about, for He has done all for us, and God asks nothing now but our repentance and faith. . . . To open our souls to God's grace means He not only saves us from being the people we are, but changes us into those we ought to be.[5]

—STANLEY VOKE

📖 Read Galatians 5:6. What is the only thing that counts? What do you think Paul means by that?

_____

_____

_____

_____

The things we do for Christ that make us feel good about ourselves, that represent some effort and even pain, are included in this verse as things that don't count. Our "being good" only happens when by faith we are changed into loving women.

Look at the context of this verse. In verse 4, Paul says, *"You have been severed from Christ, you who are seeking to be justified by law."* He is talking to Christians who want to be justified by their obedience to the law, and he is saying that we don't get points with God by obedience. Both our justification and our sanctification are the work of Christ's grace, by His Spirit's work in us. Verse 5 says, *"For we through the Spirit, by faith, are waiting for the hope of righteousness."* We should not strive to do it ourselves. Our prayers, Bible reading, and worship do count if they are done in faith and are expressions of love—but they don't count if they are fleshly attempts to produce some credit on our accounts in heaven. The wise men who wrote the Westminster Confession of Faith saw clearly that both our justification and sanctification are acts of God and not something we do to be good or obtain righteousness.

How does legalism dishonor God and His Word? Why did Jesus come down hardest on the Pharisees?

_____

_____

_____

_____

Doctrine
JUSTIFICATION

Justification is an act of God's free grace, wherein he pardons all our sins, and accepts us as righteous in his sight, only for the righteousness of Christ imputed to us, and received by faith alone.

Doctrine
SANCTIFICATION

Sanctification is the work of God's free grace, whereby we are renewed in the whole man after the image of God, and are enabled more and more to die unto sin, and live unto righteousness.

🛑 APPLY Describe your own efforts to be good. Are you more prone to work hard at doing the right thing, or are your efforts in the pursuit of a deeper relationship with Christ?

_____

_____

_____

_____

What is your view of the Law, and how do you use it?

_____

_____

_____

_____

In what ways does your flesh prefer the Law to walking by the Spirit? Why?

_____

_____

_____

_____

Which *"deeds of the flesh"* listed in Galatians 5:19–21 are most visible in your life?

_____

_____

_____

_____

What *"fruit of the Spirit"* has been produced in you?

_____

_____

THE FRUIT OF REPENTANCE

Oswald Chambers once said, "The entrance into the kingdom of God is through the sharp, sudden pains of repentance colliding with man's respectable 'goodness.' . . . This new life will reveal itself in conscious repentance followed by unconscious holiness, never the other way around."[6] This is true not only for the new Christian, but for all of us. Growth occurs as we repent of our self-righteousness. As long as we live in denial about our sin, or in pride about how well we are doing, we don't need Christ and do not depend upon the Holy Spirit. The "goodness" we display is self-deception. Holiness (or true goodness) is always the fruit of repentance. If we confess our self-righteousness, He cleanses us and gives a new heart and grace to obey (see 1 John 1:9). If we repent He produces fruit in us. True goodness is unconscious because it is His doing, not ours. Our focus needs to be on recognizing our need more than offering our obedience. Thomas Watson, a famous Puritan, described repentance as seeing our sin, sorrowing over it, confessing it, being ashamed of it, hating it, and turning away from it.[7] True repentance is often a painful process, but it leads to joy and fruitfulness.

📖 Read Hosea 14:1–8. What kind of words (verse 2) do you think we take with us? In what way do we see the work of our hands as a god? Where does real fruit come from, according to verse 8?

_____

_____

_____

_____

_____

"This new life will reveal itself in conscious repentance followed by unconscious holiness, never the other way around."

—Oswald Chambers

Verses 1 through 3 are words of repentance. They acknowledge our iniquity as well as our need for forgiveness and cleansing. They admit our need for mercy and grace. They admit no one else can save us. They confess legalism and self-righteousness as false gods and promise to forsake idolatry. Verses 4 through 8 give God's response to the words of repentance. After His promise to heal, love, and forgive them, He prophesies fruitfulness, beauty, and renown for His chosen ones. Verse 8 makes it clear our fruit comes from Him and is not the work of our hands.

📖 Read 2 Corinthians 7:9–11. What is the difference between the sorrow of the world and true repentance? What does God produce in people who repent, according to verse 11?

_____

_____

_____

_____

Think through the list you have just written of things godly sorrow produces and try to come up with examples of each one. How might they describe true repentance in contrast to the sorrow of the world? I could always tell when my children were just sorry they had been caught and not truly repentant, when their sorrow had no earnestness, no eagerness to convince me they would never do it again, no fear that they might be tempted, no longing that it would be different next time. When they were truly repentant they accepted punishment as part of justice and realized the sorrow they were experiencing would help them say no to future temptation.

📖 Read Psalm 51:17 and Isaiah 57:15. How are our spirits broken? Is there anything we can do to break them? What do you think the promise that He dwells with those who are lowly and contrite means? What comes from that cohabitation?

_____

_____

_____

_____

JESUS, OUR PERFECT RIGHTEOUSNESS

How easy it is! The only way to get rid of sin is to admit it! Why is this so hard? Surely because it means letting go our own righteousness which is the very thing we do not like doing. Yet how can we have Christ's perfect robe of righteousness if we insist on keeping our own? It is impossible. Jesus is our perfect righteousness. When we come to Him, we need no other. The struggle for righteousness is over, and He becomes our reputation and glory.[8]

—STANLEY VOKE

I wonder if this verse calls a broken spirit a sacrifice *of* God rather than *to* God because we cannot break our own spirit. God is the only One who can break our spirits. We must pray for the gift of repentance. We must long to be broken. We must come to the realization that though it is painful and difficult, brokenness is our best hope this side of heaven. For it is in that place of brokenness that God will come and dwell with us. And when we dwell with Him we become fruitful.

🛑 APPLY Why is letting go of your own righteousness so difficult?

_____

_____

_____

_____

Have you ever seen the work of your hands as a god?

_____

_____

Does your church or small group give regular opportunity for public confession and repentance?

_____

Remember times in your life when God has brought you to true repentance. How did you experience both the pain and joy of it?

_____

_____

_____

_____

Why do we fight so hard against being broken?

_____

_____

_____

THE GOOD SAMARITAN

Scripture can be confusing when it seems to be saying two opposite things. Maybe God's purpose is to keep us in balance by calling us to live in a tension between the two. So, although we are taught that only **knowing Christ** will make us "good," there are also many verses that give us the responsibility of **doing good** works. At first glance there would seem to be a discrepancy here—is it our responsibility to produce good works or Christ's responsibility? Luke 10 teaches that both we and Christ are responsible. In verses 38–42 of this chapter, Jesus tells Martha she should sit at His feet and not get distracted by her focus on meeting people's needs, but in the verses preceding those (25–37) He tells a lawyer through the story of the Good Samaritan that he should be more concerned about meeting the needs of others. So do we follow Jesus' instructions to Martha or to the lawyer? Some churches emphasize one to the virtual exclusion of the other. But, obviously, we have to follow both instructions, because they are both Jesus' words. There may be times when He would say one thing to us, and there may be other times and situations where He would say what seems to be the opposite. Actually, good works cannot be produced without the effort of both responsible parties—God and those who follow Him. No one can produce good works without the Spirit of God working in that person, and no one can truly know God and have His Spirit dwelling within and not produce good works.

📖 Read Philippians 2:12–13. Do we work out our salvation by doing good works, or does He work in us to do good works?

_____

_____

_____

_____

If we try to understand this rationally, we are tempted to emphasize one over the other, because we think both can't be true. But Paul teaches both, and we have to believe both.

📖 Read Hebrews 10:19–24. How does this passage help us see the necessity of both sitting at His feet and doing good deeds? What is the proper progression? What happens when we mix up which produces which?

_____

_____

_____

_____

_____

This is another passage that discusses both God's work in and for us and our own good works, but don't miss the progression of sitting at His feet first and then doing good deeds. Be sure not to get the order mixed up and think you have to do the good works in order to enter His presence. Also, notice it is not just a matter of waiting for the good fruit to be produced, but we have a responsibility to stimulate one another to do it, as well.

📖 Read 2 Timothy 2:19–22. Does the Holy Spirit cleanse us or do we? Isn't effort on our part being implied? If this is mystery, can we leave it in that realm?

_____

_____

_____

_____

_____

LIFE'S CHOICES

Being a Christian should mean that our trajectory is toward need, regardless of danger and discomfort and stress. In other words, Christians characteristically will make life choices that involve putting themselves and their families at temporal risk while enjoying eternal security. . . . We are admonished, "Do not grow weary in doing good."[9]

—JOHN PIPER

Again in these verses we see the other side of the tug of war. We have been saying Christ makes us good and the Holy Spirit sanctifies us, so we pursue Him, and goodness follows as a result. But these verses clearly say we are to pursue righteousness (another word for goodness) and that we cleanse ourselves. Our responsibility cannot be denied. Effort on our part is specifically implied. So what do we do with this? Does it negate all we have said? Can both be true? Does God do it or do we?

We cannot come up with a clear answer. The Bible teaches both are true. God does a sovereign work in us that makes us good, and we have a responsibility to cleanse ourselves in preparation for a pursuit of righteousness.

There will never be a clear answer regarding exactly who does what. Some of this must remain in the realm of mystery. We can't balance the books because our finite minds can't comprehend God's math. We just have to accept both. He will make us good and we have a responsibility to be good. We must **rest** in Him, but we also must make every **effort.** We just can't take one side too far and ignore or deny the other side of the truth. We must somehow fully embrace both resting and doing.

Look again at verse 22. Are we to pursue righteousness by ourselves? What is the significance of doing it with others? Is there any way of being good outside of relationships?

_____

_____

_____

_____

_____

_____

As in Hebrews 10:24, there is an implication in verse 22 that the pursuit of righteousness is best accomplished in community. It is impossible to be good when you are isolated from others if the bottom line is love for God and others.

Read Luke 6:43–45. How does Jesus clarify the debate regarding God's responsibility and our responsibility?

_____

_____

_____

_____

_____

Being good is first and foremost a matter of the heart. If our hearts have not been changed by the divine work of the Holy Spirit, all the fruit we produce will be artificial. However, if we claim to have new hearts and are not producing good fruit, there is really no reason to believe the change has actually occurred. Both the priest and Levite in Jesus' parable of the Good Samaritan considered themselves righteous, but their behavior proved otherwise. They had no real love.

There may be times when we feel our wells have gone dry, when our faith is low and our hearts find it difficult to love. These are the times when we must remember self-effort will not suffice. We can't just try harder to do something we don't really want to do, just so we can be good. The dry well is an indicator that we have not spent enough time at Jesus' feet. The "one thing needful" (see Luke 10:42) has been overlooked again. The _"good part"_ has been taken away by our choices and priorities. The good treasure of our hearts needs to be replenished. Thankfully, the promise of a sufficient supply is always there for us. Our part is to come to Him. His part is to fill our hearts with good treasures and to produce the fruit in us. At times we need to exert the effort to "bring it forth" (see Luke 6:45)—let the Holy Spirit be your coach and encourager as you push new life into your world.

> **"Pursue righteousness, faith, love and peace, with those who call on the Lord from a pure heart."**
>
> **2 Timothy 2:22**

_____

_____

Does it bother you that Christ tells you to do good to your neighbor but also to sit at His feet? Does this confuse you?

_____

_____

How do you pursue righteousness with others?

_____

_____

_____

_____

With what is your heart filled?

_____

_____

_____

_____

What good works is He producing in you? How are you bringing them forth?

_____

_____

_____

_____

_____

Spend some time in prayer.

 Dear Father in heaven, hallowed be Your name. Praise You for Your perfect righteousness. I exalt You in Your infinite holiness. I praise You for Your plan of salvation and sanctification. Thank You for Your gracious work in me to make me more like Christ. Thank You for making Your church a "tub of love."

Most merciful Father, I confess my own self-righteousness. I repent of all my attempts to be good in Your sight apart from Jesus Christ. I know that, in and of myself, I can produce nothing more than filthy rags. Please forgive my pride and all my efforts to be good without faith.

I pray for people I know who are still in bondage to the law. They are trying so hard to live lives that look good to others, and even please You. Help me to explain Your grace and show them by my faith, hope, and love that there is a better way to live. May they soon know the freedom found in Christ.

"For I am confident of this very thing, that He who began a good work in you will perfect it until the day of Christ Jesus."

Philippians 1:6

Father, I pray for Your protection from the lies of the enemy, who would keep me in bondage to sin and the law. May Your truth prevail. May Your grace be found greater. May Your kingdom come. Amen.

Take some time to write your own prayer or journal entry in the space provided below.

_____

_____

_____

_____

_____

_____

_____

_____

_____

_____

_____

_____

_____

_____

_____

_____

_____

_____

_____

_____

Notes

11

False Submission

I met Kathy over thirty years ago in Norfolk, Virginia. We lived in a townhouse community, and both of us had little baby girls, just a week apart in age. I was canvassing the neighborhood to find women who might be interested in a Bible study. Kathy was a new Christian, eager to learn, and I was given the privilege of discipling her. We became close friends, as we shared the Word and our lives together for almost three years. When she moved to Colorado, we continued to stay in touch and visited each other every few years. After my husband left me, my children and I moved to Colorado so I could attend graduate school. A big factor in the choice of a school in Colorado was the opportunity to live closer to Kathy once again, and this time, to be discipled by her. In the intervening years, her passion for Christ and ability to hear His voice gave her the kind of relationship with Him that I longed for. The Lord provided a house just a couple of blocks away, and we had another three years of living close together.

Kathy's husband Jack was not a Christian for the first twenty-four years of their marriage. Her heart yearned for him to know Christ and to be the spiritual leader of their home. In the midst of her waiting, God graciously took Kathy to a deeper level of trust and dependence on His leading. Her example of careful listening for the Holy Spirit's direction taught me much about submission and helped me identify what was false in me.

Kathy...

...a humble disciple

I remember the day we were walking together along Bear Creek, and I was confessing how much hidden control had undermined my feeble attempts at submission in my marriage. She commented at that time that she thought fear was the biggest factor keeping her from submission. Those few words opened up a "Pandora's box" of my own suppressed fears. I found that my denial systems went deep into my subconscious. I knew I was controlling but had never looked at the fears that fueled my need to control. I had convinced myself I was afraid of very little, yet, the deeper I dug, the more I saw how my inability to trust my husband came from an underlying distrust of God and a fear that He wasn't as good or as powerful as I said I believed. Recently, Kathy was talking about how important it is to get at the root of our sins and allow God to dismantle them. Her pastor's wife taught that we chop at the fruit of our sins but rarely get to the root.

"Submission is not the final goal," she pointed out, "it is only part of the process of sanctification. We must be aware of our motives. At times we must step aside and observe what we are doing and ask ourselves why. We must look at the things that hinder truth and freedom. When we become aware, God can teach us how He wants to change us. As victims of brokenness we need to come to the Father each day and trust Him to uncover whatever He wants to deal with that day, in order to bring us to wholeness." Kathy's humble reliance on God to change her and lead her makes her the kind of disciple I want to be.

Control Behind a Façade

To understand why submission is so difficult for us as women, we need to go all the way back to the beginning of time. After the fall into sin, God put a curse on the woman which is recorded in Genesis 3:16:

> To the woman He said, "I will greatly multiply your pain in childbirth,
> In pain you shall bring forth children;
> Yet your <u>desire</u> shall be for your husband,
> And he shall rule over you."

The great tension between the man and the woman began there. A hint regarding the meaning of "*desire*" can be found by comparing its usage in the next chapter, Genesis 4:7:

> Then the LORD said to Cain, "Why are you angry? And why has your countenance fallen? If you do well, will not your countenance be lifted up? And if you do not do well, sin is crouching at the door; and its <u>desire</u> is for you, but you must master it."

Taken together, these verses suggest the fuller meaning of the word "desire"—"desire to control." These verses show the tension between two opposing forces that are striving for control. They identify the two basic conflicts in which we all struggle. The most basic is our struggle between choices of good and evil. We desire to do good, but sin desires to control us. Sin must be mastered in order to choose good. The second conflict occurs in marriage when a woman desires to control her husband, but he rules over her. Women who are in denial regarding their sin of controlling often prac-

"Older women likewise are to live priestly lifestyles, not to be malicious gossips, nor should they have any addictions, but should be teachers of beauty, so that they can **train the younger women** to love husbands, to love children, to be of sound mind, to be pure, to be keepers of the home, to be good and **to be submissive to their own husbands** that the word of God may not be dishonored."

Titus 2:3–5 (AUTHOR'S PARAPHRASE)

tice a false submission, which is merely an outward show. But if the desire to control is not dealt with (continually confessed, forgiven, and cleansed) no amount of behavior modification will bring us to true submission. Hiding control is not submission.

📖 Read Genesis 3:16–24. Discuss what it must have been like for Eve after having lost the comfort of Eden and the security of sinless love. Why would control be important to her?

_____

_____

_____

_____

_____

Control became the issue as soon as sin entered the world. When Adam and Eve ate of the tree of the knowledge of good and evil, they immediately lost the blessing and security of living in a loving environment. Eve no longer felt the security of Adam's love and care for her. She was now married to a sinner, who was more focused on his own selfish concerns. He wanted to rule over her to insure that his needs were met. Because she had lost the security of Adam's love, she felt she needed to provide her own security. She did this by attempting to take control, just like so many other women who are born into this fallen world.

📖 Read Numbers 12. What was Miriam after? How did she go about getting it? Why do you think God punished her with leprosy but not Aaron?

_____

_____

_____

_____

In Numbers 12, Miriam seems to be trying to create a position of authority for herself, and it is obvious that God is not pleased with her. In verse 3, Moses is commended for his meekness—a commendation all women who truly understand submission should desire. In contrast, Miriam was not meek and therefore was punished with leprosy.

📖 Read Mark 6:17–28. Relate how Herodias used control to get what she wanted but did it in such a way that looked submissive.

_____

_____

_____

_____

_____

Herodias is an example of a controlling woman who puts on a façade of submission. She gets her way but has to manipulate a lot of people to accomplish it. Our goal is not to look submissive, but to have truly submissive hearts.

Word Study
BEING SUBMISSIVE

The Greek word translated *"being subject to"* (NASB) or *"being submissive"* in Titus 2:5 is *hupotássō*. *Hupotássō* is a combination of two root words, *hupó*, which means "under,"[1] and *tássō*, which means "to arrange."[2] In the context of marriage, the literal meaning is for wives to choose positions under their husbands. John Piper defines it as, "the divine calling to honor and affirm a husband's leadership."[3]

"Things are out of control because you are in control. God is challenging us to relinquish management of our lives so we can be out of control—and love it."[4]

—Lisa Bevere

"Beware of the leaven of the Pharisees, which is hypocrisy."

—Luke 12:1

Read Luke 12:1–2 and 1 Corinthians 5:7–8. What was it about the Pharisees that Christ hated? Why are sincerity and truth so important? How does sincerity apply to our relationships with our husbands?

_____

_____

_____

_____

_____

_____

_____

Hypocrisy is worse than control. Our husbands aren't fooled by our pretense, and Christ is not honored. Sincerity and truth should be our goals, even if the sin of control is revealed. Christ our Passover has provided the payment for those very sins, so why not let them surface—then we can confess, repent, and be cleansed. Hiding our desire to control behind a pretense of submission will only prolong the agony and keep our relationships shallow. It is better to be honest about our sinfulness and bring it to the Cross.

APPLY How aware are you of your own need to control? Have you identified control as one of your major sin issues?

_____

_____

How do you hide your control? Or are those around you (husbands, friends, etc.) so passive you can get away with obvious control?

_____

_____

_____

_____

In what ways do you project a façade of submission?

_____

_____

_____

_____

False Submission

DAY TWO

DENIAL-BASED CONFORMITY

Conforming to a husband's desires when our hearts tell us something different is not true submission. If our conformity requires a denial of the truth or leads us into silence, we are practicing a false submission. Some women pretend to obey or agree with their husbands in order to keep the peace. They may think their silence is submission, but it is not. It is a lie.

I was a pro at this kind of false submission in my twenty-five years of marriage. My husband tended to be more passive, and I tended to be more controlling. So we both worked hard at pretending. He knew he was to be the leader, so he tried to deny his passivity and conform to leadership behavior. I knew I must be the submissive wife, so I tried to convince everyone that I was not in control. I compared my outward behavior to other women I knew who honestly let it all hang out, and congratulated myself on how well I was doing. But all of the efforts both of us displayed made it difficult to find the help and encouragement we needed to deal with our sinful hearts. We were both in denial. Our marriage was a failure because we never learned to speak the truth in love.

📖 Read Acts 5:1–11. Verse 2 tells us the decision Ananias made was *"with his wife's full knowledge."* What kind of false submission do you think Sapphira was using? What did it get her?

_____

_____

_____

_____

_____

The text does not tell us why Sapphira did what she did, but it does tell us she had full knowledge, so she either agreed with it or decided to submit without voicing her disagreement. Either way, God punished her for her deceit and suppression of the truth. Peter offered her the chance to speak the truth apart from her husband, revealing God's justice in giving her the opportunity to stand on her own. But she chose compliance with her husband over and above truth. When we comply with sinful leadership without speaking our disagreement or standing for the truth, we are held accountable. Too many women think submission is their ticket to immunity from responsibility for their actions, but their silence and denial is not as innocent as they may hope.

📖 Read Ephesians 4:25–27. Would you agree "falsehood" includes silence? Do you sometimes let the sun go down on unspoken anger? What kind of an opportunity does that give the devil? When we live in denial, to whom are we being false?

_____

_____

_____

_____

_____

When we are silent we give the devil the opportunity to speak whatever lies he would about what we think and feel. He is especially active in marriages that lack good communication. I would maintain that more people practice falsehood by failing to speak the truth than by speaking a lie. Equating submission with silence is a dangerous idea.

PSEUDO SUBMISSION

Pretending to go along with things on the outside that you don't support on the inside is not submission, nor is it humility. It is dishonesty—and probably a spiritualized sugar-coating over seething anger, as well. Giving up your own dreams, your ideas, your very identity in order to earn the approval of another is not submission, nor is it real spirituality. It is a tragedy. Living this way will make you sick.[5]

—JEFF VANVONDEREN

Read Ephesians 4:15. Study the diagram below and answer the questions pertaining to each quadrant of the diagram. The questions below are targeted to married women; however, for those of you who are single, the principle of submission still applies, as we all have to submit to someone sometime, and, of course, we all must submit to God.

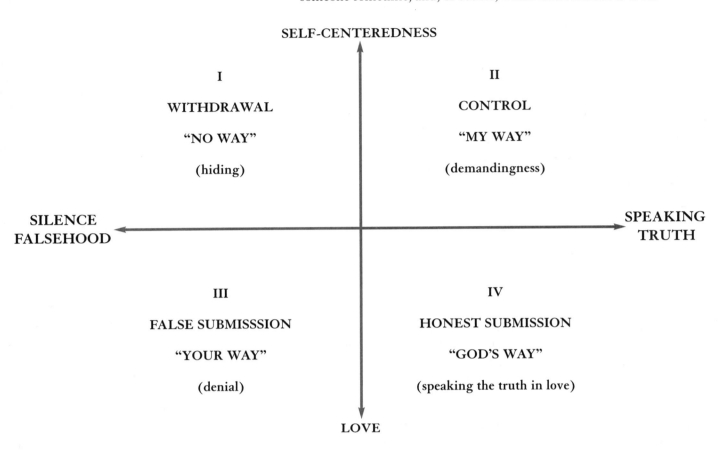

SELF-CENTEREDNESS

I

WITHDRAWAL

"NO WAY"

(hiding)

II

CONTROL

"MY WAY"

(demandingness)

SILENCE
FALSEHOOD

SPEAKING
TRUTH

III

FALSE SUBMISSSION

"YOUR WAY"

(denial)

IV

HONEST SUBMISSION

"GOD'S WAY"

(speaking the truth in love)

LOVE

I   For those of you who are married, what is it like for you when you feel very little love for your husband and don't want to talk to him? Does your personal security ever seem more important to you than your marriage relationship? Do you "shut down" when you are angry?

_____

_____

_____

_____

_____

II   How often do you demand your own way and talk your husband down? Do you see your husband as weak and easily controlled? Are you lonely?

_____

_____

_____

_____

THE STRENGTH TO SPEAK

Women obscure the image of God when they refrain from speech. . . . Feminists blame a patriarchal culture for the silencing of women, and implore women to speak so that they no longer sacrifice themselves. This is where I disagree. I believe women are silent because they do not understand the nature of love [and submission]. . . . Extravagant love, born of desperation, gives the strength to speak and live truth even at great cost.[6]

—SHARON HERSH
(words in brackets mine)

III Have you ever fallen prey to the temptation to bite your tongue when you think just letting your husband have his way will keep the peace? Do you think submission *means* letting him have his way? Do you even know who you are, what you feel, and what you need?

_____

_____

_____

_____

IV Why is speaking the truth in love the best way? Do you understand your position under your husband's leadership in no way negates your responsibility to speak the truth? How would you describe submissive confrontation?

_____

_____

_____

_____

> ## "But speaking the truth in love, we are to grow up in all aspects into Him, who is the head, even Christ."
> ### Ephesians 4:15

Ephesians 4:15 gives us a key principle of submission. Paul states that we "grow up in all aspects into Him, who is the head, even Christ" as we "speak the truth in love." Our growth is inextricably tied to His headship. The more we know Him as our "head" and are in Him as His submissive body, the greater our growth. Growth is also tied to speaking the truth in love. Speaking the truth is honest communication. It is sometimes confrontation. It involves laying aside falsehood, silence, and denial. True submission never means we don't speak; it only means our speech comes from a meek and quiet spirit and is spoken from a position that honors authority and leadership.

APPLY Do you ever think of your silence as submission?

_____

_____

Do you become more verbal or less verbal when you disagree with someone?

_____

_____

_____

_____

How much of your "submission" is simply denial?

_____

_____

How much of your denial is a cover-up for sin?

_____

_____

What are some of the things that keep you from speaking the truth?

_____

_____

_____

_____

Have you ever been convicted by Ephesians 4:25–26? Why is silence usually seen as a virtue? When does it become a vice?

_____

_____

_____

_____

How could an older woman help you learn to speak the truth submissively?

_____

_____

_____

_____

False Submission

DAY THREE

FEAR-INDUCED COMPLIANCE

Another type of false submission is one that is motivated by fear. In the best of marriages submission is a resting place where the wife not only trusts in God, but where she can also trust in the loving care of a faithful husband. In stark contrast are abusive marriages in which wives fear for their safety, and at times their lives, if they do not do whatever their husbands want. Then there are all the marriages in between. According to Dr. Susan Forward and Joan Torrance, "Abuse is defined as any behavior that is designed to control and subjugate another human being through the use of fear, humiliation, and verbal or physical assaults. In other words, you don't have to be hit to be abused."[7] A helpful tool to measure where you are on that continuum is your fear. There is no fear in love (1 John 4:18) and there should be no fear in submission. Fear comes from the enemy.

Read 1 Peter 3:6. Why do you suppose Peter included the phrase "_without being frightened by any fear_" at the end of his discourse about submission? What are some fears that keep women in false submission?

_____

_____

_____

_____

Peter defined submission in a way that excluded fear. He knew fear would be a likely motive for submission and he wanted to discard any notion that submission should be a byproduct of our fears. If our submission involves any fear, other than the fear of God, we need to talk to someone who understands true submission and identify the work of the enemy in our lives and in our marriages. Any church that expects a woman to submit in fear has a false view of submission.

📖 Read 1 Samuel 25. How did Abigail deal with her abusive husband? Do you think she was submissive to him? How was her submissiveness revealed to David? Can a woman be bold and submissive at the same time?

_____

_____

_____

_____

_____

_____

Think what might have happened if Abigail had been in a church that taught women they must submit to their husbands no matter what. The story proves that God was pleased with the way she handled things—and so was David. Her submissiveness towards David showed she had a submissive heart, but her discernment about her husband gave her the wisdom to do what was right in a bold and courageous way. This clearly establishes a precedent against submitting to abuse and folly. And though we are generally called to speak the truth, there are times it is right to refrain from speaking.

📖 Read 1 Timothy 1:5. What are Paul's *goals* for his *instruction*? What is the opposite of *"love from a pure heart"*? What is the opposite of *"a good conscience"*? And of *"a sincere faith"*? Can you see how Satan's goals are just the opposite of Paul's? How might each of these goals help define true submission?

_____

_____

_____

_____

_____

_____

_____

_____

_____

> **"But the goal of our instruction is love from a pure heart and a good conscience and a sincere faith."**
>
> **1 Timothy 1:5**

Love is the ultimate motive for submission. Submission that comes out of a pure heart, not one mixed with fear, pretense, or denial, is far better than false submission. Second Timothy 1:7 (KJV) says, *"God has not given us a spirit of fear but of power and love and a sound mind."* We must recognize that it is the enemy who gives a spirit of fear. His goal is to force us into either control or a false submission. When we identify any of these fears within, we can submit to God and resist the devil (see James 4:7). If we know it is a matter of spiritual warfare, we can seek reinforcements and ask our sisters to stand with us against the enemy and to pray for a spirit of power, love, and a sound mind. Satan's goal is to isolate us so he can use fear to control us. The battle is never simply between a husband and wife. It is also in the heavenlies. We need others to fight this battle with us. We need "older women" to teach us how to overcome, repent of our fears, and find true submission.

APPLY With which of the following fears do you identify:

☐ fear of insignificance
☐ fear of the fallibility of your husband
☐ fear of the consequences of your husband's bad choices
☐ fear of not knowing what will happen if you relinquish control
☐ fear of not being heard
☐ fear of not realizing personal potential
☐ fear of abuse
☐ fear of abandonment
☐ fear of conflict
☐ fear of chaos
☐ fear of the consequences if you speak up
☐ fear of God's displeasure or retribution
☐ fear of a legalistic church

(What are Satan's lies behind those fears?)

_____

_____

_____

How can you deal with your fear?

_____

_____

_____

_____

False Submission

DAY FOUR

SUBJECTION TO UNGODLY AUTHORITY

Any man who demands obedience from his wife totally misunderstands Paul's teaching on servant leadership. God never forces us to obey Him, nor does He give authority to men so they can force women to obey them. There is no teaching in Scripture that even implies a man should see to it that his wife is submissive. That is wrong and ungodly. The authority man is given is for the purpose of wise direction, provision, and protection. Self-sacrificing love is the only description of how that authority is exercised. Prideful and demanding authority is not a part of the gospel. Allowing this kind of subjection is not submission. It needs to be lovingly confronted.

📖 Read Ephesians 5:23–33. Think of how Christ's love is not only self-sacrificing but is also focused on the needs and glory of His bride, the Church. What specific parallels can you think of that you would find in a godly marriage?

_____

_____

_____

_____

_____

Christ loves us so much, He died that we might be made beautiful and experience the joy of being cherished by the King of kings. A husband who gives no thought to his wife's spiritual well-being, emotional nourishment, or psychological soundness knows little of Christ's agape love. Men who think all they are required to do is bring home the paycheck are sadly mistaken. All women long to be cherished, but only some experience a fulfillment of that longing in this life. Too many men are more focused on their work, their games, or their own pleasures than they are on the needs of their wives. They can see how their wives' submission is there to meet their needs but fail to see their call to sacrificial love is to ensure that their wives' needs are met as well.

📖 Read Matthew 20:25–28. How did Jesus teach His disciples to exercise authority?

_____

_____

_____

_____

Jesus knew how often power is corrupted by sinful man, and so He specifically taught His disciples how to use their authority, and why they were given authority to begin with. For followers of Jesus, the more authority He gives, the more servanthood He expects. His own example of humility to the point of death for those He loves is given as the supreme example.

📖 Read Ezekiel 34:2–16. How does God react to under-shepherds (those He gives authority) who use their authority to satisfy their own needs and desires?

_____

_____

_____

_____

CULTURE OF ABUSE

Is male headship in any and all forms a death sentence? No, but a distortion of it often is. Widespread abuse of male power is both anticipated and condemned in Scripture. . . . Due to inborn depravity, males often need little or no training to abuse their power. . . . Physical and sexual abuse by men is shockingly prevalent in our culture. Domestic violence…is the greatest single cause of injury to American women.[8]

—STEVEN TRACY

Men who *"eat the fat and clothe themselves with the wool"* without giving their wives and children the nourishment they need are no better than the corrupt shepherds of Israel. Hurting wives who experience the neglect of their husbands will someday be delivered by the love and care of God Himself, and the husbands will face His judgment.

_____

_____

_____

_____

> ## "Thus says the Lord God, 'Woe, shepherds of Israel who have been feeding themselves! . . . I will feed My flock and I will lead them to rest.' "
>
> ## Ezekiel 34:2, 15

If a woman allows ungodly leadership to go unchallenged, she is enabling her husband's sin and helping to destroy his chances for a crown of glory. Part of our responsibilities as help-meets is to help our husbands see their sin. Submission is never a matter of allowing men to subject you to their compulsion, domination, or pride.

APPLY Think of examples of men you know who lead their wives in a godly way. Think of others who are more dominating. Where would you put your own husband on that scale?

_____

_____

_____

_____

What would you say to a younger woman whose husband is trying to force her into submission? How should Matthew 18:15–17 be carried out in that situation?

_____

_____

_____

_____

_____

_____

False Submission

DAY FIVE

MUTUAL SUBMISSION THAT DENIES GENDER DIFFERENCES

Some misguided theologians handle the submission question by suggesting that equality and mutual submission (see Ephesians 5:21) totally eliminate authority structure and gender roles. In his commentary on the fall of mankind, Ray Ortland dispels the myth of blurred gender roles: "Eve usurped Adam's headship and led the way into sin" while Adam "abandoned his post as head." He then asks the question, "Isn't it striking that we fell upon an occasion of sex role reversal? Are we to repeat this confusion forever?"[9] Blurring sexual distinctness can water down submission to the point of meaninglessness. We dare not allow the pendulum to swing that far in the opposite direction just because some interpret submission as yielding to domination.

📖 Read Genesis 3:1–6. Where was Adam all this time? Why did he say nothing? What could he have said or done to prevent the fall?

_____

_____

_____

_____

_____

Adam's sin was that he said nothing. He should have protected Eve from the serpent. He should have verified for Eve exactly what God had said. He should have refused the fruit and told Eve not to eat it. But he said nothing. As Ray Ortland puts it, he abandoned his post as head. The vacuum created by Adam's refusal to lead was filled by Eve's tendency to talk. How often that pattern is repeated in our lives. Mutual submission creates a similar vacuum, giving our sin natures freedom to exercise their propensities for control (for the woman) and withdrawal (for the man). This teaching takes the truth of our equality beyond the limits God has set by the bounds of headship and submission.

📖 Read Romans 5:12–21. Whom does Paul blame for our fall? Why doesn't Paul blame both Adam and Eve? Why does God call out to Adam, _"Where are you?"_ (Genesis 3:9)? Why doesn't God summon both Adam and Eve to account together?[10] What roles and responsibilities are implied?

_____

_____

_____

_____

_____

_____

God holds responsible those He sets in authority. The fact that God held Adam accountable implies He gave the responsibilities of leadership to the man from the beginning. It was His intention that Eve be the one to follow, and in that role she would not carry the burden of responsibility.

📖 Read Ephesians 5:21–23. How is our mutual submission described and prescribed?

_____

_____

_____

_____

We revisit this passage to make it clear, as Paul does, that our mutual submission takes different directions for each gender. He begins to describe the way a husband and wife submit to one another in the two verses after his statement about mutual submission. The husband submits by his sacrificial leadership, and the wife submits by taking a position under her husband. Mutual submission that does not include the humility and sacrifice typified by the Cross is devoid of meaning. Our gender differences created by God

CONSEQUENCE OF CONFUSION

Confusion over the meaning of sexual personhood today is epidemic. The consequence of this confusion is not a free and happy harmony among gender-free persons relating on the basis of abstract competencies. The consequence rather is more divorce, more homosexuality, more sexual abuse, more promiscuity, more social awkwardness, and more emotional distress and suicide that come with the loss of God-given identity.[11]

—JOHN PIPER

and our gender roles ordained by Him are gifts we should embrace and enjoy rather than reject and rebel against.

APPLY How often do you experience the pattern set by Adam and Eve in your marriage?

_____

_____

_____

What do you believe about "mutual submission"?

_____

_____

_____

_____

Are you totally confused by all the false submission that abounds in our society and churches and ready to discover exactly what Scripture teaches about true submission?

_____

_____

_____

_____

Spend some time with the Lord in prayer.

 Father in heaven, I give You praise for being a perfect Husband, one I can submit to without fear. I am safe under Your wings. I praise You for Your loving care and faithfulness. Thank You that I can totally trust You and give You the honor due Your name. I praise You for Your sovereign control over all things and for Your plans for me that are for my good and Your glory. Help me to submit to You and in that find it easy to submit to my husband.

I confess I have lived out of a false idea of submission, and found myself often in a place of denial and pretense. I have been silent when I should have spoken, and have spoken when I should have kept silent. Too often, I am motivated by fear of man or what others think, and try to act submissive when my heart is in rebellion. Although I try to hide my desire to control, it is ever with me. Please forgive me, and change my heart. Fill me with the Spirit of Christ, that I may walk humbly with You and with my husband.

Lord, I pray for my sisters who are married to abusive men. I pray that You would fill them with the knowledge of Your will through all spiritual wisdom and understanding. Help them to establish safe boundaries and know when to distance themselves from abuse. Please strengthen them with all power that they may live a life worthy of You, Lord, to please You in every way. Help them to see when pleasing their ungoldly husbands is not pleasing to You. May they bear fruit in every good work, growing in the knowledge of You.

Lord, I pray you would protect those in my study group from the evil one. I know he is out to destroy us and our marriages. Help us to know when he is tempting us to rebel against Your ways or to pretend we are obedient when we know we are not. Protect us from his lies and accusations. Help us to know Your will and to walk in Your ways, for Your glory and honor. Amen.

Write your own prayer or journal entry in the space provided below.

_____

_____

_____

_____

_____

_____

_____

_____

_____

_____

_____

_____

_____

_____

_____

_____

_____

_____

_____

Notes

True Submission

Christ set an example by the way He submitted to His Father, and He expects His disciples to follow it. He said, *"My sheep hear My voice, and I know them, and they follow Me."* Kathy has consistently been an example to me of one who reflects Christ's submission as she follows Him. Her ability to hear His voice and to obey what she hears comes from years of prayer. The time she has spent in the presence of her Lord has changed her to be more like Him. Once she learned to follow Christ, He began teaching her to submit to her husband.

While Jack and Kathy's son was in high school, she felt the Lord saying to her, "You must no longer be the spiritual head of your home. I am going to begin to teach Jack to lead." The Lord also instructed her to share this with Jack and to tell him that she would be praying for him. Kathy shared the news with Jack, though neither of them understood at the time. In hindsight, it is evident that God was also teaching Kathy to give up control. About a year later, she felt the Lord leading her to give Jack the full responsibility of the discipline of their son. Again, she felt instructed to relate this to Jack and to support him in prayer. For Kathy, the crux of the matter was not just submitting to Jack in this area, but trusting Jesus to give Jack wisdom. Only believing in God's utter faithfulness could keep her obedient and on the sidelines.

The next two years were filled with their son's deception and drug use, and Jack handled each incident with wisdom and love.

Kathy...

...reflecting submission

True Submission

Kathy continued to pray. In their son's senior year, he was suspended from school for using drugs on school property. Both parents realized that they were fighting for the life of their son. God gently placed Kathy in the corner of the situation and did just as He had promised. God was leading Jack and revealing to him his own spiritual condition. Jack understood for the first time that if he were to lead his son, he would first have to open himself up to God. As he shared all this with Kathy, she found it difficult not to take over his spiritual journey out of sheer excitement. The Lord reminded her again to trust Him, to pray, and not to lay her hands on it. Jack began reading Chuck Colson's book, *Born Again*. The more he read of Colson's story, the more he knew that he also needed Christ in his life. The week before Christmas, Kathy invited Jack to come to church with the family. He tenderly took her into his arms and apologized for waiting for her to ask him. He said, "I wanted to tell you I would like to go with you before you asked."

I'll never forget that Christmas afternoon. Kathy knocked on our door just after we finished eating our meal. She burst into the room with the biggest smile on her face. "I just had to come over and tell you the good news," she exclaimed. "Jack responded to the pastor's invitation to accept Christ, this morning!" Even my guests who didn't know Kathy had tears in their eyes as we rejoiced together over the wonderful news she had been waiting so long to hear.

A GIFT OF HONOR

True submission is a gift we give to our husbands that will bring honor to them and give honor to God. It is important to limit the scope of submission to marriage. We are not called to give this gift to every man. Women are not told to submit to men just because they are men. The notion of unlimited subservience to the male gender is yet another false interpretation of the meaning of submission.

Part of the confusion about who we are to submit to may come from the fact that the Greek words for man (*anér*) and woman (*guné*) are the same words for husband and wife, and thus can be translated either way. Because we are limiting our study to submission in marriage, we will consistently consider each passage that uses *anér* and *guné* in reference to husbands and wives. You may find this one difference in translation may bring clarity to passages that have confused you before.

We freely choose to take positions under our husbands to honor their leadership. Our submission is a gift we offer that will not only meet their needs but also will allow them to meet some of our needs. The first passage we will study is one of those controversial passages we normally try to overlook because it can be so confusing. Hopefully, inserting the words *husband* and *wife* for *man* and *woman* will make it clearer for you.

📖 Read 1 Corinthians 11:3. Fill in the blanks below concerning headship:

_____ is the head of every husband

_____ is the head of his wife

_____ is the head of Christ

What can we learn about the purpose of submission from these correlations? What does it mean that Christ is the head of the Church (see Ephesians 5:23)? How did Christ submit to God the Father in John 8:28–29 and Philippians 2:5–8? How does God share His authority with Christ in John 5:19–24?

_____

_____

_____

_____

_____

We can learn both why and how to submit by seeing why and how Christ submits to the Father and the church submits to Christ. Studying and discussing passages that describe how the Son relates to the Father give us a picture of what marriage should look like. The reverse is also true—marriage can give us a picture of how God relates. God established the relationship between men and women in marriage as an illustration for us of the relationships within the Trinity and the kind of relationship He desires with us.

We must get past the childish questions of "Who's the boss?" and see the bigger picture Paul is presenting here. Philippians 2 tells us to have the same attitude Christ took. As wives, we have the opportunity to follow His example of obedience and humility even though equality with our husbands is our true position. We don't need to grasp our equality, but can voluntarily lay it aside in order to honor our husbands and reveal to others the glory God gave them in the role He set for them.

📖 Read 1 Corinthians 11:7 and 15. Fill in the blanks below concerning glory:

_____ is the glory of God when he reflects His image

_____ is the glory of her husband

_____ is the glory of a wife

What do you think *glory* means? How do we honor someone by giving that person glory?

_____

_____

_____

_____

_____

_____

Man's glory is that he reflects the image of God the Father by being the protector, provider, and leader of his family. The woman is the glory of man in that, as her husband relates to and cares for her, her submission reflects the essence of who he is. The process of submission and bringing glory to our husbands also reflects what God is like. When we honor our husbands by submission it gives them glory. It also gives them the distinction of reflecting the splendor of God.

Also, a symbol of our submission (long hair in that culture) will give us glory. When we deny our God-given responsibilities or try to change God's creative order, we not only deny His will but also destroy our own glory and the relationship God intended to reflect the love of the Godhead.

📖 Read John 17:9–10. Who is bringing Christ glory according to these verses?

_____

_____

📖 Read 2 Corinthians 3:16–18. How does Christ's glory come to us? How does this correlate with submission in the marital relationship?

_____

_____

_____

_____

_____

Christ's glory starts coming to us the minute we turn to Him (verse 16), and as we seek to know Him more, we become more like Him. We are being transformed into His image (and glory) as we walk in His Spirit. When we submit to His Spirit's leading in our lives, His glory is reflected in us. The same is true in our marriages. As we walk with our husbands and submit to their leadership, our unity brings glory to both of us.

📖 Read 1 Corinthians 11:3–15. Why are wives instructed to cover their heads while husbands are not required to do so? What does covering symbolize according to verse 10? How would our willingness to wear a symbol of submission bring honor to our husbands? How does covering benefit us?

_____

_____

_____

_____

_____

_____

The submissive symbol of covering one's head used in Paul's day is not the issue. This passage is not really about hats, scarves, or long hair. It is about God's original purpose in making man in His image, both male and female, and how the way they relate to one another reflects the glory of the Godhead.

To understand the reason a woman needs covering, we must go back to origins and creation, as Paul implies in verses 8, 9, and 12. Consider the possibility that man was created to reflect the Father's role, and women to reflect both the role of the Son in His relationship to the Father and the Church in her relationship to Christ. Just as Christ needed to submit to His Father's will in all things in order to carry out His ministry here on earth, we as women need to submit to the authority of our husbands when we are involved in ministry of _"praying or prophesying"_ (verse 5). The _"covering"_ the Father pro-

> ## "Those whom Thou hast given Me; for they are Thine. . . . and I have been glorified in them."
>
> ### —John 17:9, 10

vided for the Son was His provision, His direction, His encouragement, and His blessing. We need the same kind of covering for ministry from our husbands or the leadership of the Church. The symbol of that submission to authority is not the same in our culture as in Paul's day. For us, a hat is only a fashion statement. We need to discover how we can reflect an attitude of submission that makes a statement to our culture of our willingness to take a position under our husbands both for their honor and for our covering.

Paul is not saying in verse 15 that long hair is beautiful and that all women should let their grow. In his day, and to some extent in many cultures, how a woman wears her hair symbolizes something of her character, position, and attitude toward her husband. Think about how an attitude of submission and seeking this kind of covering will lead to glory for women. Unlike radical feminists who seek glory in taking on the roles and responsibilities of men, we need to see how God's design brings glory, not only to Him, but also to us, His image-bearers.

Submission brings God glory as we reflect His image in biblical manhood and womanhood. Submission brings our husbands glory as we honor their positions as leaders and trust God's grace in them to provide for, protect, and sacrifice for us. Submission brings us glory as we fit into the design God has established. True beauty is reflected when we are cleansed from the natural control, fear, and anger that clouds and mars the essence of femininity.

APPLY How does your husband respond when you give him the gift of honor?

_____

_____

_____

_____

What does it do to his self-esteem?

_____

_____

What motivates him more—nagging or honor?

_____

_____

_____

Why is it harder to give honor than to complain? How does discontentment lead to usurping authority?

_____

_____

_____

_____

BLURRING THE DISTINCTIONS

The women in Corinth, by prophesying without a head covering, were sending a signal that they were no longer submitting to male authority. Paul sees this problem as severe because the arrogation of male leadership roles by women ultimately dissolves the distinction between men and women. Thus, this text speaks volumes to our culture today, because one of the problems with women taking full leadership is that it inevitably involves a collapsing of the distinctions between the sexes.[4]

—THOMAS SCHREINER

THE ESSENCE OF FEMININITY

A young woman is visited by an angel, given a stunning piece of news about becoming the mother of the Son of God. Unlike Eve, whose response to God was calculating and self-serving, the virgin Mary's answer holds no hesitation about risks or losses or the interruption of her own plans. It is an utter and unconditional self-giving: *"I am the Lord's servant. . . . May it be to me as you have said"* (Luke 1:38). This is what I understand to be the essence of femininity. It means surrender.[5]

—ELISABETH ELLIOT

"Stand by the ways and see and ask for the ancient paths, where the good way is, and walk in it; and you shall find rest for your souls."

Jeremiah 6:16

A RESTING PLACE

We also take positions under our husbands to find rest and covering. Just as Mary, the mother of Jesus, rested in God's plan for her, we can find rest in His plan for us. We are prone to fret and worry when things are out of our control, but there is great rest in trusting that God working in and through our husbands will make everything come out good. Our ultimate resting place is in His arms, but He graciously gives to some of us the arms of a husband as well. Submission to a husband is like practice in resting. May we all get to the place of saying with Mary, *"Behold the bondslave of the Lord, be it done unto me according to your word"* (Luke 1:38).

📖 Read Psalm 91. Though we are constantly tempted to find security in control, where is it really? Discuss why we need covering in order to rest. How does God cover us? In what ways should a husband offer similar covering?

_____

_____

_____

_____

Just like a blanket can make a child feel warm and secure for her nap, we can rest under the shadow of God's wings. Although these verses speak only of the rest that is available in God's care, think of the parallel covering a wife is to find in her husband's care. There is a presumption in Scripture that there is safety and security in submission. If a husband totally fails to offer this kind of covering, there is reason for church discipline. Ultimately, the woman is safe in God's care, but the man is missing the opportunity to experience the glory of reflecting God's image.

📖 Read Jeremiah 6:16. What do you think the "ancient paths" are? Why is there no rest if we are on a path of our own will? How sad is it that Jerusalem refused?

_____

_____

_____

_____

The "ancient paths" are the road map God has given to man since the beginning of time. For us, they are found in Scripture. In Jeremiah's day, God's Word and will were passed down primarily by word of mouth. Although God's people had His direction, they often refused to walk according to it. Their example and the consequences of their disobedience make Jeremiah's words all the more compelling for us. Our souls will never find rest if we walk on our own paths. We will be like the world—totally stressed out, wondering if our next move is the right one. One of God's clear directives for us is submission to husbands. If we will choose this ancient path, we will find rest for our souls.

📖 Read Matthew 11:28–30. Why do we get weary and heavy laden? What is Christ's yoke? Would you consider submission to be part of His yoke?

_____

_____

_____

_____

A yoke is the wooden frame that joins two oxen together so they can work side by side. It is sometimes used as a metaphor to describe one individual's subjection to another. The yoke is a symbol of submission. Christ is telling us there is rest in submission to Him, and the parallel would be that there is rest in our submission to our husbands if it is done in the right way.

Christ does not tell us why we are weary, but it is clear He expects that we will be weary. I think we get weary when everything depends on us. Jesus offers a better way. It is the way He took with the Father. He was humble in heart—He willingly wore the yoke that kept Him joined to His Father (see John 5:19). He is telling us it is easier to be led by God, to walk in His ways, to learn from Him than to go our own way. One of the reasons He came to earth was to show us how submission is done.

🛑 APPLY — We cannot rest without trust, and we cannot trust without God's grace and the work of the Holy Spirit. Consider this quote from Jan Meyers, and ask yourself where you are in feeling the "rest" that results from submission.

> It simply isn't possible, this side of the Fall, to trust like that without the Spirit of God. So every time we trust, we worship. Every time we let go, we abandon ourselves to the Spirit's keeping. Every time we relinquish our pettiness in order to bring pleasure to others, we die, let resurrection power have its way, and then we rest.

> Think of what it takes to have good sex. Good sex is not possible unless both partners are willing to relinquish their needs for the moment, so that the needs of the other can be fulfilled. Timing is everything. As both people give completely, needs that could never be articulated are mysteriously met. . . . What it takes for a moment of true ecstasy is death. We have to die to ourselves, surrender control completely. We have to give ourselves up wholly for the sake of the other. Death gives us a taste of heaven. Relinquishment gives us moments of satisfied stillness.[7]

What is it that you deeply long for? What are you willing to relinquish in order to see that longing fulfilled? How does that help you understand this particular reason for submission?

_____

_____

_____

_____

_____

_____

_____

_____

"The reclaiming of submission as the heart of love, is without a doubt the single most demanding, dangerous, and important task that Christian couples have before them in the modern ages."[6]

—Mike Mason in The Mystery of Marriage

REST IN SUBMISSION

In the grave of Jesus, in the fellowship of His death, in death to self with its own will and wisdom, its own strength and energy, there is rest. As we cease from self, and our soul becomes still to God, God will arise and show Himself. "Be still and know that I am God."[8]

—ANDREW MURRAY

AN EXPRESSION OF TRUST

We take positions under our husbands to express our trust in them. They need us to believe in them. Mike Mason, in *The Mystery of Marriage*, points out that we submit to God because He is perfect, but we submit to husbands because they are not perfect. Our submission is the humble service of our love, because they so desperately need it.[9] We submit to build them up and encourage them to be strong leaders and godly men.

There is no question that it is difficult to trust someone who is imperfect, but trust can grow. Just as faith comes by hearing the word of Christ (see Romans 10:17), our trust grows as we listen to the words and the hearts of our husbands. To truly know another person and learn to trust him with our submission, we must be willing to communicate our inner thoughts, feelings, motivations, and values to each other. Trust is born of commitment. It grows in an atmosphere of faithful reassurance. It thrives in open and honest communication. We need to pursue intimacy in order to build trust.

📖 Read Proverbs 3:5–6. This describes our trust in God. Does it teach us anything about trust and submission in general? How do trust in man and trust in God differ?

_____

_____

_____

_____

📖 Read Isaiah 30:15. Where is a woman's real strength? Why do we try to find strength in control rather than in trust?

_____

_____

_____

_____

For most of us, repentance, rest, quietness, and trust are the hardest positions to attain. Our default setting is control. We feel strong when we are able to manage our lives and surroundings and things are going our way. We hide our weaknesses and sins and use our verbal acumen to wield whatever authority we can grab.

📖 Read Isaiah 30:16–21. How did Israel respond to God's words? How can we avoid their mistakes? What are we ultimately longing for?

_____

_____

_____

_____

_____

_____

TRUST IN THE LORD!

You have trusted Him in a few things, and He has not failed you. Trust Him now for everything and see if He does not do for you exceeding abundantly.... It is not hard, you find, to trust the management of the universe, and of all the outward creation, to the Lord. Can your case then be so much more complex and difficult than these, that you need to be anxious or troubled about His management of you? Away with such unworthy doubtings! Take your stand on the power and trustworthiness of your God, and see how quickly all difficulties will vanish before a steadfast determination to believe.[10]

—HANNAH SMITH

A woman's strength is in her trust. Sometimes that trust is tested by delay. Waiting with longing is such hard work. We are far more prone to get on our swift horses and hurry into the battle, but it never gets us anywhere. We must learn to wait until we *"hear a word behind* [us], *'This is the way, walk in it.'"* Only when we are quiet can we hear that still small voice. This is what trusting often comes down to. It is so with husbands as well as with God. Some women are in a greater hurry than their husbands, and submission for them often is manifested in their waiting.

Read 1 Corinthians 14:34–36. What kind of trust is implicit in our choice to keep silent at times and let the men do the talking, especially in public? How did Eve reveal our propensity as women to take control and disgrace our husbands by speaking up when they are silent? Why is it so hard to hold our tongues and allow them to speak? What does trust have to do with it?

_____

_____

_____

_____

_____

_____

_____

We express our trust in our husbands' ability to speak the truth when we allow them to speak for us in public settings. We express trust in our husbands when we ask them questions at home that will draw them out. We express trust when we encourage them to seek answers to those things they may not already know, rather than putting them down for not knowing. A wife who does all the talking for her husband disgraces him and tells everyone she cannot trust him to know what to say.

APPLY Have you experienced God's leading through the direction given by your husband? Have you also known times when you needed to help him see a different, more godly direction?

_____

_____

_____

_____

Can you articulate the difference between true submission and false submission and what part trust has in each?

_____

_____

_____

_____

_____

How would you rate the level of commitment and communication in your marriage?

How difficult is it for you to be silent in church? Why? What do you think is the real purpose and point of the suggestion Paul gives in 1 Corinthians 14?

_____

_____

_____

_____

True Submission

DAY FOUR

A REVELATION OF BEAUTY

We submit to our husbands to reveal our true beauty. Most of us are repelled by loud, controlling, obnoxious women. There is something ugly and unfeminine about them. We often try to avoid them in our circle of acquaintances. The world tells us our beauty is seen in how we look, but Scripture makes it clear it is revealed in our submissive spirits. Feminine beauty is that which reflects God's beauty, reveals Christ in us, and expresses the fruit of the Spirit to others.

Part of the beauty of Christ was His submission to the Father. It is this meek spirit that is precious in the sight of God. Submissive beauty is the beauty He looks for in us and found in Jesus. Psalm 149:4 promises He will beautify the meek with salvation (KJV). Meekness and submission are synonymous. Like submission, meekness has lost its meaning and acceptance in our culture. Most of the modern translations choose the word "gentleness" instead of "meekness." But by doing that they lose the power and impact of the deep commitment which says, *"Not my will, but Thine be done."*

📖 Read 1 Peter 3:1–4. Discuss the contrasting sources of beauty described in verses 3 and 4. What makes a meek and quiet spirit beautiful?

_____

_____

_____

God's idea of beauty is very different than the world's. Peter contrasts our preoccupation with clothing, hair, and jewelry with God's focus on our hearts. He is looking for meek and quiet spirits in His search for feminine beauty. We need to understand the biblical definition of meekness and discuss why modern translations avoid using the word. Common dictionaries define it with words such as: "enduring injury with patience and without resentment . . . deficient in spirit and courage" (Webster's definition). Definitions such as these seem more like the false submission we discussed last week. Contrast Webster's definition of the word "meek/meekness" with that of the Bible dictionary printed in the side margin of this page.

Word Study
MEEKNESS

The high place accorded to meekness in the list of human virtues is due to the example and teaching of Jesus Christ. Rarely was it commended by pagan writers, who paid greater respect to the self-confident man. . . . In the New Testament meekness refers to an inward attitude . . . it is part of the fruit of Christ-like character produced only by the Spirit. The meek do not resent adversity because they accept everything as being the effect of God's wise and loving purpose for them . . . knowing that these are permitted by God for their ultimate good.[11]

—J. C. CONNELL

How significant is the difference between the two words that describe our behavior (verse 2), and the two that describe our spirit (verse 4). What dangers would we face in confusing these four words?

_____

_____

_____

_____

_____

_____

I believe it was a misinterpretation of this passage in 1 Peter 3 that helped to destroy my own marriage. It was the combination of the phrase in verse 1, *"without a word"* and the end of verse 4, *"a quiet spirit,"* that caused confusion for me. I thought this meant I was not to speak a word—I was to be quiet and simply let my husband continue in his disobedience without any confrontation from me. In my legalistic view of things, I thought God was guaranteeing that if I did my part in silent submission, He was promising to do His part in somehow changing my husband's heart. I'm here (without a husband) to tell you it doesn't work that way.

I now believe Paul's meaning in these verses is that our lives as Christian women who have submissive, gentle, quiet spirits can be a living word (that includes loving words) which will continue to hold before our husbands the truth even when they are ignoring God's Word. The quietness comes from our spirits and not necessarily from our tongues. I realized too late that while I was biting my tongue, my spirit was raging. I was screaming and yelling inside, both at my husband and God, but controlling my words in a way that was denying who I was and what I was feeling. I wasn't really fooling anybody but myself. God knew my spirit was not submissive, and my husband could tell my quietness was only skin-deep. I was hard and cold and very controlled—far from an ability to speak the truth in love. I was not revealing any kind of beauty by my false submission.

📖 Read 1 Peter 3:7–9. Discuss how the fulfillment of these verses in your home would enable you to freely submit and feel beautiful in doing it. Why is the final phrase in verse 8 so vitally important? How does it affect both a woman's submission and a man's love for his wife?

_____

_____

_____

_____

_____

We freely choose to take positions under our husbands to learn humility. The process of becoming humble is often painful, but it is designed to happen in a relationship of love and commitment, which cushions and softens it. It is our pride that refuses to put aside our own glory, pitiful as it is. It is our pride that keeps us from admitting our weakness, vulnerability, and need. It is pride that refuses to submit. Yet in God's perfect plan, He calls us to humility and gives us, as women, the command to choose the place of

> **"To sum up, let all be harmonious, sympathetic, brotherly, kind-hearted, and humble in spirit."**
>
> **1 Peter 3:7**

THE GIVE AND TAKE OF MARRIAGE

In marriage it so happens that the Lord has devised a particularly gentle means for helping men and women to humble themselves, to surrender their errant wills.... Marriage cannot help being a furnace of conflict, a crucible in which these two wills must be melted down and purified and made to conform.... Marriage turns out to be through and through an act of acquiescence, a willing compliance both with God and with one other person, in the difficult process of one's own subdual and mortification.... No marriage can succeed unless it is permeated, saturated, with this spirit of acquiescence, of continual giving in, of gracious and willing compliance.[12]

—MIKE MASON in
The Mystery of Marriage

submission in marriage as our training ground. (The training ground for a man is the challenge to understand, honor, and love his wife sacrificially.)

📖 Read Romans 10:15 and John 13:5, 14–15. What can we learn from these passages about feet? How can something as ugly as feet become beautiful? How is humility connected with beauty?

_____

_____

_____

_____

When we submit to God's call to carry the gospel to all the world, our feet take us there. Our feet are beautiful because humble submission is beautiful. Likewise, when Jesus (as the Head) humbly washed His disciples' feet (the most humble part of the body), He showed how sacrificial service to those who were in submission to Him could also be a beautiful thing.

APPLY Are you tempted to call your denial and tendency to keep silent a good thing rather than repenting of it?

_____

_____

Do you consider your spirit to be meek and quiet? What can you do to make it more so?

_____

_____

_____

_____

Do you see your own pride getting in the way of submission?

_____

_____

What does pride have to do with your propensity to control?

_____

_____

_____

_____

Can you think of a better way for God to choose to deal with your pride, rather than calling you to submission? Would you prefer sacrifice? If so, what does that indicate?

_____

_____

_____

_____

A Place to Experience Freedom

We choose to take positions under our husbands as an expression of our own freedom as well as to give them freedom. The goal for those experiencing good marriages is to give their spouses freedom to be who they are and to fulfill the calling God puts on their lives. God calls women to submission to their husbands, but if men demand submission it cannot be freely given. He calls men to love their wives sacrificially, but if a woman demands the sacrifice it cannot be freely given. Freedom is an integral component of true submission.

Think about how God deals with us. He risked the possibility of sin entering the world because He wanted to give us the freedom of choice. He could have made us like robots and wired us to do only His will. But because He wanted our love for Him to be freely given, He chose the way of freedom. Because we fell to the temptation of sin, God had to make the ultimate sacrifice of love in order to redeem us back into His love. The cost of freedom is always high, but the possibility of true love is worth it.

📖 Read Ephesians 5:21–31. When is it hard to submit? How can we do it? Why should we even try?

_____

_____

_____

_____

> **"And be subject [hupotásso] to one another in the fear of Christ."**
>
> **Ephesians 5:21**

This is the classic text dealing with submission, and though we have looked at it previously in dealing with both false and true submission, let's look at it one final time to see how our obedience to the principles given here will take us into real freedom in the marital relationship.

First, I want to make a comment about the phrase in 5:21 that we should submit *"in the fear of"* or *"in reverence to Christ."* Jesus knows how difficult this submitting can be—especially when a husband is not loving his wife sacrificially. It is precisely at this critical point that we need to recognize that the submissive spirit must come from our relationship with Christ and be motivated by conviction that His way is far better than what our human nature demands. Our "fear of Christ" must become stronger than our natural fears. We can and will submit when we are totally convinced of the truth and love He has for us. And, again, our submission will not look like fearful silence, but bold speech that puts that truth and love into words.

Second, we need to remember what we studied in the beginning of chapter 11 about false submission from Genesis 3—that we are called to submission and our husbands are called to sacrificial love in order to counteract the curse. The two parts of the curse for women were that we would have pain in childbirth and that our husbands would rule over us, even though it would be our desire to control them. In our redeemed state, we are promised preservation through the child-birthing process (see 1 Timothy 2:15) and freedom from our sinful desire to control by the exercise of a submissive heart. As we follow Christ in His humility, we are freed from our sinful tendencies. Christ came to conquer the evil one and to free us from the evil within—counteracting the effects of the Fall. As we submit to Him and to one another, this is accomplished in our lives.

Finally, freedom is experienced when we are more and more made into the likeness of Christ. Even though, to the world, submission looks like bondage, we who know Christ understand the wisdom of God is often surprising to the human mind. Our husbands are called in this passage to love us like Christ does. We are called to freely choose the position of submission, even though our equality is not in question, in order to carry out God's purposes both in us and in our husbands. When we do this, we are following Christ's example given in Philippians 2. Both husband and wife are made in His image yet reflect that image in different ways.

📖 Read 1 Timothy 2:8–15. If this passage is talking about husbands and wives (see Word Study in the side margin of Day 1), what does it tell us about the responsibilities of each one? What propensities to sin does the passage imply about each of them?

Husbands:

_____

_____

Wives:

_____

_____

Verse 8 implies the husband's responsibilities of protection and provision and warns against anger, withdrawal, or abuse. Verse 12 implies a husband's responsibility to teach and lead his wife. Verses 9 and 10 imply the wife's responsibility to cultivate beauty defined by inner qualities that produce good deeds. Her propensities to control and to talk too much are tempered by Paul's admonition to submissive quietness (see verse 11). (Please read the word study on *hēsuchía*.)

I believe Paul's choice of the word *hēsuchía* is significant; he is saying wives should *rest* in their husband's leadership and have a *peaceful* spirit that enables them to speak the truth in love. Paul could have chosen the word, *sigáō* if he meant women should be silent, or *siōpáō* if he meant they should hold their tongues. I am convinced he did not mean to muzzle (*phimóō*) all women and keep them from exercising their God-given gifts in the church. Rather, he is dealing with the relationships between husbands and wives *"in every place"* (verse 8).

How can submissiveness free us from the traps of the world that bind us to fashion, materialism, feminist propaganda, deception, and pain? Would you agree there is more freedom and joy in following God's design than in seeking after the ways of the world?

_____

_____

_____

_____

Word Study
QUIET

The Greek word for "quiet," or peace, *hēsuchía,* is only used four times in the New Testament: twice in 1 Timothy 2:11–12, and again in Acts 22:2 and 2 Thessalonians 3:12. Two other words from the same root are also helpful in discovering Paul's intended use of this word. *Hēsúchios* is translated as *"peaceable"* in 1 Timothy 2:2 (NKJV), and Peter uses the same word in 1 Peter 3:4 (*"quiet spirit"*). *Hēsucházo* is translated *"rested"* in Luke 23:56, *"quiet"* in 1 Thessalonians 4:11, and *"quieted down"* in Acts 11:18. It is interesting to note that the Christian leaders who held their peace in Acts 11 continued to speak the truth.

Think about how one person's freedom and responsibility are always limited by another person's freedom and responsibility. How does a wife who tries to exercise authority or teach her husband get in the way of his carrying out his responsibilities?

_____

_____

_____

_____

How do these verses in 1 Timothy free us from taking responsibility that is not meant to be ours? If our freedom were not limited by submission, where would our natural tendency to control take us?

_____

_____

_____

_____

_____

Why does Paul bring Adam and Eve into the discussion? What does this inclusion of the first family do to the argument that submissiveness was just a part of Paul's culture?

_____

_____

_____

_____

Notice Paul takes us back again to the garden and the Fall. The reason it is necessary for the wife to quietly submit is not based on the culture of Paul's day. It is the created order which reflects God's original design. When we try to "wear the pants" we are falling again, just like Eve fell. We are being deceived by the enemy into thinking we will be more secure if we are the ones in control. Verse 15 clearly tells us our true security lies in *"faith, love, and sanctity."* Naturally we are afraid of the pain life brings to us, but God promises He will preserve us through it all. In many ways, our experience in childbirth is the ultimate symbol of life. There is plenty of pain in the process, but, at the end, there is great joy and celebration of new life.

Read 1 Timothy 2:15 again, meditating on the last four words. These words can be translated as *"faith, love, purity, and a sound mind."* How do they summarize the topics in Titus 2:3–5?

_____

_____

_____

_____

Faith, love, purity, and soundness of mind are the primary themes we have been studying. We have touched on one or more of them in every chapter. Maybe the Holy Spirit put these thoughts in Paul's mind as a way of help-

THE GIFT OF FREEDOM

We connect ourselves to God's work in this world when we do what He came to do: offer others freedom by confronting and accepting them just as they are for Jesus' sake, with the intention of inviting them into repentance and grace. Freedom is perhaps the most precious gift we offer [other human beings] . . . freedom to be who they are without trying to make them change. We will long for them to become more Christ-like and we'll confront them when they're not, but we won't take responsibility for making it happen.[13]

—NANCY GROOM

ing us focus on our unique call as women to minister to other women, as well as to our husbands and children.

APPLY In its effort to obtain freedom for women, how has the Church followed the feminist agenda? What has that done to dishonor the Word?

_____

_____

_____

_____

Have you experienced freedom?

How have you experienced freedom, or the lack of it?

_____

_____

_____

_____

Of the six reasons to submit (honor, trust, rest, beauty, humility, and freedom), which is most compelling for you? Why?

_____

_____

_____

_____

Which is most difficult? Why?

_____

_____

_____

Spend some time with the Lord in prayer.

 I praise You my Father for these special verses given as specific instruction for me as a woman. I thank You for the time You have given me to study them with others. I praise You for all Your Word teaches me and for the comprehensive guide it is. I thank You especially this week for Your call for wives to submit to their husbands. Even though I may not understand all the reasons You have set things up this way, I know Your plan is best, and I praise You for it. I thank You for the rest that comes when women submit to You and to their husbands.

Lord, I confess that I do not trust You completely. I always hold back a reserve of control. Please forgive me and continue to help me see when I am controlling. Grant me the repentance I need to hate this sin in myself and truly long for a meek and quiet spirit.

Lord, it is hard to believe that I have reached the end of this study. I pray that this study will be just the beginning for all members of my study group of living according to the Titus 2 model. I pray that the discussions and search for truth continue in our homes, in our offices, in ministry situations, and in friendly encounters. May we all continue to become women of ministry, and encourage and train others to join us.

Father, please deliver me from the pressures in our culture to conform to the world around me. May I be different because of my relationship with You and with others. May Your kingdom come into my life in a way that radically changes the way I think and live. Give me a sound mind, a pure heart, a loving relationship, and the faith I need to walk in Your paths. Do this I pray for Your name's sake, that I might bring honor and glory to You. Amen.

Write your own prayer or journal notation in the space provided below.

_____

_____

_____

_____

_____

_____

_____

_____

_____

_____

_____

_____

_____

_____

_____

Credits

Throughout this Bible study workbook, various quotations have been excerpted from other sources in an effort to supplement the study. The author and the publisher of this study are very grateful to the publishing houses and ministries who gave permission to quote from their resources.

Side margin quote on page 7 titled "Thoughts on the Priesthood" comes from *Worship His Majesty* by Jack Hayford, ©1987. Used by permission of Gospel Light/Regal Books, Ventura, CA 93003.

Side margin quote on page 48 is reprinted from pages 50–51 of the title *Repentance—The Joy-Filled Life* by the late M. Basilea Schlink (available through The Evangelical Sisterhood of Mary 602-996-4040 or info-us@kanaan.org). Used by permission of The Evangelical Sisterhood of Mary.

Block quote at the top of page 59 is excerpted from *Why Beauty Matters* by Karen Lee-Thorp and Cynthia Hicks. © 1997 by Karen Lee Thorp and Cynthia Hicks. Used by permission of NavPress (www.navpress.com). All rights reserved.

Side margin quote on page 78, is reprinted by permission of Thomas Nelson Inc., from the book entitled *As for Me and My House*, copyright date 1990 by Walter Wangerin. All rights reserved.

Block quote on page 80 is reprinted from *Intimate Issues*. Copyright © 1999 by Linda Dillow and Lorraine Pintus. WaterBrook Press, Colorado Springs, CO. All rights reserved.

Side margin quote on page 115 is excerpted from *The Allure of Hope* by Jan Meyers. © 2001, by Jan Meyers. Used by permission of NavPress (www.navpress.com). All rights reserved.

Side margin quote on page 118 is reprinted from *Bright Days, Dark Nights,* by Elizabeth Skoglund. ©2000 by Elizabeth Skoglund. Published by Baker Book House Company, Grand Rapids, Michigan. Used by permission.

Quotations on pages 124, 138, 142, 145, 149, 152, and 154 are excerpted from *The Mystery of Marriage* ©1985 by Mike Mason. Used by permission of Multnomah Publishers, Inc.

The Dan Allender quote on page 130 is reprinted from *The Healing Path*. Copyright © 1999 by Dr. Dan B. Allender. WaterBrook Press, Colorado Springs, CO. All rights reserved.

First side margin quote on page 144 is reprinted from *The Power of a Praying Parent*, Copyright © 1995 by Stormie Omartian. Published by Harvest House Publishers, Eugene, Oregon. Used by permission.

The Larry Crabb quotes on page 159 are reprinted from *The Pressure's Off*. Copyright © 2002 by Lawrence J. Crabb Jr., Ph.D., P.C. WaterBrook Press, Colorado Springs, CO. All rights reserved.

Side margin quote on page 166 is from *The Roots of Endurance: Invincible Perseverance in the Lives of John Newton, Charles Simeon, and William Wilberforce,* by John Piper, copyright © 2002, pages 20–21. Used by permission of Crossway Books, a division of Good News Publishers, Wheaton, Illinois 60187.

Side margin quote on page 175 is reprinted from *Families Where Grace Is in Place,* by Jeff VanVonderen. ©1992 by Jeff VanVonderen. Published by Bethany House Publishers, a division of Baker Book House Company, Grand Rapids, Michigan. Used by permission.

Works Cited

LESSON 1
1. W. E. Vine, *Expository Dictionary of New Testament Words* (Old Tappan, NJ: Fleming H. Revell Company, 1966), 3:135.
2. Ibid., 1:43; 2:20.
3. Robert Young, LL.D., *Analytical Concordance to the Bible* (Grand Rapids, MI: Eerdmans Publishing Company), 487.
4. *Strong's Exhaustive Concordance* #4241 p. 60 of Greek Dictionary.
5. Jack Hayford, *Worship His Majesty* (Dallas, TX: Word Publishing, 1987), 87–88.
6. Jerry Cook, *Love, Acceptance & Forgiveness* (Ventura, CA: Regal Books, 1979), 45, 47–49.
7. Gary Thomas, *Sacred Pathways* (Grand Rapids, MI: Zondervan, 1996), 135.
8. Andrew Murray, *With Christ in the School of Prayer* (Old Tappan, NJ: Fleming H. Revell Co., 1977), 8.
9. Hannah Hurnard, *God's Transmitters* (Wheaton, IL: TyndaleHouse Publishers, Inc., 1978), 18.
10. Oswald Chambers, *My Utmost For His Highest* (Westwood, NJ: Barbour and Company, 1935), 5 February.

LESSON 2
1. W. E. Vine, *Expository Dictionary of New Testament Words* (Old Tappan, NJ: Fleming H. Revell Company, 1966), 4:39.
2. Gary Collins, *Christian Counseling* (Dallas, TX: Word Publishing, 1988), 307.
3. Sharon Hersh, *Brave Hearts* (Colorado Springs, CO: Waterbrook Press, 2000), 84.
4. Larry Crabb and Dan Allender, *Encouragement, The Key to Caring* (Grand Rapids, MI: Zondervan Publishing House, 1984), 22.
5. Ken Sande, *The Peacemaker* (Grand Rapids, MI: Baker Books, 1991), 25.

LESSON 3
1. W. E. Vine, *Expository Dictionary of New Testament Words* (Old Tappan, NJ: Fleming H. Revell Company, 1966), 1:139.
2. Sharon Hersh, "The Desperation of God—A Reflection on the Feminine Desire for Relationship," Mars Hill Review 9 (Fall 1997): 27.
3. Mrs. Charles Cowman, *Streams in the Desert* (Grand Rapids, MI: Zondervan 1925, 1965), 313.
4. Gerald May, *Addiction and Grace* (San Francisco, CA: Harper and Row Publishers, 1988), 94.
5. M. Basilea Schlink, *Repentance—The Joy-Filled Life* (Minneapolis, MN: Bethany House Publishers, 1984), 50–51.

LESSON 4
1. Robert Young, LL.D., *Analytical Concordance to the Bible* (Grand Rapids, MI: Eerdmans Publishing Company), 428.
2. C. S. Lewis, *The Weight of Glory and Other Addresses* (New York, NY: Touchstone, 1975), 29.
3. *Webster's Seventh New Collegiate Dictionary,* s.v. "beauty".
4. Henry Drummond, "The Changed Life," in the appendix to *Soul Care,* by Peter Lord, (Grand Rapids, MI: Baker Book House, 1990), 251.
5. John Piper, *Desiring God* (Portland, OR: Multnomah Press, 1986), 78.
6. Macrina Wiederkehr, "Many Come in Darkness" The Mars Hill Interview, *Mars Hill Review* 9 (Fall 1997) 40.
7. Thomas Kinkade, *Lightposts for Living* (New York, NY: Warner Books, 1999), 94–108.
8. Edith Schaeffer, *Hidden Art* (Wheaton, IL: Tyndale House Publishers, 1971), 28.
9. Ibid., 14.
10. Ibid., 22.
11. Karen Lee-Thorp and Cynthia Hicks, *Why Beauty Matters* (Colorado Springs, CO: Navpress, 1997), 237–38.
12. Lewis, 37.
13. Karen Lee-Thorp, "Is Feminine Beauty Dangerous?" *Mars Hill Review* 9 (Fall 1997): 48.
14. Joni Eareckson Tada, *Heaven* (Grand Rapids, MI: Zondervan Publishing House, 1995), 50.

LESSON 5
1. W. E. Vine, *Expository Dictionary of New Testament Words* (Old Tappan, NJ: Fleming H.Revell Company, 1966), 3:21–22.
2. Ibid.
3. Gary Chapman, *The Five Love Languages* (Chicago, IL: Northfield Publishing, 1995).
4. Janelle Hallman, address presented at "Love Won Out Conference," November 4, 2000. Available through Christian Audio Tapes. 1–888–CA TAPES.
5. John Townsend, *Hiding From Love* (Grand Rapids, MI: Zondervan Publishing House, 1991), 34.

6. Mike Mason, *The Mystery of Marriage* (Portland, OR: Multnomah Press, 1985), 138, 142.

7. Walter Wangerin, Jr., *As For Me and My House* (Nashville, TN: Thomas Nelson Publishers, 1990), 18–19.

8. Linda Dillow and Lorraine Pintus, *Intimate Issues,* (Colorado Springs, CO: Waterbrook Press, 1999), 111–12

9. Larry Crabb, *Marriage Builder* (Grand Rapids, MI: Zondervan Publishing House, 1982), 57.

10. David Augsburger, *Caring Enough To Forgive* (Scottdale, PA: Herald Press, 1981), 74.

LESSON 6

1. John Charles Ryle, *The Duties of Parents* (Conrad, MT: Triangle Press, 1993), 12.

2. Miriam Adeney, *A Time for Risking* (Vancouver, BC: Regent College Publishing, 1987), 112–16.

3. Nancy Friday, *The Power of Beauty* (New York, NY: HarperCollins Publishers, 1996), 275.

4. "Mighty Warrior" by Debbye Graafsma ©1983 Integrity's Hosanna! Music (Administered by Sovereign Music, UK).

5. Pat Springle, *Trusting* (Ann Arbor, MI: Servant Publications, 1994), 13.

6. Ross Campbell, *Relational Parenting* (Chicago IL: Moody Press, 2000), 139, 142.

7. Jan Meyers, *The Allure of Hope* (Colorado Springs, CO: Navpress, 2001), 17.

8. C. John Miller & Barbara Juliani, *Come Back, Barbara* (Phillipsburg, NJ: Presbyterian and Reformed Publishing, 1997), 60, 120.

LESSON 7

1. W. E. Vine, *Expository Dictionary of New Testament Words* (Old Tappan, NJ: Fleming H. Revell Company, 1966), 4:44.

2. Ibid.

3. Frederick Buechner, *The Longing for Home: Recollections and Reflection* (San Francisco, CA: HarperSanFrancisco, 1996), 109.

4. Charles Spurgeon, quoted by J. I. Packer, *Knowing God* (Downers Grove, IL: InterVarsity Press, 1973), 13–14.

5. Jan Meyers, *The Allure of Hope* (Colorado Springs, CO: Navpress, 2001), 15, 16, 18, 21, 24, 26.

6. Ibid, 33–34, 47, 52, 86, 90, 122, 130, 175.

7. Ibid.

8. Elizabeth Skoglund, *Bright Days, Dark Nights* (Grand Rapids, MI: Baker Books, 2000), 90.

LESSON 8

1. W. E. Vine, *Expository Dictionary of New Testament Words* (Old Tappan, NJ: Fleming H. Revell Company, 1966), 1:183.

2. Harry Schamburg, *False Intimacy* (Colorado Springs:CO: Navpress, 1992), 197.

3. Dan Allender, *The Healing Path* (Colorado Springs, CO: Waterbrook Press, 1999), 105.

4. John White, *Eros Redeemed: Breaking the Stranglehold of Sexual Sin* (Downers Grove, IL: InterVarsity Press), 39, 45.

5. Charles Kraft, *Deep Wounds, Deep Healing* (Ann Arbor, MI: Servant Publications, 1993), 59.

6. Mason, *The Mystery of Marriage* (Portland, OR: Multnomah Press, 1985), 124.

7. Ibid., 150.

8. Ibid., 144.

LESSON 9

1. W. E. Vine, *Expository Dictionary of New Testament Words* (Old Tappan, NJ: Fleming H. Revell Company, 1966), 2:236.

2. Ibid., 228.

3. Ibid.

4. Stormie Omartian, *The Power of a Praying Parent* (Eugene, OR: Harvest House Publishers, 1995), 14.

5. John Murray, *The New Bible Dictionary* (Grand Rapids, MI: Eerdmans Publishing Co., 1973), "Covenant."

6. Dorothy Patterson, "The High Calling of Wife and Mother in Biblical Perspective," in *Recovering Biblical Manhood and Womanhood* (Wheaton, IL: Crossway Books, 1991), 367.

7. Karen Mains, *Open Heart, Open Home* (Colorado Springs, CO: David C. Cook Publishing Co., 1976), 25–26.

8. Richard Foster, *Celebration of Discipline* (San Francisco, CA: Harper & Row, 1978), 80.

LESSON 10

1. W. E. Vine, *Expository Dictionary of New Testament Words* (Old Tappan, NJ: Fleming H. Revell Company, 1966), 2:163.

2. Carolyn James, *When Life and Beliefs Collide* (Grand Rapids, MI: Zondervan Publishing House, 2001), 38, 40.

3. G. Walters, *The New Bible Dictionary* (Grand Rapids, MI: Eerdmans Publishing Co.), "The Holy Spirit."

4. Larry Crabb, *The Pressure's Off* (Colorado Springs, CO: Waterbrook Press, 2002), 1.

5. Stanley Voke, "The End of the Struggle" from Personal Revival, Operation Mobilization Literature. Quoted in *Sonship* (Philadelphia, PA: World Harvest Mission, 1999), Lesson 4–21.

6. Oswald Chambers, *My Utmost for His Highest*.

7. Thomas Watson, quoted by Rick Downs in a sermon entitled "Repentance." The three passages used in the questions were also used in his sermon. In *Sonship* (Philadelphia, PA: World Harvest Mission, 1999), Lessons 7–9, 12.

8. Voke, 4–21.

9. John Piper, *The Roots of Endurance* (Wheaton, IL: Crossway Books, 2002), 20–21.

LESSON 11

1. W. E. Vine, *Expository Dictionary of New Testament Words* (Old Tappan, NJ: Fleming H. Revell Company, 1966), 4:86.

2. Ibid.

3. John Piper, "A Vision of Biblical Complimentarity—Manhood and Womanhood Defined According to the Bible," in *Recovering Biblical Manhood and Womanhood* (Wheaton, IL: Crossway Books, 1991), 53.

4. Lisa Bevere, *Out of Control and Loving It* (Lake Mary, FL: Creation House, 1996), 15.

5. Jeff VanVonderen, *Families Where Grace Is in Place* (Minneapolis, MN: Bethany House Publishers, 1992), 155.

6. Sharon Hersh, "The Desperation of God, A Reflection on the Feminine Desire for Relationship" *Mars Hill Review* 9 (Fall 1997) 26–27.

7. Susan Forward, *Men Who Hate Women and the Women Who Love Them* (New York: Bantam Books, 1986), 43.

8. Steven Tracy, "Headship With a Heart" *Christianity Today* (February 2003) 51, 53.

9. Raymond Ortland, "Male-Female Equality and Male Headship" in *Recovering Biblical Manhood and Womanhood,* (Wheaton, IL: Crossway Books, 1991), 107.

10. Ibid.

11. Piper, "A Vision," 33.

LESSON 12

1. W. E. Vine, *Expository Dictionary of New Testament Words* (Old Tappan, NJ: Fleming H.Revell Company, 1966), 4:86.

2. Ibid.

3. John Piper, "A Vision of Biblical Complimentarity—Manhood and Womanhood Defined According to the Bible," in *Recovering Biblical Manhood and Womanhood* (Wheaton, IL: Crossway Books, 1991), 53.

4. Thomas Schreiner, "Head Coverings, Prophecies and the Trinity," in *Recovering Biblical Manhood and Womanhood* (Wheaton, IL: Crossway Books, 1991), 139.

5. Elisabeth Elliot, "The Essence of Femininity," in *Recovering Biblical Manhood and Womanhood* (Wheaton, IL: Crossway Books, 1991), 398.

6. Mike Mason, *The Mystery of Marriage* (Portland, OR: Multnomah Press, 1985), 184.

7. Jan Meyers, *The Allure of Hope* (Colorado Springs, CO: Navpress, 2001), 130–31.

8. Andrew Murray, *Waiting on God* (Chicago, IL: Moody Press), 129.

9. Mason, 181.

10. Hannah Whitall Smith, *The Christian's Secret of a Happy Life* (Old Tappan, NJ: Fleming H. Revell Co., 1976), 54.

11. J. C. Connell, *The New Bible Dictionary* (Grand Rapids, MI: Wm. B. Eerdmans Publishing Co., 1973), "Meekness."

12. Mason, *The Mystery of Marriage,* 139.

13. Nancy Groom, *Bondage to Bonding* (Colorado Springs, CO: Navpress, 1991), 176.

Appendix

Venues for Training

Obviously, I believe studying the Bible together and engaging in meaningful conversation about our struggles in life are primary ways to carry out the Titus 2 mandate. But there are many other ways to train in addition to small-group Bible studies. Each church and each individual need to seek the Holy Spirit's guidance to find the place and form their ministries will take. It will depend on what their gifts are, how things are structured, when time can be reprioritized, and who wants to be involved. My hope is that this Bible study will help us think through the Titus 2 mandate and find ways to carry it out.

Bible Study

A church-based Bible study with both older and younger women working together to understand and apply the Word of God to their lives is probably the ideal venue for carrying out the Titus 2 mandate. I say this for four reasons.

✓ A group study brings more of the mind of Christ as each woman adds the perspective Christ has given her to the combined understanding.

✓ Our personal experiences and gifts equip us to speak to a few topics, but none of us can do it all alone. Becoming women of ministry will take a concerted effort. Like an orchestra, every woman must play her part to produce the music of ministry. The uniqueness of the body of Christ is that each particular church is given all of the gifts needed to carry out its ministry. But the Church needs every woman to offer and use the gifts she has been given.

✓ A Bible study keeps our conversation and training focused on the Word.

✓ Group settings offer opportunity to confess our sins to one another and pray for one another.

Mentoring or Discipling

There are times when we need personal training in a certain area, or there may be situations when there are only two women called to study together. Mentoring has become a popular concept in our day. I believe discipleship is the biblical word for mentoring. Discipling is planting truth in the life of another in a one-on-one relationship. It is training focused on things we experience together. It is speaking truth to one another and expressing love for one another. It is building one another up in faith. It is relevant application of the truths of Scripture to particular circumstances of life.

Apprenticeship

A similar term used in the business world can help us understand what is needed. In an introduction to the book of Philippians, Eugene Peterson writes:

None of the qualities of the Christian life can be learned out of a book. Something more like apprenticeship is required, being around someone who out of years of devoted discipline shows us, by his or her entire behavior, what it is. Moments of verbal instruction will certainly occur, but mostly an appren-

---

> **A church-based Bible study with both older and younger women working together to understand and apply the Word of God to their lives is probably the ideal venue for carrying out the Titus 2 mandate.**

tice acquires skill by daily and intimate association with a "master," picking up subtle but absolutely essential things, such as timing and rhythm and "touch."

Apprenticeship can be as informal as two women cooking together or as formal as a counseling internship. Because our culture doesn't have built-in opportunities for apprenticeship, we have to intentionally create them.

Work Parties

Why not meet from house to house simply to work together. As we work, we talk. The work can be as simple as folding laundry, or sorting photos, or some of those more daunting tasks like painting the nursery or planting a garden. If there are small children to care for, invite enough mothers so you can take turns watching the kids or do something that involves the kids.

Hospitality

Hospitality ranges from opening your home to share a cup of coffee with a neighbor to moving out of your master bedroom so a woman dying of AIDS can learn how to live. The bottom line is an open heart—one that is willing to give to others what Christ has given you. This can be the most effective venue because it multiplies opportunities for connection, observation, training, and love.

Counseling

Even though I believe a vital Titus 2 ministry will eventually diminish the need for counseling, there will always be some cases that need extra care and expertise. One thing I like about the counseling model is the consistent timing. Usually, a client will come once a week for an hour-long session. I used to say I quit counseling because I couldn't love people just one hour a week. But it is better than nothing. At least it gave me opportunity to talk with other women, and permission to go to those deeper places we usually avoid. The thing I didn't like about counseling was the relational dynamic that made me the expert and the other woman the client. I prefer the idea of two disciples on the road together. One might be ahead aways, shedding light on the path, but not expected to have all the answers. Only Christ has all the answers, and we need to encourage one another to seek Him.

Third Chair Counseling

Something I recommend to professional counselors who are working with a woman who is part of a good church is to suggest the new client bring an older woman from her church with her to her counseling sessions. This accomplishes a number of goals. The older woman offers co-counsel, accountability, and community perspective. She may also benefit like an apprentice, learning how to help this particular woman and many more like her. The client gets two for the price of one, and has on-going support of a discipler not bound by rules regarding dual relationships. (Professional counselors are not to relate to their clients in any way outside the counseling office. In contrast, Scripture calls us to relate to one another in many different ways.) The referring church receives the opportunity to be part of the healing process and can be assured of the biblical content and godly directions the sessions take. The counselor is not limited to information coming only from her client. The added perspective and wisdom of the older woman can greatly enhance the effectiveness of the counseling process. Matthew 18:16 suggests taking one or two with you when dealing with someone struggling in sin, and Titus 2 identifies the major issues

> **Even though I believe a vital Titus 2 ministry will eventually diminish the need for counseling, there will always be some cases that need extra care and expertise.**

---

*Eugene Peterson, *The Message,* (Colorado Springs, CO: Navpress, 1995), 414.

that come up in this process. Working together, we can see God's word being honored by the ministry we offer.

RETREATS

The beauty of the retreat venue is the opportunity to escape busyness, to refocus and reprioritize life, to connect and spend time together. It is not necessary to bring in a special speaker to do the ministry; sometimes, all we need is opportunity to minister to one another.

FORMAL TEACHING

Of course, there are times when formal teaching is appropriate and necessary. Conferences, seminars, workshops, special speakers, and so forth, can all be very helpful. My point is that they are not the only venues for ministry, and should not be the primary ones.

FRIENDSHIP

The give and take of a good friendship will always include ministry to one another. Sometimes, one will be speaking as an older woman, while, at other times, the other one will. The goals of encouragement, speaking the truth in love and strengthening faith in one another, will not only enrich the relationship, they will build up the church.

MOTHERING

Those who have daughters would naturally need to talk about all these categories with them. There may need to be special opportunities created to cover some more thoroughly. Women who have already raised their daughters can use their mothering skills for young women who need spiritual mothering or re-parenting.

PRAYER PARTNERSHIPS

My relationship with Lucille began when I, as a younger woman, asked her to pray for me on a regular basis. This may be the easiest venue for ministering to one another. It not only gets us talking about issues of the heart, it takes us to the throne of grace, where we both find the help we need. This may be a primary venue to maintain relationships formed in the Bible study and to continue the ministry started as you studied the Word together. Hopefully, the ice has been broken and the hurdles to getting to deeper issues have already been overcome so you can be more honest with one another.

THE QUESTION OF PURSUIT

I am often asked if the younger woman or the older woman should pursue the relationship. My answer is that **you** should. All women long to be pursued, not only by a good man, but also by other women. Even though we dream of being "the chosen one," or someone's best friend, or a woman of ministry that others long to talk with—the reality is: if we all wait to be pursued, no one connects. If you are asking the question, you at least understand something of the mandate, so just do it. You may share in Christ's suffering by being rejected by some you pursue, but most women will be thrilled that you care. So ask an older woman to pray with you or ask a younger woman to ride along with you on your next errand. Invite a troubled woman over for a cup of coffee. Or plan a retreat. Just begin connecting, taking advantage of every opportunity you can imagine and every time the Holy Spirit nudges.

I am often asked if the younger woman or the older woman should pursue the relationship. My answer is that you should.